How the Working Class Can Help the Middle Class

For my ten—and perhaps more later—great-grandchildren.
May their world be harmonious

HOW THE WORKING CLASS CAN HELP THE MIDDLE CLASS

Reintroducing Non-Majority Collective Bargaining to the American Workplace

BY CHARLES J. MORRIS

NEW ENGLAND INSTITUTE
OF TECHNOLOGY
LIBRARY

7/11 #1119748398

HOW THE WORKING CLASS CAN HELP THE MIDDLE CLASS
Reintroducing Non-Majority Collective Bargaining to the American Workplace

Charles J. Morris

Published by:

Vandeplas Publishing, LLC – August 2019

801 International Parkway, 5th Floor
Lake Mary, FL. 32746
USA

www.vandeplaspublishing.com

Copyright © 2019 by Charles J. Morris
All rights reserved.

No part of this book may be reproduced, stored in a retrieval system, or transmitted by any means, electronic, mechanical, photocopying, recording, or otherwise, without written permission from the author.

ISBN 978-1-60042-501-1

PREFACE

This book represents the capstone of my seven decades of trying to maintain or help bring to fruition Senator Robert Wagner's goal of making democracy in the American work place a reality through the medium of collective bargaining. The culmination of those efforts are contained in this book, which arrives at a time when it is most needed, when the nation has reached a critical economic crossroad where, in order to move forward, the right road ahead is the one where the middle class, on which an advanced democratic economy depends, must receive a push from the bottom up rather than a trickle from the top down. And this outcome cannot be achieved without a healthy labor movement, for in order to counteract the inequality that pervades the American economy, a significant increase in the actual earnings of millions of workers is required, and in our free enterprise system only labor unions can make that happen. This means that the democratic capitalism that we hope to foster must again include strong labor unions, just as we had strong unions and an enviable economy for many decades following World War II.

Unfortunately, union membership today is the lowest in recent history, with only 6.4 percent of employees in the private sector now represented by unions. Although there are many reasons why union representation is now so low, the principal reasons are the long-standing impediments, some legal and some illegal, which American employers and their political allies have managed to impose as preconditions of union representation. Fortunately, the means to correct that condition and revive the collective bargaining process already exists. No additional legislation is required, for the corrective change is already contained in unambiguous but long overlooked language in existing, but still vital, provisions of the original National Labor Relations Act that Senator Wagner introduced and guided to passage. Those provisions provide an available unionizing process, but one that hasn't been recently used. It is members only, nonmajority collective bargaining, which was a procedure that was heavily and successfully employed during the first decade following passage of the Act in 1935. In fact, it was that less-than-majority members-only means by which the steel and automobile industries were unionized. It's now needed again, and I and this book propose its reintroduction and reconfirmation.

Seventy years ago, as a young union lawyer in Dallas, Texas, following my graduation from Columbia Law School, I began my efforts to help make Senator Wagner's collective-bargaining goal come alive, especially for working people in the South and Southwest. Nineteen years later, in my new role as a professor of Law at Southern Methodist University in Dallas, I continued those efforts to advance the collective-bargaining process. When some students asked me whether I was pro-union or pro-employer I honestly replied, "neither, I'm pro-collective bargaining." Indeed, that neutral position continues to this day; and it was evidenced in my work as a labor arbitrator when I was jointly chosen by both employers and unions in more than 300 arbitration cases. Although my career, which included visiting professorships at Cornell University, the University of San Diego, and Monash University in Melbourne, Australia, and my numerous law review and book publications and also speeches, might qualify as useful continuations of my chosen goal of spreading the word about collective-bargaining, it is the implementation of the contents this book that would represent the happiest culmination of that process.

Accordingly, the most important thing that I can now do to advance that cause—not just to further the practice of collective bargaining, but to help keep that practice from becoming virtually irrelevant—is to publicize and promote the proposed long-forgotten process of non-majority collective bargaining. This will make union representation easier to achieve. That's particularly important now because several efforts in recent years to bring this issue to the Labor Board for consideration, including rule-making procedures instituted by more than a dozen large national unions, never reached the Board for decision-making because of indirect but highly effective employer opposition. The Board's General Counsel twice improperly refused to bring the issue to the Board for decision-making, and political opposition regarding confirmation of President Obama's Board appointments caused indefinite, but non-prejudicial, postponement of the rule-making consideration. Thus, the Board has yet to rule on the issue. Now—at a time when the countervailing power of a robust labor movement is needed to reverse the curse of economic inequality—we may be faced with the last realistic opportunity in foreseeable years to move significantly toward revival of a strong and healthy labor movement and a better middle-class life. This book says that time is now.

Charles J. Morris, June 2019

Table of Contents

CHAPTER 1.
AN OVERVIEW OF A RESPONSE TO A NATIONAL NEED

I. CONVENTIONAL WISDOM AND ITS CHALLENGE

In February, 2019, Justin Rashad Long, a warehouse worker at Amazon's Staten Island warehouse was summarily fired—allegedly for a safety violation, although his union claimed to the National Labor Relations Board (NLRB or Board)[1] that the real reason was his union activity, including his having publicly asserted that during the peak holiday season "Amazon required him and other workers to work 12-hour shifts five or even six times a week with few breaks."[2] Although simple due process should have provided a fair and reasonably prompt means to resolve that issue, such a process is not available in the United States except where there's a union contract. Notwithstanding statutory language in the National Labor Relations Act (NLRA or Act) that's supposed to mandate that private-sector employees have a right to union-representation,[3] the NLRB does not effectively guarantee such a right, and its records indicate that even its successful remedies for unlawful discharges usually take from one to two years.[4] It's unlikely that Justin Long's union can either obtain or win an NLRB election, for Amazon has already created the perception among affected employees that favoring a union might lead to loss of one's job, and that company's general hostility toward unions has thus far been totally successful, for "[t]here are no unionized Amazon warehouses in the United States."[5] Nevertheless, notwithstanding employer opposition, there is a reliable way for pro-union employees to obtain union representation. That is what this book is all about.

It's about rebuilding the American labor movement by reintroducing a presently available but long-forgotten procedure that could provide employees like

---

1 29 U.S.C. § 153(a).

2 See Noam Sheiber, *Amazon and Union at Odds Over Fired Worker,* N.Y. Times (March 21, 2019).

3 *See* chap. 4 *infra* at notes 7-14.

4 *See* Charles J. Morris, *A "Tale of Two Statutes Redux: Anti-Union Employment Discharges Under the NLRA and RLA, with a Solution, 40* BERKELEY J. EMP. & LAB. L. __(2019) (hereinafter *Two Statutes*).

5 *Id.*, nn 71-73.

Justin and his union colleagues with a union with whom the employer—by law—must engage in good-faith collective bargaining. This book points to a methodology that could create a strong and vital union movement in the private sector—which is an important ingredient for a healthy middle class. I assert in this book that the way to achieve that lofty objective is by reintroducing the process of *members-only non-majority collective bargaining (NMCB)*, which is an historically proven but almost forgotten unionizing procedure. Although this is a process upon which the NLRB has not yet definitively ruled, one member of that Board did correctly recognize it in an unopposed concurring opinion in a little-noticed 2016 "sleeper" case, which held that majority union representation under existing law was not a prerequisite for the right to engage in protected collective bargaining.[6] Furthermore, the last outgoing General Counsel of the Board conceded that the NMCB process was based on a "plausible"[7] interpretation of the Act. This rebuilding of organized labor is needed to help restore a strong middle class, which is an essential ingredient for a truly democratic capitalist system. It will also provide further recognition that union rights are human rights.

Although logic and a natural desire for human fulfillment should offer sufficient incentive for union decision-makers and other pertinent parties to begin initiating this members-only collective bargaining process, recent economic phenomena encourage the creation of new means and opportunities that point in that same direction. The renewal of an old form of union organizing and bargaining that's here proposed thus fits well into Jeremy Heimans's and Henry Timms's description of "new power," which they compare to "old power" concepts, emphasizing that it operates differently: "like a current, it is made by many. It is open, participatory, and peer driven. It uploads, and it distributes. Like water or electricity it's most forceful when it surges. The goal is not to hoard it but to channel it." Indeed, that's how members-only bargaining is expected to function. Heimans and Timms appropriately thus remind us to use today's peer-driven tools to channel peoples' increasing thirst to participate, stressing that individuals place a higher value on what they term the "IKEA effect" on objects and experiences that they are personally able to shape, and "[n]ew power models, at their best, reinforce

6 Member Kent Hirozawa's unopposed concurring opinion in *Children's Hospital and Research Center of Oakland*, 364 NLRB No. 114 (2016). *See* chap. *2 infra* at notes 35 & 76 and chap. 4 *infra* at notes 1, 29-32 & 113.

7 General Counsel Richard F. Griffin, Jr., letter regarding SCA Tissue North America, LLC., Case 03-CA-132930. *See* chap. 2 *infra* at note 34 & chap. 6 *infra* at notes 41 & 42.

the human instinct to cooperate rather than compete"[8]—all of which are characteristics found in the NMBC process here proposed. It provides the means for virtually all private sector employees, regardless of their economic status, to actively engage as a real partner in determining the nature and benefits that should be derived from their labor.

It is common knowledge that the American middle-class is in severe jeopardy. There is, however, a workable key which could substantially aid in its improvement, although rebuilding the labor movement is generally not considered to be that key. More likely to be considered, or proposed, are other familiar proposals, such as trickle-down relief from the lowering of high-end and corporate taxes, taxing high-end wealth, improving educational and health programs, hoped-for resurgence of American manufacturing, elimination of poverty by providing low-earners with modest basic income, or the creation of new and fanciful forms of employee organization, or the fanciful suggestion that corporate executives should voluntarily share the wealth with their employees. Yet, none of these approaches reach the underlying problem. Insufficient middle-class income cannot be solved by any of these or other commonly proposed means, or even by increasing the gross number of jobs. Simply put, a realistically available solution must produce substantially higher wages for the working class. This is the critical ingredient for true success in improving middle-class income—in fact it's an absolute requirement. And only a strong labor movement can make that happen. While this may seem to many as an unpopular choice, acceptance should come with success. But inasmuch as organized labor is presently so exceedingly weak, how can any union-related solution be the missing key? Or how can weak unions become strong unions? Those are the questions which this book seeks to answer.

I am pleased to confirm that the previously noted NMCB is that appropriate key and that it can be made reasonably available. It's a key that can significantly assist in rebuilding a strong and effective labor movement. It's the missing force that's needed to pump increased income into the middle class. But, as I have indicated, it's not a new key; it's actually old and remotely familiar; though it must now be treated as if it were new. What's important is that it is genuine—it's not just a pie-in-the sky proposal. And despite organized labor's current state of malaise and typical lack of courage, attaining this key is achievable. In my view, it's the only realistically available key that has any chance of

8 *See* JEREMY HEIMANS & HENRY TIMMS, NEW POWER, 2, 7, 126, & 21 (2018).

significantly boosting the national economy and thus delivering a fair share of national income to a major part of the American population.

Nevertheless, conventional wisdom would suggest the contrary. Although there are a few exceptions worth highlighting, most mainstream economists and economic journalists have not seriously considered emphasizing the labor-union potential. They may view organized labor as too old or too weak, or some might even believe too corrupt, to remake itself into a dynamic and viable national player in today's high-tech global economy; or they might simply be following the general business view that any and all union representation should be avoided.

Edwardo Porter is an interesting example. Writing for the New York Times *Economic Scene*, he first asserted that it's "fanciful" to consider "American workers' collective bargaining power, among the weakest in the rich industrialized world [as a solution for] the struggling working class;" yet more recently, in voicing a need for "the American economy to recover some of its lost dynamism" he asserted that for workers to reap a larger share of the spoils of growth, "they must claw back the bargaining power they lost." While he doesn't view that goal as impossible, he urges that it requires pushing back against a view that government should not stand in the way of corporate America's forward march,[9] whereupon, he touts Jared Bernstein's *Hamilton Project* proposal[10] which recommends a forward-looking program that—no surprise—does not include a means to rebuild the labor movement.[11]

And Oren Cass, a conservative Manhattan Institute scholar, although deemed "out of step with most conservative views," asserts that "American

9 Edward Porter, *Reviving the Working Class Without Building Walls*, N.Y. TIMES, Mar. 9, 2016. Edward Porter, *Pay Raises are Back, but Are They Here to Stay?* N.Y. TIMES, Feb. 28, 2018.

10 Jared Bernstein, *The Importance of Strong Labor Demand*, HAMILTON PROJECT OF BROOKINGS INSTITUTION (2018), in which he offers a four-part proposal to increase labor demand along with earnings and employment opportunities: "(1) reform the monetary policy framework to accommodate more monetary stimulus and reduce the risk of hitting the zero lower bound, (2) develop a Full Employment Fund to reduce labor market slack, (3) support direct job creation programs to boost labor demand, and (4) design international trade policies to safeguard aggregate demand and mitigate the negative effects of trade deficits."

11 *See Income inequality and labour income share in G20 countries: Trends, Causes* p.8, INTERNATIONAL LABOUR ORGANIZATION INTERNATIONAL MONETARY FUND, ORGANISATION FOR ECONOMIC CO-OPERATION AND DEVELOPMENT, WORLD BANK GROUP. (Prepared for the G20 Labour and Employment Ministers Meeting and Joint Meeting with the G20 Finance Ministers, Ankara, Turkey, 3-4 September 2015.)

"labor policy. . . is out of sync with a pro-work agenda. . . ." [12] He contends that "[I]f we give workers standing, if we make their productive employment an economic imperative instead of an inconvenience, the labor market can reach a healthy equilibrium."[13] To achieve this, however, he recommends a wholly utopian system of what he calls "co-ops," which—despite his strongly expressed opposition to American unions—would seem to have virtually the same authority that unions presently possess under the NLRA once they succeed in winning an employer-required election.[14] He cites, among his models, the examples of Denmark and Sweden, yet he ignores the fact that unions and collective bargaining in those countries are universally accepted and not opposed by management. Cass's harsh criticism of unions under the NLRA exposes his failure to understand the flexibility inherent in the NLRA's broadly worded collective-bargaining text,[15] which American employers and their Republican cohorts—not unions—have consistently sought to limit.[16] The following are a few additional examples of his illogical conclusions: His pointing to the hyper-adversarialism that prevails under the NLRA to the disadvantage of workers, "producing only short-term 'gains' that over time reduce workers' value and opportunities;" however, he fails to recognize that such a condition was not instigated by unions but by employers, for they sought a more narrow concept of bargainable subjects.[17] And he fancifully asserts that his proposed co-ops would be voluntary organizations, which "[u]nlike with unions, membership and dues payments

---

12 Jason Willick, *Conservatives and the Politics of Work: Interview with Oren Cass,* WALL STREET J., Nov. 24-25, 2018.

13 OREN CASS, THE ONCE AND .FUTURE WORKER: A VISION FOR THE RENEWAL OF WORK IN AMERICA, 5 (2018).

14 *See* Linden Lumber Div., Summer & Co., 190 N.L.R.B. 718 (1971), *enforcement denied sub nom.* Truck Drivers Local No. 413 v. NLRB, 487 F.2d 1099 (D.C. Cir. 1973), *rev'd sub nom.,* Linden Lumber Div., Summer & Co. v. NLRB, 419 U.S. 301 (1974).

15 Section 8(d), 129 U.S.C. describes that flexible scope: "to bargain collectively is the performance of the mutual obligation of the employer and the representative of the employees to meet at reasonable times and confer in good faith with *respect to wages, hours, and other terms and conditions of employment,* or the negotiation of an agreement, or any question arising thereunder. . . ." (Emphasis added.)

16 *See,* eg., First National Maintenance Corp. v. NLRB, 452 U.S. 666 (1981); Allied Chemical & Alkali Workers Local 1 v. Pittsburgh Plate Glass Co, 404 U.S. 157 (1971); Westinghouse Electric Corp. 150 NLRB 1574 (1965). *See generally* Charles J. Morris, *How the National Labor Relations Act was Stolen and How it can be Recovered: Taft-Hartley Revisionism and the National Labor Relations Board's Appointment Process, 33 BERKELEY J. OF EMP. & LAB. L. 1* (2012).

17 *Id.*

would always be voluntary"[18] yet—somehow—still be authoritative. He cites for an example of model apprenticeship programs, which he advocates, the experience of American building trades unions, although he complains that "these arrangements come with the baggage of an NLRA union, such as when a union at a top rated company "committed the unforgivable sin in the eyes of the union, of refusing a demand to forego secret ballot elections and permit organization via card check,"[19] which the union obviously desired for its very survival. Cass, nevertheless, cites with apparent approval the absence of union elections in Sweden and Denmark,[20] and he wholly ignores the fact that American employers, who usually oppose unions, would likely also seek to prevent co-ops from having a say in determining their workers' conditions of employment.

There is, however, one economist, Paul Krugman, who encouragingly reports that there is "a growing though incomplete consensus among economists that a key factor in wage stagnation has been workers' declining bargaining power—a decline whose roots are ultimately political."[21] He asserts that

> Technological disruption . . . isn't a new problem . . . What's new is the failure of workers to share in the fruits of that technical change. . . . The decline of unions has made a huge difference. Consider the case of trucking, which used to be a good job but now pays a third less than it did in the 1970s, with terrible working conditions. What made the difference? De-unionization was a big part of the story. . . American workers can and should be getting a much better deal than they are.[22]

They are certainly entitled to a better deal. Although it is encouraging that economists are increasingly recognizing the need to strengthen the labor sector, most of their recommendations fall short of proposing a means to achieve that objective. Collective-bargaining is required to accomplish the heavy lifting that the economy needs. With the means which this book advocates, that goal is achievable.

---

18 *Supra* note 9 at 157.

19 *Id.,* at 52-53.

20 *Id.,* at 150.

21 Paul Krugman, *Don't Blame Robots for Low Wages,* N.Y. Times (3/15/2019).

22 *Id.*

It's also encouraging that international attention is being given to finding a way to reverse or mitigate the too-common world-wide problem of income and wealth inequality. One such sought-after approach posits "that pro-equity policies, especially those that target the middle class and poor, can also be pro-growth if properly designed and implemented."[23] That's exactly the objective which should be the goal for the United States. This book attempts to point in that direction.

Now to reconfirm the identity of the missing key, i.e., the union-related answer that's been lost, or at best misunderstood even by many who actively support collective-bargaining and urge improving the plight of the middle class. For example, the *Center for American Progress* (CAP) in its 2014 report, *The Middle-Class Squeeze,*[24] accurately described what has happened to the American middle class and posited a comprehensive description of what was needed to reverse or slow that decline. However, its proposals contained only a few boilerplate clichés to define the desired role of unions in that process. Although that report noted that the steady decrease in the middle-class's share of income correlated strongly with the decline in union membership, its only proposed solution was a benign recommendation that the nation should "strengthen unions and empower workers."[25] It's thus no surprise that well-meaning groups have tended to concentrate their proposals to aid the middle-class with familiar progressive measures that don't relate directly to unions, such as that early CAP proposal of revising tax policy, extending federal unemployment insurance, raising the minimum wage, strengthening the earned income-tax credit, developing paid family and medical-leave, improving health and education programs, workforce-development plans, and rebuilding the nation's infrastructure.

In its 2016 report, however, *The Future of Worker Voice and Power,*[26] CAP evidenced an increased awareness of the potential role of organized labor in

---

23 *Income inequality and labour income share in G20 countries: Trends, Causes,* p.8, International Labour Organization International Monetary Fund, Organisation for Economic Co-operation and Development, World Bank Group. (Prepared for the G20 Labour and Employment Ministers Meeting and Joint Meeting with the G20 Finance Ministers, Ankara, Turkey, 3-4 September 2015.)

24 The Middle-Class Squeeze: A Picture of Stagnant Incomes, Rising Costs, and What We Can Do to Strengthen America's Middle Class, Center for American Progress, (Jennifer Erickson ed., 2014).

25 *Id.,* at 23. *But see generally,* Unions Make the Middle Class: Without Unions, the Middle Class Withers, Center for American Progress (David Walter & Nick Bunker eds., 2011).

26 David Madland, *The Future of Worker Voice and Power,* Center for American Progress, https://

helping to restore a strong middle-class, but it failed to propose a realistic means to reach that objective. David Madland, its author, correctly observes that achieving the goals of worker voice and power "has been largely off the table," notwithstanding that "[f]ew things are as well supported by economic research as the fact that collective voice for workers raises wages and reduces inequality . . . ."[27] Whereupon, he provides solid support for the proposition—which I share—that "a strong and growing middle class is necessary for a strong and growing economy"[28] and that "[s]trengthening worker voice is among the most important elements required to raise wages and reduce inequality."[29] To achieve that objective he asserts that "a new and better labor relations system is needed."[30] But here we part company, for in his proposed solution he wholly departs from reality. He recommends a near-utopian labor-relations system consisting of regional and industrywide collective-bargaining supported by happy employers who bargain with free-rider unions whose membership would be voluntary; and within individual establishments there would be German-type works-councils supported by happy employees—in other words, an example of pure pie-in-the-sky not unlike Cass's co-op system. Furthermore, Madland's fairytale-like proposal would require an abundance of federal regulation and a huge governmental role in both the procedural and substantive aspects of his idealized collective-bargaining process. Considering America's multifaceted business structures and eclectic corporate- and employee-relations systems, such a plan would have no chance of ever being accepted.[31]

A few other commentators—notwithstanding their abundance of skepticism—have cautiously voiced limited recognition that a resurgence of unionism might be needed to help save the middle class. For example, New York Times columnist Nicholas Kristof, who had previously "been wary of labor unions," more recently recalled that "[h]istorically the periods when union membership were highest were those when inequality was least," so he could now say: "I was wrong. At least in the private sector, we should strengthen unions, not try

---

cdn/americanprogress.org/wp-content/uploads/2016/10/0605/1753/WorkerVoice2pdf .

27 *Id.*, at 2.

28 *Id.*, at 19.

29 *Id.*, at 39.

30 *Id.*, at 40

31 For a similar well-intended proposal, *see* William E. Forbath & Brishen Rogers, *New Workers, New Labor Laws,* N.Y. Times (Op-Ed) Sept. 4, 2017 (hereinafter Forbath-Rogers).

to eviscerate them."[32] And law professors William Forbath and Brishen Rogers perceptively observe: "We can't hope to build a more equitable economy unless working people have strong organizations of their own."[33]

Another observer whose analysis seized my attention—for an obvious reason—is Thomas Geoghegan. In his book, *Only One thing Can Save Us,*[34] he first argues that what's needed is a different kind of labor movement, preferably something like German works counsels—which, I must interpose, despite their efficiency have no chance whatever of being generally accepted in the United States, as events at the Volkswagen plant in Chattanooga, Tennessee have already demonstrated.[35] But for his final proposal— which I welcome—he argues that although organized labor is "the only way to deal with the fault lines in our country's economy,"[36] to achieve that objective he advocates a system of *members-only minority-union collective-bargaining.* That naturally aroused my interest, for, as he explains, that was exactly my analysis and conclusion in my 2005 book, *The Blue Eagle at Work,*[37] which I am here and now again strongly proposing. This is the missing key to the rebuilding of the American labor movement.[38] It's a proposition that's very much alive for, as I noted at the beginning of this chapter, it quietly received, without fanfare, an endorsement in a 2016 concurring-opinion in a little-noticed NLRB decision; and it was also designated as a "plausible reading" of the Act by General Counsel Richard F. Griffin, Jr.[39] Both of those expressions will be discussed later.

---

32 Nicholas Kristof, *The Cost of a Decline in Unions,* N. Y. TIMES, Feb. 19, 2015.

33 Forbath-Rogers, *supra* note 31.

34 THOMAS GEOGHEGAN, ONLY ONE THING CAN SAVE US: WHY AMERICA NEEDS A NEW KIND OF LABOR MOVEMENT (2014) (hereinafter GEOGHEGAN). *Cf.* STANLEY ARONOWITZ, THE DEATH AND LIFE OF AMERICAN LABOR: TOWARD A NEW WORKERS MOVEMENT (2014)

35 *See infra* at note 76.

36 GEOGHEGAN *supra* note 28 at 237.

37 CHARLES J. MORRIS, THE BLUE EAGLE AT WORK: RECLAIMING DEMOCRATIC RIGHTS IN THE AMERICAN WORKPLACE (2005) (hereinafter BLUE EAGLE).

38 *See* chap. 4 *infra* for its legal basis.

39 Children's Hosp. and Research Center of Oakland, *supra* note 2, concurring opinion by Hirozawa and General Richard F. Griffin, Jr., letter regarding SCA Tissue North America, LLC., Case 03-CA-132930. See *supra* at note 3 and chap. 4 *infra* at notes 29-32 & 113.

II. WHAT THE MIDDLE CLASS AND ORGANIZED LABOR JOINTLY NEED

Why has organized labor's present-day impotence, as well as its hidden potential, not been more adequately addressed by the economics community? The answer to that question, at least in part, is because professional economists who may assume they know so much about the economy generally know so little about the real content of American labor law and its possibilities. As a knowledgeable source recently observed: "Economists must think broader—or risk becoming irrelevant."[40] And, regrettably, even many top union leaders (but with some notable exceptions), have been slow to recognize and advocate available legal opportunities under the existing Act,[41] although they have willingly spent large amounts of money and energy seeking unobtainable legislative agendas, such as *The Employee Free Choice Act (EFCA).*[42]

With popular culture viewing unions as only minor movers in the national economy, organized labor, despite its ability to exercise considerable political clout, has become the forgotten player on the economic stage, no longer deemed relevant to the development of the nation's long-term fiscal problems. As this book will demonstrate, however, one need not shy away from acknowledging the positive economic role that unions can play in helping to rebuild the middle class, for—notwithstanding conventional wisdom to the contrary—a robust labor movement that a healthy economy requires is a goal within reach. In fact, it may be the only politically achievable goal that has any chance of bringing about adequate improvement in middle-class income.

Would it make any difference to the economy if unions were to remain weak? With the problems that unions bring to the economic table, why should we look to organized labor for a way to help mitigate the plight of the middle class? Because there's no alternative available. Furthermore, increased union participation will be healthy for the economy and our democratic values. There are, of course, additional valid reasons to support a strong labor movement,[43]

---

40 Mohamed El-Erian, *Economists must think broader—or risk becoming irrelevant,* GUARDIAN (U.S. edition) March11, 2019.

41 *See* e.g., Charles J. Morris, *Undercutting Linden Lumber: How a Union Can Achieve Majority-Status Bargaining without an Election,* 35 HOFSTRA LAB. & EMPL. L. J. 1 2017) (hereinafter Morris *Linden*).

42 35 H.R. 1409, S. 560, 111th Cong. (2009). *See* Jon O. Shimabukuro, Cong. Research Serv. RS21887, *The Employee Free Choice Act,* (2011).

43 *See e.g.,* notes 57-59 *infra* and chap. 2 *infra* at note 42.

but history and international comparisons tell us that there's no other available mechanism that can offer a credible means to address the insufficiency of middle-class *income*, which is the heart of the problem.[44] What the middle-class needs most is more *earning* power. Although the "trickle-down" theory has been consistently disproved by its past failings, even typical progressive proposals for economic and political solutions—such as those recommended by such organizations as the Center for American Progress noted above[45]—fail to adequately address the underlying problem of the inadequacy of employee earnings.

Twentieth-century history and the example of industries under the Railway Labor Act (RLA)[46]—the other national labor statute that regulates labor relations on the airlines and railroads—plus the success of advanced industrialized democracies elsewhere, support the proposition that a robust labor movement would provide major support for the type of economic stimulus that's essential for reducing economic inequality.

A. A Lesson from History

Historical evidence that verifies the importance of a strong labor movement in a healthy democratic capitalist economy is illustrated by the role labor unions played during the several decades following World War II, which created an American middle class that was universally admired. As labor historian Dorothy Sue Cobble records, "[t]he newfound bargaining power of workers in the post-World War II decades was certainly among the factors contributing

44 For a description of the magnitude of the nation's economic inequality, which continues, see the following:

> The top 10 percent of families own 75.3 percent of the nation's wealth—a percentage that has been steadily rising—whereas the bottom half of families own only 1.1 percent and the families in between those two groups own 24.6 percent. Federal Reserve *Survey of Consumer Finances* report for 2013.
>
> Gains may be finally trickling down to those at the bottom of the ladder. But the numbers still offer a lopsided picture, with a gargantuan share of income rising to the top. While the bottom fifth of households increased their share of the nation's income, by the census's definition, to 3.4 percent from 3.3 percent, the richest 5 percent kept 21.8 percent of the pie, the same as in 2014." Edward Porter, *America's Inequality Problem: Real Income Gains Are Brief and Hard to Find*, N.Y. Times Sept. 13, 2016.
>
> Despite last year's gains, the bottom 60 percent of households took a smaller share of the income pie than four decades ago. The bottom 20 percent took in only 3.4 percent of all income — compared with 5.6 percent in the mid-1970s. The richest 5 percent of Americans, by contrast, have done much better for themselves — taking in about 22 percent of the nation's income, 6 percentage points more than they did in 1975." Eduardo Porter, *America's Inequality Problem: Real Income Gains Are Brief and Hard to Find*, N.Y. Times Sept. 13, 2016.

45 *See supra* at note 20.

46 45 U.S.C. §§ 151-88.

to the economic prosperity and the dramatic decline in economic stratification during the 'long New Deal,' from the 1940s to the 1970s."[47] During that period, collectively-bargained wages and other labor-related economic benefits set the pattern for labor-relations generally, not just for unionized employees but also for employees in many nonunion companies that routinely increased wages whenever they were raised in comparable or competing union establishments.[48]

Those were the days when the most common means for a nonunion company to remain union-free was by granting "tandem" or "copy-cat" benefits roughly comparable to union benefits, which meant that as compensations increased at major union establishments, they tended likewise to increase at other workplaces, i.e., nonunion establishments.[49] In that extended post-war period, wage-competition thus produced higher wages and other improved employee benefits—a phenomenon that contrasts sadly with recent and current practices of companies under NLRA jurisdiction. Today, wage-competition too often doesn't mean competition to retain employees but rather means a race to the bottom to suppress wages, which naturally has an adverse effect on middle-class income. To remain union-free today, many employers resort to discouraging union-organizing by employing aggressive scare tactics, both legal and illegal.[50]

In the national search for ways to counteract income inequality, the positive role that unions and collective bargaining played following World War II are rarely presented as models—which is understandable inasmuch as union membership in recent years has been in free-fall. Only 6.4 percent of the nation's private-sector non-supervisory employees are currently union members,[51] whereas

47 Dorothy Sue Cobble, *The Intellectual Origins of an Institutional Revolution,* 26 A.B.A. J. Lab. & Emp. L. 201, 204 (2011).

48 For a perceptive portrayal of that union-non-union interplay, see the following description by Joseph W. Garbarino, *Income Policy and Income Behavior,* in Employment and the Labor Market 56, 81 (Arthur M. Ross ed. 1965):

> The negotiated settlements cover only the minority of the labor force organized in unions, but the realities of industrial relations require that similar adjustments be granted to other employees—for such reasons as a desire to be equitable, a need to maintain morale and efficiency, or a desire to discourage the spread of organization. In industries in which manual workers are organized, "tandem" increases to unorganized workers are likely to be immediate, but even the rare industries that are largely unorganized dare not tempt fate and the union organizer by getting very far out of step, although they may delay getting into step.

49 *Id.*

50 *See infra* at notes 63 & 85.

51 Bureau of Labor Statistics, *Economic Release,* Jan. 18, 2019.

in the post-war years of the 1950s and '60s almost a third of the workforce was unionized.[52] It's a paradox that while current union membership is at a low point, the nation's support of labor unions has been steadily rising. As a recent Gallup Poll reports, "61 percent of adults say they approve of labor unions."[53]

Regardless of present facts and opinion regarding labor unions, the major role that unions played in creating and implementing strong middle-class income during the post-World War II years is beyond question.

B. A Lesson from the Railway Labor Act.

Although the view that unions now play only a minor role in the American economy is generally accurate, it overlooks one area in American life where the opposite is true. Unlike the absence of union presence in most of the private sector, there is one area of that sector where union membership is high and unions are strong, i.e., in the airlines and railroads,[54] where labor relations are governed by the Railway Labor Act, an entirely different statute..[55] Unlike most of the private sector, union density under that statute is relatively high.

As previously described, general union density in the private sector in the United States has been steadily declining.[56] Some of that decline is due to the fact that most unions have been unable to regenerate new members sufficiently to make up—even partially—for losses caused by a multiplicity of economic forces. One might assume, as many do, that the primary reason for that organizational failure is that most American workers prefer to retain their nonunion status and have little desire for union representation, whatever their reason. If this were an accurate assessment of employee attitudes, one would expect to find a similar decline in union membership throughout the private sector. That is not the case, however, for the record of both union density and successful union organizing in the two industries covered by the RLA remains exceedingly high.

52 Working Life, *Union Membership: Overall* (1948-2004); Union membership in 1954 was 35 percent. *Labor Unions in the United States,* Wikipedia (2017).

53 Jaclyn Diaz, *Can Unions Capitalize on Increasing Approval Rating?,* BNA Daily Lab. Rep., 9/01/2017, 169 DLR 17.

54 *See infra* at notes 49-53.

55 The Railway Labor Act, *supra* note 46.

56 *See* notes 44-45 *supra..*

The National Mediation Board (NMB),[57] the federal agency under the RLA that administers the union representational process and assists the parties in collective bargaining with mediation and arbitration, reports that for years 2011-2012 the combined union density for both railroads and airlines was 62 percent[58]—a far cry from the low density for the private sector as a whole. It further reports that in 2012 among the 146 air carriers with a total of 540,000 employees, union density was 56 percent,[59] and that among the nation's 567 railroads with a total of 176,000 employees, union density in 2011 was 83 percent.[60] There's no reason to believe that those percentages have changed adversely since that time.

Thus, despite the fact that profitability in the airline industry has been elusive and highly irregular,[61] union membership and collective bargaining in that industry are well established and ever-growing, which presents a striking example of how strong union representation translates into higher wages. Based on information supplied by the U.S. Bureau of Transportation Statistics, "compensation in the airline industry remains relative[ly] high and a sizable union wage premium continues to exist."[62] In fact "average compensation for airline employees since 2000 has grown at an annual rate of 4.5 percent, as compared with the civilian workforce of 2.8 percent.[63]

Airline labor relations also provides revealing examples of what employee-life is like in a union atmosphere; these are conditions which today merit highlighting because union workplaces have become relatively rare. During the

57 45 U.S.C. §§ 154-55.

58 NMB response to Freedom of Information Act (FOIA) request, file No. F-1656, March 23, 2015. "This percentage is calculated as 56% of the airline employees plus 83% of the railroad employees divided by the total number of employees." For slightly lower estimates, *see* David Walsh, *Where Have They Landed? Observations On U.S. Airline Labor Relations,* 21 PERSPECTIVES ON WORK (LERA) 18, 19 (2017), (hereinafter Walsh) where the authors estimated that in 2016 39.2 percent of air transportation workers were union members, and 41.3 percent enjoyed union representation, drawing from data supplied by Barry T. Hirsch & David A. MacPherson, eds, *Union Membership and Coverage Database from the CPS.* www.unionstats.con (hereinafter Hirsch & MacPherson)

59 *Id.,* from "Airlines for America, formerly The Air Transport Association."

60 *Id.* "This figure is calculated as the total of class 1, other local or small railroads based on the average number of craft and classes per category of railroad times the number of railroads in the respective category. The average of craft and classes is based on an average of 7 Class 1 and 2 small or local railroads. The total of Class 1 is 196 (28 times 7) and local railroads is 1,078 (539 times 2). Local railroads are all class 2, 3 and 4 carriers."

61 Walsh, *supra* note 58 at 18.

62 *Id.*, at 21, *citing* Hirsch & MacPherson, *supra* note 585.

63 *Id., citing* U.S. Bureau of Labor Statistics.

decades following World War II, finding a unionized company to serve as a model of healthy labor relations, where both the employing company and the employees visibly benefited from that relationship, was relatively easy, for such workplaces were common. But today there are fewer such workplaces and most must compete with nonunion companies. It is thus easier today to find outstanding examples of model labor relations under the RLA where most employees are covered by union agreements.[64] This is not to say, however, that labor relations always runs smoothly under that statute, for its early history contained some extreme examples of poor employment relations.[65] Currently, however, the airline industry can boast of numerous examples of carriers where mutual benefits for both management and unionized employees are commonplace. My favorite example of such a carrier is Southwest Airlines. That company serves well as a model of what can be achieved in a union environment. Joe Harris, Southwest's now retired labor-relations attorney—whom I well remember from my days as an active labor arbitrator when I decided several grievance cases at Southwest—briefly recorded the inside story of the kind of labor relations to which I hope this book will help point the way. Here are excerpts from what he wrote:

> Often, when people would learn that I represented Southwest Airlines, they would ask, "How does Southwest manage to remain non-Union?" I would chuckle and explain that, in fact, Southwest is the most heavily unionized airline in the industry. (We currently have ten collective bargaining agreements covering 85% of our approximate 34,000 Employees.
>
> But why was I so often asked this question? I believe it is because there has been so little labor strife at Southwest. But what is the explanation for such a remarkable labor relations history? I believe it is attributable to two factors: (1) commitment to positive labor relations at the highest level of Leadership; and (2) our positive Employee Culture. . . . Lamar Muse, the first operating CEO and President of Southwest, . . . expressed the opinion. . . that if Unions were voted in by our Employees, we could build and manage successful relations with them. Herb Kelleher, recently retired [now deceased][66] Chairman of the Board at Southwest, believed that it was important for our

64 *See supra* at notes 51-55.

65 *See* Jody Hoffer Gittell, The Southwest Airlines Way: Using the Power of Relationships to Achieve High Performance, 165-82 (2003).

66 Died on Jan. 3, 2019.

> employees to have a voice. He also strongly believed that we should not be adversaries, but rather partners, with any labor organization representing our employees.

***

> At Southwest, our Employees come first; our Customers come second; and our stockholders come third. The rationale is pretty simple. If we treat our Employees right, they're going to treat our Customers right. If our Customer are treated right, they will come back and our stockholders will benefit. Moreover, if we are committed to the proposition that we are going to treat our Employees right, then it follows *a fortiori* that we should treat the labor organizations that represent them no differently. . . . In summary, we value the relationship we have with our Employees and the labor organizations that represent them. We believe that this relationship has contributed to the remarkable success of Southwest Airlines. [67]

Need I say more? I submit Southwest Airlines as a model of what companies under the NLRA can achieve after the American labor movement becomes strong again.

C. A Lesson from Abroad

Although the foregoing historical and RLA comparisons are illustrative of the positive role that a strong union presence can play in lessening income inequality, additional proof of that role can also be found in other advanced democratic countries. It's the *direct effect* on income distribution which strong labor movements have had in such countries as France, Germany, the Netherlands, and all of the Scandinavian countries, and also Australia, to name a few where income inequality is much less than it is in the United States. These countries are living examples of the macro effect which a strong union presence has on the distribution of income among their populations.

---

67 Joe Harris, Labor Relations at Southwest Airlines, Aug. 2008, http://www.blogsouthwest.com/labor-relations-southwest-airlines/ (last accessed 6/13/15). *See also* David Macaray, *The Secret of Southwest Airlines*, April 1, 2010, http://www.counterpunch.org/2010/04/01/the-secret-of-Southwest-Airlines/ (last accessed 6/20/2013).

It's not my purpose to speculate here as to the kinds of unionization that best contribute to a reduction in economic inequality, for the union structures in those other countries differ considerably from each other. It suffices to simply point to the economic role that strong unions play in these other advanced industrial democracies, for that role adds further evidence of what strong unions could achieve here in America. A comprehensive study conducted by the International Monetary Fund in 2015 is, however, noteworthy.[68] It expressly concluded that "where unions are strong, firms tend to engage in consultations with worker representatives allowing them to have some influence over the size and structure of top executive compensation."[69] That study's findings "suggest that the weakening of unions contribute[s] to the rise of top earners' income shares and less redistribution, and eroding minimum wages increase[s] overall inequality considerably."[70]

III. THE STATE OF THE UNIONS

So why is union membership in the United States now so low? What caused this decline? Proffered reasons typically include some combination of the following: Intense employer opposition to unions expressed through both legal and illegal means—which Steven Greenhouse, an expert labor observer. contends "is by far the leading factor behind labor's decline."[71] There's also the major factors of exporting jobs to low-wage countries abroad, substantial down-sizing and robotizing of unionized heavy industry, plus changes in patterns of employment and increased reliance on temporary, contract, and gig or platform labor. Furthermore, there are fewer employees today who are directly familiar with unions or who want to become union members.

68 60 Florence Jaumotte & Carolina Osorio Bultroni, *Inequality and Labor Market Institutions,* 8 INTERNATIONAL MONETARY FUND RESEARCH DEPARTMENT (2015).

69 *Id.*, at 8.

70 *Id.*, at 27.

71 SEVEN GREENHOUSE, THE BIG SQUEEZE: TOUGH TIMES FOR THE AMERICAN WORKER, 296 (2008). *See also* John Schmitt & Ben Zipperer, *Dropping the Ax: Illegal Firings During Union Election Campaigns,1951-2007,* CENTER FOR ECONOMIC AND POLICY RESEARCH (2009), ("Our findings provide significant support for the view that an important part of the decline in private-sector unionization rates . . . is that aggressive—even illegal—employer behavior has undermined the ability of workers to create unions at their work places." p. 1). *See also* chap. 2 *infra* at note 14.

While all of those reasons are in varying degrees correct, they fail to acknowledge another major factor, which is that most established labor unions—though with some notable exceptions[72]—have failed to sufficiently engage in efforts to organize at traditionally nonunion companies and industries. That failure has been the result not only of lack of incentive, but also because union organizing has become highly expensive, a factor caused mostly by the intense and often massive anti-union opposition that employers typically mount to remain union-free.

Nevertheless, as this book will demonstrate, the lofty goal of unions again achieving substantial membership gains is conceivable because the National Labor Relations Act contains a rich source of long-forgotten union power and authority that can still be made available—though belatedly—to restart organized labor's once-powerful economic engine. By their past reliance on traditional organizational methods, unions failed to reach the success needed to return collective bargaining to anywhere near the role it played during several decades following World War II. A different and more direct approach to organizing is therefore in order. Although some union leaders have been outspoken in recognizing this problem, the problem remains. For example, Bob Martinez, president of the Machinists Union (IAM) warned in 2016—but to no avail—that "The way we have been organizing is based on a model that is 30 years old. We must be bold enough and confident enough to come up with *new organizing strategies*."[73] Which was reminiscent of AFL-CIO President Richard Trumka's acknowledgement a few years earlier that the "basic system of workplace regulation is failing [, therefore] the labor movement must embrace *new models of representation* that exist outside of traditional unionism,"[74] However, such strategies and new models have yet to be adopted. Accordingly, it was no surprise when the IAM lost its critical 2017 election at the Boeing plant in Charleston, North Carolina,[75] nor was it a surprise when three other major union elections were also lost

72 *E.g.*, Service Employees International Union (SEIU); International Brotherhood of Teamsters (Teamsters); United Steel, Paper and Forestry, Rubber, Manufacturing, Energy, Allied Industrial and Service Workers International Union (Steel Workers); and United Automobile, Aerospace and Agricultural Implement Workers of America (UAW).

73 *See* Tyrone Richardson, *Machinists Union Leaders Overhaul Spending, Organizing*, BNA Daily Lab. Rep. 172 DLR. A-12 (9/6/16). Emphasis added.

74 Michael Bologna, *Trumka Calls on Labor Movement to Adapt to New Models of Representation*, BNA Daily Lab. Rep., 45 DLR. A-12, 3/7/2013 (hereinafter Bologna). Emphasis added.

75 Julie Johnson & Josh Eidelson, *Boeing's South Carolina Mechanics Reject Union in Blow to Labor*, BNA Daily Lab. Rep. 33 DLR. A-9 (2/16/17)

in other Southern "right-to-work" (RTW) states: by the United Automobile Workers (UAW) at the Volkswagen plant in Chattanooga, Tennessee,[76] and at the Nissan plant in Canton, Mississippi,[77] and by the Steel Workers Union (USWA) at the Kumho Tire plant in Macon, Georgia.[78] Such losses need not continue. This book is designed to aid in reversing the downward trend in union representation and influence which those losses typified.

Now a brief word about the organization of this book's remaining chapters. Chapter 2 spells out the general nature of the non-majority collective-bargaining process, and Chapter 3 provides a working description of that process plus many of its variations. These are presented at that early stage because some readers before confronting technical legal materials might wish to learn just how members-only organizing and bargaining will be expected to function. It is Chapter 4, however, that contains the basic treatment of known legal issues with appropriate legal analyses that provide not only pertinent statutory text and intensive legal evaluation, but also supporting legislative history plus post-enactment legal history. Chapter 5 reviews the relationship of relevant human-rights concepts in American labor law and corresponding obligations under international compacts to which the United States is a party. Chapter 6 reviews past efforts to obtain Board confirmation and recommends several validation processes, including various judicial methods, to implement the book's propose. The Appendix depicts prior unsuccessful efforts to bring non-majority collective-bargaining to the Board's attention and notes the common objections that have been raised against this concept together with the comprehensive legal and fact-based refutations that demonstrate the invalidity of those objections.

---

76 *See* Ben Penn, UAW Files Objections Over VW Election With NLRB, Alleges Third-Party Coercion, BNA DAILY LAB. REP. 35 DLR. AA-1 (2/21/14)

77 *See* Brent Snavely, *Where UAW goes now after rejection by Nissan workers in the South*, DETROIT FREE PRESS (8/5/17). See chap. 2 *infra* at note 32

78 *See* Jaclyn Diaz, *Kumho Tire Workers Reject Steelworker Representation*, DAILY LAB. REP. 198 DLR. 10 (10/16/17).

CHAPTER 2.
AN INTRODUCTION TO NON-MAJORITY COLLECTIVE BARGAINING

I. THE FORECAST

It's now time to formally introduce the "*organizing strategy*" and "*representational model*" that union leaders have long sought. That model is the elusive "key" that was inquired about in the opening chapter, which I am proposing in this book. It's the proven concept of *non-majority collective-bargaining (NMCB)* that was first elucidated in my previously noted 2005 book, *The Blue Eagle at Work.*[1] As this book shall explain later in detail, collective bargaining is a basic right which the Supreme Court in its initial review of the National Labor Relations Act (NLRA or Act) labeled "a fundamental right."[2] Among the NMCB features, the legal aspects of which are described in Chapter 4, is the historical fact that the Act's unambiguous statutory "guarantee" of collective bargaining does not always require employees to be part of a majority in an appropriate bargaining unit. This is not a recent observation. It's an established historical fact that during the first decade following passage of the Act in 1935 non-majority members-only collective bargaining was not only commonly recognized,[3] it was widely practiced.[4] However, inasmuch as that hasn't been the practice since that time, it must now be re-validated by the NLRB and/or the judiciary. This minority-union process has a critical role to play in rebuilding the American labor movement.

Had this NMCB concept been in effect when the four lost elections referenced in the preceding chapter[5] were held in three Southern "right-to-work"

1 Charles J. Morris, The Blue Eagle At Work: Reclaiming Democratic Rights in the American Workplace (2005) (hereinafter Blue Eagle).

2 NLRB v. Jones & Laughlin Steel Corp., 301 U.S. 1, 33 (1937).

3 E. G. Latham, *Legislative Purpose and Administrative Policy under the National Labor Relations Act,* 4 Geo. Wash. L. Rev. 433, 453-54 & n. 65 (1936).

4 *See infra* at notes 114-117.

5 See chap.1 *supra* at notes 75-78.

(RTW) states, it's quite possible that those elections would not have been conducted. It's likely instead that at least some—and possibly a majority—of the employees at those plants would have already been organized with bargaining rights obtained the same way that the United Automobile Workers (UAW) in the late 1930s organized General Motors and Chrysler and how the early Steel Workers Union (USWA) organized U.S. Steel. All of that crucial unionization was achieved with minority-union collective-bargaining and members-only contracts, as will be described later in this chapter and in Chapter 4.

It's a sad fact, however, that by virtue of those four above lost elections, the several hundred employees who voted for union representation"[6]—like other disappointed pro-union voters in other lost elections—were being denied a basic human right, i.e., their right to voluntarily belong to a labor union and engage in collective bargaining, which is a right not only under the NLRA itself—where it's only partially enforced—it's also a right under two international compacts to which the United States is a party.[7] In the aforesaid elections, by denying hundreds of minority union employees their right to union representation, the non-union voters were effectively discriminating against their pro-union colleagues.

Although organized labor should experience a resurgence in membership as a result of the proposed NMCB process, that will not fully replicate the high wages that prevailed when the American manufacturing sector was strong; nevertheless it will make a substantial difference. Despite large-scale shrinkage in domestic manufacturing employment of which certain work, including some highly mechanized jobs, are now returning or being recreated—there are millions of existing underpaid service-sector jobs, such as in food service, health care, retail sales, and warehousing, which require skills comparable to that of those millions of ordinary assembly-line workers who during the last century

---

6 *Id.*

7 The United States is a party to two international compacts which support the right of all employees to freedom of association, including the right to belong to a trade union and to bargain collectively: INTERNATIONAL COVENANT ON CIVIL AND POLITICAL RIGHTS, S. Exec. Doc. E, 95-2 (1978), 999 U.N.T.S. 171 (adopted in 1966, entered Into force in 1976, ratified by U.S. in 1992), and Arts.1, 2, & 22; 42 U.S.C. §1983 (2012); INTERNATIONAL LABOUR ORGANIZATION DECLARATION ON FUNDAMENTAL PRINCIPLES AND RIGHTS AT WORK, International Labour Conf., 86th Sess. (June 1998); reprinted in 144 CONG. REC. S6909-10 (daily ed. June 23, 1998). *See also* Charles J. Morris, *Jack Pemberton Lecture, Collective Rights as Human Rights: Fulfilling Senator Wagner's Promise of Democracy in the Workplace—The Blue Eagle Can Fly Again*, 39 U.S.F. L. REV. 701 (2005) ("Collective rights are human rights because in the economies of today a meaningful exercise of democratic freedom necessarily includes the right of individuals to join with others in a common effort to achieve a lawful goal." *Id.*, at 701). *See generally* JAMES A. GROSS, A SHAMEFUL BUSINESS: THE CASE FOR HUMAN RIGHTS IN THE AMERICAN WORKPLACE (2010). For full treatment of this issue, *see* chap. 5 *infra.*

were able to enter a lower but comfortable level of the middle class because they were represented by unions. There's no compelling reason why today's semi-skilled jobs in the service-sector would not under this newly rediscovered NMCB system likewise yield wages, adjusted for inflation, that would be roughly comparable to the decent union wages of semi-skilled assembly-line workers of earlier years. As a consequence, more union-represented employees, especially service-sector workers, could eventually become secure lower echelon members of the American middle class. That achievement may require robust but lawful economic action by their unions, however, but that's the way democratic collective bargaining works. And if we add to this mix the potential power of additional highly skilled new union employees working in robotized manufacturing and cyberspace industries, plus other employees who want but have been unable to obtain onion representation,[8] a strong labor movement should result.

II. ORGANIZED LABOR AS A COUNTERVAILING POWER

This nation now needs what was once recognized as the countervailing power of such a strong labor movement. Such a development could once again produce an economic impact similar to what economist John Kenneth Galbraith described in the early years following World War II when he wrote that "[t]he operation of countervailing power is to be seen with the greatest clarity in the labor market where it is . . . most fully developed."[9] He contended that the reason the strongest unions at that time were to be found in industries "where markets are served by strong corporations''[10] was because the repressive conduct of those corporations toward their employees "made it necessary for workers to develop the protection of countervailing power,"[11] which gave them the opportunity to "share in the fruits of the corporation's market power."[12] He concluded that "as an explanation

8 *And see* chap. 1 *supra* at 71 and chap 4 *infra* at note 14.

9 John Kenneth Galbraith, American Capitalism: The Concept of Countervailing Power 114 (1956 ed.).

10 *Id,*. at 115.

11 *Id.*

12 *Id.*

of the incidence of trade-union strength in the American economy, the *theory of countervailing power* clearly fits the broad contours of experience."[13]

Although the current exploitation of workers by nonunion employers may bear only slight resemblance to the repression to which Galbraith referred, its main difference is in the fear-generated control which many employers now exert to prevent their employees from experiencing union representation and collective bargaining.[14] It's my hope, however, that such a degree of control will eventually be lessened after workers succeed in unionizing widely, particularly in accordance with this book's proposal. If and when large-scale organizing and collective-bargaining do occur, unions should once again be able to exert a significant measure of the type of countervailing power that Professor Galbraith described, which is what the economy needs.

Such power would thus become a critical means for increasing middle-class income. The long-term impact of America's widening income inequality has been well documented. Construing what that data shows, Nobel economist Joseph E. Stiglitz points out that "America has the distinction of being the most unequal of the advanced countries."[15] And he has opined that "our middle class is too weak to support the consumer spending that has historically driven our economic growth."[16] Accepting that deduction, that income inequality and its consequences seriously threaten the nation's economic future, and also recognizing that such a condition is accompanied by political and social consequences that are innately anti-democratic and even a violation of internationally recognized, but rarely enforced, rights to which the United States is obligated,[17] it is my contention that the program which this book recommends would contribute

---

13 *Id.* at 116. Emphasis added.

14 As Professor James Brudney accurately observes, "[t]here is powerful evidence that the American workplace today features widespread employer practices of lawful and unlawful resistance to unionization." James J. Brudney, *Isolated and Politicized, the NLRB's Uncertain Future,* 26 COMP. LAB. L. & POL'Y J. 221, 225, & n. 17 (2005). *See also* Anne Marie Lofaso, *The Persistence of Union Repression in an Era of Recognition,* 62 ME. L. REV. 199 (2010); Kate Bronfenbrenner, *No Holds Barred: The Intensification of Employer Opposition to Organizing,* ECONOMIC POLICY INSTITUTE AND AMERICAN RIGHTS AT WORK EDUCATION FUND (2009).

15 Joseph E. Stiglitz, interview by Farakeed Zakaria on CNN TV, Mar. 21, 2019. *See generally* JOSEPH E. STIGLITZ, PEOPLE, POWER, AND PROFIT: PROGRESSIVE CAPITALISM FOR AN AGE OF DISCONTENT (2019).

16 Joseph E. Stiglitz, *Inequality is Holding Back the Recovery,* N.Y. TIMES (Op-Ed) Jan. 19, 2013.

17 *See* chap. 5 *infra.*

significantly to a more effective enforcement of the NLRA and hence to a reawakening of organized labor with a resulting positive effect on the national economy.

If a stronger labor movement with ensuing higher wages and other benefits eventually develops, American inequality will be substantially reduced and the middle class will have become a source of consumer-spending that Professor Stiglitz found missing.

III. THE *BLUE EAGLE* AND LABOR'S NEED

As Thomas Geoghegan recognized in the preceding chapter, the specific key to achieving a strong labor movement was to be found in my earlier book, *The Blue Eagle at Work: Reclaiming Democratic Rights in the American Workplace.*[18] That book derived its name from the *Blue Eagle* icon that symbolized compliance with New Deal regulations, which included union recognition and collective-bargaining and also embraced members-only minority-union bargaining.[19] Indeed, that *Blue Eagle* is almost ready to land as an integral part of the American labor movement. Although the United States Chamber of Commerce presciently advised that "*The Blue Eagle Has Landed,*"[20] it hasn't landed yet, but it can soon be ready to land. A principal feature of labor's resurgence will be the availability of a different and alternative method of organizing and bargaining collectively from which unions may choose and still achieve traditional majority-exclusive unionism. This should be a welcome change, because the nature of work itself has changed and traditional methods of union-organizing have failed to adequately respond to the needs and desires of the majority of workers who would eagerly unionize if the process were easier.

This upcoming effort at large-scale unionization will represent a restoration of a procedure that was commonly employed during the first decade following passage of the NLRA in 1935. And—believe it or not—the means of this renewal and its timing can rely heavily on an approach to interpreting statutory text that applies a teaching of the late Justice Antonin Scalia—but not his political

18 *Supra* note 1.

19 *Id.*, at chap. 1

20 *The Blue Eagle Has Landed: The Paradigm Shift from Majority Rule to Members-Only Representation,* U.S. Chamber of Commerce (2014). See appendix *infra* at notes 103-107 and related text.

philosophy. In fact, such reliance will be based not only on that specific teaching, but also on his actual statutory reading in a case where he employed that same approach in interpreting another provision of the NLRA.[21]

The timing of this revival of American unionism is especially appropriate in view of the coinciding of several phenomena: to wit, the abysmal state of union membership, the endemic nature of employer opposition to unions,[22] and the heated political atmosphere that prevails before and after the 2020 national elections in which the matter of income inequality is and will be a frontal matter of concern. And inasmuch as the role and condition of organized labor should be of national interest, the issue of the kinds of persons who ought to be selected for appointment to the NLRB should be a major subject for consideration by Presidential and Congressional candidates.

The union representational process here proposed will appreciably change some of the ways in which workers organize and deal with their employer. It will be at least an alternative process. That process is usually labeled either *members-only minority-union collective bargaining* or *non-majority collective bargaining.* Both designations are used in this book, together with the acronym of the latter designation: NMCB. This heretofore unfamiliar process should be especially welcomed by workers who crave a more accessible kind of union representation and one that can better cope with their current economic and employment conditions. Many such workers have during the last several years been publicly calling for a means to improve their wages and working conditions. And sizeable numbers of them—including many who are employed, partially employed, and unemployed—have frequently assembled publicly and demonstrated in groups—that activity being their only means of visibly protesting in favor of improvements in their workplaces.[23]

The widespread scope of these protests can be captured by a sampling of media-headlines that accompanied some of the stories of those frustrated non-union workers who were attempting to bring their inferior wages and working condition to the attention of both their employers and the public. To illustrate that prevailing need, here's a sampling of those headlines: *Nonunion Wal-Mart*

21 *See* NLRB v. Kentucky River Community Care, Inc., 325 U.S. 706 (2001), discussed in chap. 4 *infra* at note 37.

22 *See* note 14 supra and chap. 1 *infra* at note 71.

23 *E.g., see* some of those protests recorded at notes 24-28 *infra.*

Workers Launch Protest In Four States Over Pay, Working Conditions;[24] *Fast Food, Retail Strikes Erupt in 60 Cities;*[25] *Low-Wage Workers' Push for Higher Pay;*[26] *SEIU Stages Worker Hunger Strike at 14 Airports;*[27]and *Retail Stores: Black Friday: Wal-Mart Workers Targeting Food Industry.*[28] None or very few of those protests, or hundreds more of a similar nature, were long-term successful—nor could they be—because under present law the targeted employers had no legal obligation to bargain with the protesters or their representatives—which would not have been the case had the NMCB program been in effect.

Although the NMCB program when adopted will greatly benefit low-wage earners—particularly those in such service-related industries as retail sales, warehousing, food-service, and hotel and office-building maintenance—it will also have a considerable and positive impact in areas involving better-paying jobs, particularly where special problems exist, such as in nonunion manufacturing in right-to-work (RTW) states and in the building and construction industry in most states. And digital industry workers are also among the union needy who will benefit, as we were reminded by a recent New York Times op-ed headline.[29]

IV. THE NATURE OF MEMBERS-ONLY COLLECTIVE BARGAINING—A PRELIMINARY VIEW

Organizing and bargaining will be easier under NMCB because union-recognition will be required at the pre-majority stage without the need of an election, which will be especially significant in RTW states. Professor Catherine Fisk has perceptively pointed out that such minority-union bargaining would generally

> reduce the necessity for, and acrimony of, organizing campaigns. It would allow employees who wish to form unions to bargain collectively to do so without imposing collective representation on co-workers who do not favor it. It would

24 BNA Daily Lab. Rep., 195-DLR A-11,10/09/12.,

25 BNA Daily Lab. Rep., Aug. 29, 2013.

26 BNA Daily Lab. Rep., Aug. 30, 2013.

27 BNA Daily Lab. Rep., Nov. 24, 2015.

28 *Id.*

29 Jason Schrier, *Video Game Makers Need Unions,* N.Y. Times (April 5, 2019).

> thus reduce the resources expended on elections by both employers and unions, and allow employees to exercise their section 7 rights more effectively.[30]

Thus, for example, Volkswagen at its plant in Chattanooga, Tennessee,[31] and Nissan at its plant in Canton, Mississippi,[32] would be required to recognize and bargain with the UAW at both plants—-but only for the union's less-than-majority employee-members, not for nonunion employees. This would be more than merely a foot-in-the-door because the bargaining requirement would continue regardless of the original size of the union's membership. And Boeing at its North Charleston, South Carolina, plant would likewise be required to recognize and bargain with the IAM for its less-than-majority employee members. And regarding the building and construction industry, where traditional NLRB election procedures and defining bargaining units have never fit comfortably within the fast-moving and rapidly changing hiring requirements of that multi-craft and multi-employer industry, building-trades unions will find it much easier to establish bargaining rights and expand their membership.[33] These are among the many areas where members-only unions could make a considerable difference in American labor relations, which will be discussed more extensively in Chapter 4.

Although the members-only bargaining procedure which this book proposes may seem relatively unfamiliar, unlike other currently proposed NLRB improvements this one can be made available without new legislation because its legal authority—despite its unfamiliarity—is already contained in unambiguous text of the existing statute. It thus meets the strict interpretive requirements that Justice Scalia advanced regarding interpretation of statutory text.

As previously noted, the NLRB during the Obama administration quietly provided two brief legal signals that signified positive evaluations of this program. The first occurred in the form of a relatively unnoticed—but nevertheless important—concession in a letter denying issuance of an unfair-labor-practice complaint in which General Counsel Richard Griffin characterized as "plausible"

30 Catherine Fisk & Xenia Tashlistsky, *Imagine a World Where Employers Are Required to Bargain with Minority Unions,* 27 ABA J. OF LAB. & EMPL, L. 1, 11 (2011). *See* chap. 4 *infra* at notes 8-14 for description of § 7 rights.

31 *See* chap 1 *supra* at note 76.

32 *See* chap. 3 *infra* at note 43-58.

33 *See* chap. 3 *infra* at notes 45-59.

the reading of "the language of Sections 7, 8(a)(1), and 8(a)(5)" of the Act as creating an enforceable duty to bargain with a non-majority union.[34]

The second signal arrived in a little-noticed unfair-labor-practice opinion in a relatively non-controversial NLRB case. It was contained in Member Kent Hirozawa's concurring opinion in *Children's Hospital and Research Center of Oakland*,[35] which affirmed, without objection from the other two members of the panel (one of whom was the Republican member who later became Board Chairman at the beginning of the Trump administration) that the duty-to-bargain requirement in the Act's clear statutory language[36] is not limited to majority unions only. Hirozawa's opinion was thus the Board's opening salvo in the upcoming re-validation of the program which this book highlights. The legal features of that concurring opinion are detailed in Chapter 4.[37]

This members-only bargaining program, which has the prospect of reviving the moribund organizational potential of the American labor movement, is certainly not a new concept, as previously pointed out. In fact, it's the natural way in which private organizations normally develop—which is with membership and operational roles growing concurrently. And it was that feature of union-organizing, combined with non-majority bargaining, that characterized the early history of much successful union activity during the first decade following passage of the Act in 1935. Because unions were seeking bargaining rights as quickly as possible, they relied heavily on those non-majority procedures that culminated in the signing of members-only-minority-union collective-bargaining contracts. These became commonplace in many different industries. In fact, as mentioned previously, those were the means used to organize both the automobile and steel industries.[38] Although that process received scholarly attention in 1936[39] and 1990,[40] during recent years its legal features were virtu-

34 SCA Tissue North America, LLC., Case 03-CA-132930, *supra* note 1, letter of June 5, 2015 from NLRB General Counsel Richard F. Griffin, Jr. *See* chap. 6 *infra* at notes 37-40.

35 364 NLRB No. 114 (2016).

36 *See* chap. 4 *infra* at notes 27-32 for a complete analysis. That Republican Board Member, was Philip A. Miscimarra.

37 *Id.* at 28-31.

38 *See* text accompanying notes 46-49 *infra* and BLUE EAGLE, *supra* note 1 at 82-85.

39 E.G. Latham, *Legislative Purpose and Administrative Policy under the National Labor Relations Act*, 4 GEO. WASH. L. REV. 433, 453-54 & n. 65 (1936).

40 Clyde Summers, *The Kenneth M. Piper Lecture: Unions without Majority—A Black Hole?*, 66 CHI-KENT. L. REV. 531 (1990).

ally unknown until it's re-identification in 2005 in my book, The *Blue Eagle at Work.*[41]

Now, once again, the need has arisen for restoration of this old-fashioned process—a process that's been lying dormant in the text of the Act for many decades, as if consciously awaiting re-use when needed. It's now needed. Regardless of its age, however, its organizational and bargaining methods will seem novel to many because of its difference from familiar traditional methods of union organizing and bargaining—to which most labor-relation practitioners have become accustomed. Nevertheless, this is a program that has the potential to become the blockbuster that organized labor has long been seeking. Recall that AFL-CIO's President Richard Trumka asserted a few years ago that "our basic system of workplace regulation is failing—failing miserably [therefore] the labor movement must embrace new models of representation that exist outside of traditional unionism."[42] The *old practice* of members-only minority-union bargaining can now become the *new practice* that has the capacity to reverse the downward trend of private-sector union membership.

I repeat, for emphasis, that the legal basis of that process, which will be explained in detail in Chapter 4 and confirmed in later chapters, is that its authority is imbedded in the Act's clear text and supporting legislative history. It is therefore not dependent on the Board's discretionary *permissive* construction.[43] As Justice Scalia insisted: "The text is the law, and it is the text which must be observed."[44]

But before explaining what the NMCB process is, I want to explain what it is not. In its final or mature form it's not a radical and different form of collective bargaining. Although It doesn't change the National Labor Relations Act (NLRA), it does make use of some of its forgotten guarantees in order to produce the familiar majority-based collective bargaining that Congress intended. It's thus a concept which begins with an unfamiliar procedure but winds up with a familiar majority-based exclusivity-coverage of all employees in an appropriate bargaining unit, which will be detailed in Chapters 4 and 5. And this process should not be confused with the outcome of the Supreme Court's decision in

41 Blue Eagle, *supra* note 1.

42 *See* chap. 1 *supra* at note 74.

43 *See* notes 58-59 *infra* and accompanying text.

44 Antonin Scalia, A Matter of Interpretation 22 (1997). *See also* chap. 4 *infra* at notes 35-40.

Janus v. AFSCME,[45] where the Court held that First Amendment free speech prohibits public-sector unions under state law from requiring non-member employees to pay fees for their collective-bargaining representation. (See discussion herein below.) Even if that First Amendment concept were to be later extended to private sector unions under the NLRA, the result would be quite different if NMCB procedures are in effect, for unions under that process would be better able to retain their representational function.

V. HISTORICAL USAGE

Now to explain what the NMCB is: It's a concept whereby a non-majority union, on behalf of those employees who are its members—but not on behalf of any other employees—engages in collective bargaining with their employer. This practice ordinarily continues until the union's membership reaches majority status among all the employees in an appropriate bargaining unit. When that occurs—as would normally be expected—the formerly minority-union becomes a conventional majority/exclusive union, which is then legally obligated to provide equal representation to all employees in that bargaining unit. However, if and when such majority status doesn't occur, that minority-union would continue to be the collective-bargaining representative of its union-member employees for whom the employer has a continuing duty to bargain in good faith. Chapter 3 provides a detailed description of how this process will probably function.

It's noteworthy that it was the head of a giant American corporation, Myron C. Taylor, chairman of the Board of U.S. Steel. who played a pivotal role that strongly influenced the spread of this minority-union bargaining concept.[46] Taylor was a prominent and experienced lawyer—indeed he later became a major donor to Cornell University's law school, which was thereafter located in the beautiful neo-gothic building that bears his name. During the summer of 1936, when the Steel Workers Organizing Committee (SWOC), which later became the Steelworkers Union, was busy organizing U.S. Steel employees—

45 138 S.ct 2018 (Jan. 27, 2018). *See infra* at notes 59-68.

46 The facts contained in this and the following related paragraphs are contained in *It Happened in Steel*, FORTUNE MAGAZINE Vol. XV, 91-94,176,179-80, May 1937, reprinted IN THE AMERICAN LABOR MOVEMENT 124-46 (Leon Litwack ed. 1962), and *see also* IRVING BERNSTEIN, TURBULENT YEARS: A HISTORY OF THE AMERICAN WORKER 1933-1941, 466-73 (1971).

which was activity which could easily have culminated in a gigantic strike—Taylor, with obvious reference to the compliance requirements of the newly enacted NLRA, recorded his intended response in a "hundred-word" document that later came to be known as the *Taylor Formula for Industrial Peace.* Although that "formula"—the text of which follows—may have reflected some of the company's prior experience with the Mineworkers' union, of which John L. Lewis was president, it was obviously drafted to conform to the bargaining requirements of the NLRA that applies to all employees without reference to majority-union status, which is legally explained in Chapter 4 . Here is Taylor's text:

> The Company recognizes the right of its employees to bargain collectively through representatives freely chosen by them without dictation, coercion, or intimidation in any form or from any source. It will negotiate and contract with the representatives of any group of its employees so chosen and any organization *as the representative of its members,* subject to the recognition of the principle that the right to work is not dependent on membership or non-membership in any organization and subject to the right of every employee to bargain in such manner and through such representatives, if any, as he chooses.[47]

According to *Fortune* magazine, those words "packed more dynamite than any one hundred words ever written by a United States industrialist."

Taylor and Lewis—who was the principal union leader of the massive organizing drives that were then prevailing in both the steel and automobile industries—met privately ten or twelve times. These meetings resulted in Taylor convincing Lewis to accept his members-only minority-union formula as the basis for settlement of the representation disputes then pending at both industries. Shortly thereafter, the *Taylor Formula* provided the basis for the UAW's settlement of the Michigan sit-down strikes, where the union did not represent an employee-majority. The members-only minority-union contracts that concluded that settlement became the model for the initial unionization of both the automobile and steel industries. It would thus be inaccurate to treat those agreements as examples of purely *voluntary* minority-union recognition by employers, for, as demonstrated by the *Taylor Formula,* the parties were *knowingly* complying with the minority-union requirements of the NLRA, as the pertinent text of that Act is shown to confirm in Chapter 4.

47 Emphasis added.

During those early years, NMCB contracts that resulted from pre-majority bargaining were as prevalent as majority-exclusivity contracts; and there's strong evidence that their numerical coverage of employees may have been even greater.[48] Negotiating and signing those members-only agreements in the late thirties and early forties, such as in the automobile and steel industries, as well as in other industries, represented a widely-followed pathway that almost always led to conventional majority-union status and Section 9(a) collective contracts. Those agreements became extremely popular, and almost all of the pre-majority unions under those contracts grew in membership and were later recognized as conventional majority-exclusive NLRA unions.[49]

One may logically ask: If the process of minority-union organizing and bargaining was so successful, why hasn't it been used for over half a century? Why was it abandoned in favor of representation elections? The answer to those questions should not be a surprise: The transition to NLRA majority-certification procedures was simply a matter of convenience. When unions discovered that the Board's representation-election process had become an easier, faster, and much less-expensive way to achieve majority/exclusive representation—which was the unions' ultimate goal and the Act's declared objective—reliance on minority organizing and bargaining, which had been only a temporarily suitable means to an end, gradually diminished and that slower and more expensive process fell into disuse.[50] And with the passage of time, institutional memory faded and minority-union organizing and bargaining became the subject of a distant past.

As a consequence, both employers and unions eventually came to assume that only majority unions—usually, but not exclusively, verified through the NLRB election process—have the right to bargain collectively. And that misperceived belief turned rather quickly into conventional wisdom. We now know only too well, however, what eventually happened to the election process. NLRB elections became employer-controlled battlegrounds that made union representation virtually unavailable to most workers who desired such representation.[51] So, once again, there's now a pressing need to return, at least alternatively, to

48 *Union Recognition as Shown in Contracts,* 1A L.R.R.M. (BNA) 781 (1938). For details, *see* Blue Eagle, *supra* note 1 *at 82-85.*

49 *See* chap. 4 *infra* at notes 101-105.

50 *Id.,* at note 104.

51 *See* note 14 *supra* & chap. 1 *infra* note 71.

members-only pre-majority organizing and bargaining. With the occurrence of plunging union membership and serious problems with the election system, it's again time to reactivate that process.

Unfortunately, however, that renewal process is being slowed by the power of conventional wisdom. Unlike the strong support that members-only collective-bargaining has received from labor law professors and union attorneys, some established union leaders and their advisors—but happily not all—have failed to take the first steps to move toward the more efficient unionization process that reinstituting members-only bargaining would represent. That reluctance apparently stems either from a lack of knowledge or from an unquestioning acceptance of the conventional wisdom to which they and their predecessors have long adhered. Such a belief seems to meet the modern definition of a "meme," i.e., "widely accepted information, thought, feeling or behavior"[52] that continues like a shared habit, regardless of its validity. So what has happened to this meme, to this rigid adherence to believing that the NLRA protects *only* majority-based collective bargaining? That's conduct which Rebecca Costa, the insightful author of *The Watchman's Rattle*,[53] might call a "supermeme," which she defines as

> a belief, thought, or behavior that becomes so stubbornly embedded that it contaminates or suppresses all other beliefs and behavior in a society.[54] [O]nce a supermeme takes hold, it becomes extremely difficult for people to imagine otherwise. This is the paradox of unquestioned, embedded beliefs. We continue believing something is true even when there is ample evidence to the contrary.[55]

She points out how easily a meme can spread and become confused with fact"[56] However, she also says that "this doesn't mean a supermeme can't be

52 120 Rebecca D. Costa, The Watchman's Rattle 44 (2010). The word "meme" was coined by Richard Dawkins, in The Selfish Gene 192 (2d ed. 1985).

53 Costa, *id.*

54 *Id.*, at 47.

55 *Id.*, at 48.

56 *Id.*

overcome."[57] In fact, she and I are in agreement that a "way to disarm super-memes is through awareness."[58] That's a principal reason why I wrote this book.

VI. DOES *JANUS* MAKE A DIFFERENCE?

Because the Supreme Court's 2018 decision in *Janus v. ASFME, Council 31*,[59] a public sector case, has challenged the American concept of union-management relations as no other case has in recent years, a question naturally arises as to whether it would affect non-majority collective-bargaining (NMCB), which this book proposes. The immediate answer is "no," but if the First Amendment principle developed in that case were to be applied to the private sector under the NLRA, the answer would not be that easy—though it would likely still be "no." Pursuant to the conservative justices' majority Opinion, the *Janus* Court held that the Michigan statute that permitted a public employer to allow the union that represented all employees in an employment unit to require the non-union employees to pay an agency fee to the union as compensation for the collective-bargaining benefits they receive violates the First Amendment of the Constitution.[60] In so holding the Court overruled the forty-year-old decision in *Abood v. Detroit Board of Education*.[61] According to Justice Alito's majority Opinion, exaction from non-consenting employees, employees who opposed the union and its activities, violated the free speech of non-consenting employees "for the First Amendment does not permit the government to compel a person to pay for another party's speech just because the government thinks that the speech furthers the interests of the person who does not pay."

Controverting the Court's erroneous reasoning, which Justice Sotomeyer's dissenting Opinion splendidly accomplished, would serve no further purpose here. But regarding the possibility of the *Janus* free-speech ruling being applied to private-sector union-shop and agency fees under the NLRA , a brief comment is in order. First Amendment protection applies against the abridgement of free speech *by governmental action*, not by *private action*. Therefore, inasmuch as

57 *Id.*, at 54.

58 *Id.*, at 59.

59 201 L. Ed. 2d 924, 138 S. Ct. 244, 82018 U.S. LEXIS 4028 (June 27,2018).

60 U.S. Constitution, Amendment 1.

61 431 U.S. 209 (1977).

private-sector union and/or agency shop agreements lack the comparable element of state action found in *Janus*, First Amendment application should not apply. In that regard, the *Janus* Court's rational for disparaging *Abood* actually included a telling concession to that effect. As part of Justice Alito's criticism of *Abood* to justify overruling it, he stated that

> Abood relied on *Railway Employees v. Hanson*[62] *and Machinists v. Street,*[63] both of which involved private-sector collective-bargaining agreements where the government merely authorized agency fees. *Abood* did not appreciate the very different First Amendment question that arises when a State requires its employees to pay agency fees. . . . Nor did *Abood* take into account the difference between the effects of agency fees in public- and private-sector collective-bargaining. . . .[64]

Justice Alito thus gave us reliable examples of some of the distinguishing features that demonstrate the absence of state action in private-sector union shop and agency shop agreements. However, the First Amendment issue may never come to fruition regarding those private-sector features, but should the Supreme Court nevertheless consider applying the *Janus* thesis to agreements under the NLRB, the Court might choose to rely on the canon of construction that it applied in *Catholic Bishop of Chicago*[65] and *DeBartelo II,*[66] which was that "where an otherwise acceptable construction of a statute would raise serious constitutional problems, the Court will construe the statute to avoid such problems unless such construction is plainly contrary to the intent of Congress."[67]

Regardless, even if the *Janus* concept ultimately deprived private-sector unions of collective- bargaining fees from non-union employees, NMCB union employees would be less affected than majority-9(a) employees, for they alone would be guaranteed the benefits of the collective-bargaining process, as would

---

62 351 U. S. 225 (1956).

63 367 U. S. 740 (1961).

64 201 L. Ed. 2d 924, 958.

65 Catholic Bishop of Chicago v. NLRB, 440 U.S. 490 (1979).

66 Edward DeBartelo Corp. v. Fla. Gulf Coast Bldg. & Constr. Council, 485 U.S. 568 (1988).

67 *Id.*, at 575.

also be the case presently in Right-to-work states, which is explained in Chapter 3 *infra.*[68]

VII. THE CALL TO ACTION ON THE ROAD AHEAD

The fact that under present conditions members-only bargaining provides an easier way to organize a union, and that this method is accompanied by quicker establishment of the majority-bargaining process, tells us that this long-neglected practice could once again play a critical role in helping organized to grow more swiftly, and thus regain some of the power it needs to help fight against the income-inequality that pervades the national economy. That process should therefore be re-validated.

But why now? With the Republican employer-lobby still in control of NLRB appointments (as of this writing), is this really the time to initiate steps to reinstate the legitimacy of members-only non-majority bargaining? As I have indicated, the answer to that question is "yes"—in fact a strong "yes," for notwithstanding the possibility of a pro-employer NLRB denying that result, "step one" of the Supreme Court's iconic *Chevron*[69] decision and *Justice* Scalia's standard for construing *unambiguous* statuary text,[70] should eventually save the day, if not promptly. The *Chevron* canon demands that

> [w]hen a court reviews an agency's construction of the statute which it administers, [the first] question [is] whether Congress has directly spoken to the precise question at issue. *If the intent of Congress is clear, that is the end of the matter;* for the court, as well as the agency, must give effect to the *unambiguously expressed* intent of Congress.[71]

Because minority-union collective bargaining is authorized by "unambiguously expressed" text that Congress wrote into the Act, this is a *mandatory construction* about which the English language leaves no doubt and which the

68 *See* chap. 3 *infra* at notes 59-62.

69 Chevron U.S.A. v. Natural Resources Defense Council, Inc., 467 U.S. 837 (1984). *See* chap. 4 *infra* at note 2.

70 *Supra* note 69.

71 *Chevron,* 467 U.S. at 842-43. Emphasis added.

analysis in Chapter 4 unequivocally confirms. This is not an area where *Chevron* "step two" requires the administrative agency to make "rules to fill any gap left implicitly or explicitly by Congress,[72] and not an area where "the statute is silent or ambiguous.[73] Rather, in the language of the *Chevron* Court, it's an area about which "Congress has directly spoken to the precise question at issue."[74] Furthermore, Congress has never promulgated any rule or holding requiring majority status as the sole prerequisite for bargaining, nor has the NLRB issued any such holding.

Suppose, however, that despite the legal strength of this proposition the Board's General Counsel refuses to allow this members-only pre-majority bargaining process to go forward—although even an unfriendly but legally honest General Counsel might find withholding such a complaint inappropriate in view of the clarity of the text, its supportive legislative history, and the Hirozawa concurring opinion. But what happens if there is such a refusal? My answer is that *quick and direct judicial review*— though it may have to become *indirect* review[75]— should promptly follow.

I'm well aware that this proposed scenario, including a likely period for preparation, will be time-consuming—probably lasting many months or longer. But during that time union adherents and their supporters should visibly rally around the issue and express strong backing for this proposition, especially among candidates for Congress and the presidency. That ought to be welcome activity during the age of Trump, and thus another reason not to wait for a more favorable time to launch the subject of this book—but if a more favorable political time should present itself, so much the better.

This is therefore a call to action, the legal details of which are spelled out in Chapter 4 and the tactical methodology in Chapter 6. Those steps would probably begin with a union-initiated test-case at an appropriate workplace—preferably in a friendly judicial district. The employer will likely refuse to bargain, whereupon an unfair-labor-practice charge will be filed, which will naturally begin with citation to the concurring opinion in the *Oakland Children's Hospital* case.[76] That should be viewed as the opening signal in the nation's move toward

72 *Id.*

73 *Id.* at 843.

74 *Id.*, at n. 11.

75 *See* chap. 6 *infra* at notes 57-84.

76 *See* note 6 in chap. 1 *supra* and chap. 4 *infra* at notes 1 & 28-32.

members-only collective bargaining. Thus begins the first step in the task of legally re-qualifying this process, for which a wide variety of procedures discussed in Chapter 6—both administrative and judicial—will be available.

Chapter 3. How Non-Majority collective-bargaining will function

I. INTRODUCTION

This chapter is designed to describe generally how non-majority collective bargaining (NMCB) is likely to function and how some of its anticipated variations might respond to heretofore unfamiliar procedures that are likely to prevail when that process becomes effective. As previously noted, the reason this "how-to" material is presented at this early stage is to benefit those readers who want access to a full understanding of how this unfamiliar process is expected to function prior to their consideration of the legal basis for that process, which is contained in Chapter 4. These two chapter can easily be reversed if desired.

Considering that this book is devoted to the re-introduction of minority-union collective-bargaining and its effect on American labor relations, and thus indirectly on the nation's economy, if the reconfirmation of this almost-forgotten process receives adequate enforcement it's likely that the practice of members-only bargaining will in time result in substantial advancement of the Congressionally declared policy of encouraging collective-bargaining and union-organizing required for such bargaining.[1] This should help to reestablish a labor movement that will once again make major contributions to the economic well-being of the nation, for increasing the earnings and dignity of millions of American workers will certainly contribute to broadening and strengthening the middle class.

How will this process work? The discussion that follows addresses that wide-ranging question by considering and describing some of the major labor relations changes that may be expected to follow the re-validation of this process. Although these new (i.e., renewed) organizational and bargaining processes

1 § 1, 29 U.S.C. § 151, which in pertinent part reads: "It is hereby declared to be the policy of the United States [:] encouraging the practice and procedure of collective bargaining and by protecting the exercise by workers of full freedom of association, self -organization, and designation of representatives of their own choosing, for the purpose of negotiating the terms and conditions of their employment or other mutual aid or protection."

will probably advance the collective-bargaining process in various and different ways, the principal change will probably be the development of more conventional majority-based exclusivity bargaining relationships that conform to Section 9(a) of the National Labor Relations Act (NLRA or Act), the pertinent text of which provides that

> Representatives designated or selected for the purposes of collective bargaining by the *majority* of the employees in a unit appropriate for such purposes, shall be the exclusive representatives of all the employees in such unit for the purposes of collective bargaining.[2]

This conventional outcome should occur in most NMCB relationships because members-only bargaining will usually function as simply the first step on a path that ultimately leads to traditional Section 9(a) majority/exclusive employee representation. However, notwithstanding that likelihood, there will be places and situations where members-only bargaining takes a somewhat different path that will merit our attention. Each of these paths will be examined in this chapter. What follows are my projections concerning the various ways that employee-representation might develop following validation of non-majority members-only collective bargaining..

The following portrayal of how labor relations may differ after the NMCB process achieves full recognition is divided into five general parts: *First,* a description of a likely initial stage of organizing a "members-only" union and shaping its structure while simultaneously establishing—or attempting to establish—the employer's recognition of that union and its entry into the bargaining process. S*econd,* a description of how this bargaining process is likely to be conducted. *Third,* a description of how organizing and bargaining on a members-only basis can be carried out by *building-trades* unions under conditions unique to the construction industry–a process that will be especially advanced by NMCB procedures. *Fourth,* how members-only organizing and bargaining will function in right-to-work (RTW) states with a likelihood of greater success. And *fifth,* a description of how non-traditional forms of collective bargain that might develop will function, such as in workplaces where minority-union bargaining continues for a lengthy or relatively indefinite period of time yet never achieves majority support, or where the process results in bargaining with two or more

2 29 U.S.C. § 159(a). Emphasis added.

unions, or where the process results in the creation of new and unique forms of employee representation.

Although a degree of crystal-ball gazing necessarily contributed to the making of those projections, they are based primarily on verifiable facts and law, both past and present.

II. INITIAL ORGANIZING AND EARLY BARGAINING EFFORTS

It's an accepted fact that most American employers are opposed to unions and collective bargaining and will go to great lengths to retain, or in some cases return to, a union-free workplace. They are either unaware, or don't care, that the consistent Congressionally mandated "policy of the United States [is] encouraging the practice and procedure of collective bargaining."[3] As we've seen, their longstanding opposition to unions has been hugely successful. Indeed, union membership has dropped steadily since the mid-fifties, and in 2018 was only 6.4 percent of the private sector workforce.[4] Although various factors have contributed to that decline, among the foremost causes have been the fierce opposition that most employers have reflexively mounted against any effort by their employees to unionize It's widely recognized that non-union managements routinely indoctrinate their workforces with anti-union rhetoric and frequently engage in both subtle and aggressive conduct—legal and illegal—to discourage any support for union organizing.[5] Discharges for union activity during election campaigns are commonplace.[6] As an empirical study confirmed, it has become "standard practice for workers to be subjected to threats, interrogation, harassment, surveillance, and retaliation for union activity" during National Labor Relations Board (NLRB or Board) election campaigns.[7] Election campaigns have

3 *See* note 1 *supra.*

4 Bureau of Labor Statistics, *Economic Release*, Jan. 18, 2019.

5 *See* chap. 1 *supra* at note 71 and chap. 2 *supra* at note 14.

6 *See generally* Charles J. Morris, *A Tale of Two Statutes: Discrimination for Union Activity Under the NLRA and RLA*, 2 Employee Rts & Employment Pol'y J. 317 (1998) and Charles J. Morris, *A Tale of two Statutes Redux: Anti-Union Employment Discharges Under the NLRA and RLA, with a Solution, 41* Berkeley J. Emp. & Lab. L. (2019).

7 *No Holds Barred: The Intensification of Employer Opposition to Organizing*, a study conducted by the Econ. Pol. Institute & American Rights at Work, reported in *Workers Routinely Subject to Threats Over Organizing Activity,* EPI Study Says, 94 Daily Lab. Rep. (BNA) A-9 (May 19, 2009). This study indicates that it was based on a random sample of 1,004 NLRB certification elections between

thus become battlegrounds between unions and managements that engender intense adversarial relations that frequently carry over following an election regardless of who wins the election prize. It's therefore no wonder that first contracts have become extremely difficult, and often impossible, to obtain.[8]

Although this culture of anti-unionism might be somewhat mitigated by a dedicated Board and General Counsel through the exercise of available statutory authority, this is presently unlikely. Indeed, a major turnaround in employer anti-union conduct is highly unlikely so long as a union's representational presence depends primarily on the election process. As long as employees are denied union representation unless and until their union succeeds in jumping through the hoops of a bitter and unfair election campaign, employers will have the incentive—plus the opportunity and means—to continue fighting aggressively to keep their workplaces union-free. But when a union's majority-status is no longer the *sine qua none* of its existence and right to bargain, a major reason for the employer's strong opposition to unionization will have disappeared. And when a union's presence is no longer dependent on majority support, even a union that's been defeated in an election will still be entitled to bargain–though only for its members–and thus will continue to play a conspicuous role in that workplace.

Regardless of the nature of typical employer attitudes toward unions that might persist after members-only bargaining becomes legally recognized—and hopefully widely accepted—there should be no illusion about anticipated employer reactions and attitudes immediately following validation of such bargaining. Nonunion American employers have become so accustomed to fearing and opposing unions that their bias will surely persist for a long while, and many if not most companies will probably continue to actively discourage their employees–often illegally–from seeking or retaining union representation. Henceforth, however, there will be an important difference. Anti-union activity will likely become markedly less successful–even in the early transition period. For example, employer conduct that presently succeeds in discouraging workers from signing union cards or voting for a union–thereby allowing the company

---

Jan. 1, 1999, and Dec. 31, 2003, and from an in-depth survey of 562 election campaigns.

8 Patrick Eagan-Van Meter & Ross Eisenbrey, *First-Contract Arbitration Facts: The Canadian Experience,* ECON. POL. INSTITUTE. Issue Brief #256, June 25, 2009 (One study found that between 1999 and 2004, only 38% of unions established by a majority vote and NLRB certification were successful in reaching a first contract within one year, and only 56% obtained a contract within two years, *citing* John-Paul Ferguson & Thomas Kochan, *Sequential Failures in Workers' Right to Organize.* Rep. 2008.)

to remain union free—won't have a similar effect when used against members or potential members of a NMCB union, for that union will thereafter be entitled to continue bargaining for its members regardless of the employer's conduct. Although such negative conduct may weaken the union, it won't necessarily destroy it. As long as there's a group of employee-members whose union seeks to bargain on their behalf, the employer will continue to be required to bargain. Accordingly, even though organizing on a members-only basis won't be easy, it will be easier than organizing through the current practice of first obtaining sufficient numbers of signed authorization cards and then engaging in a bitter and expensive election campaign that's inherently tilted toward the employer.

Members-only organizing will differ significantly from today's familiar pre-election organizing. Instead of soliciting for union-authorization cards,[9] organizers—whether they be active employees or outside representatives—will solicit for and offer genuine union membership. From the beginning, the organizational goal will be the building of a viable union rather than the winning of an election. And that different course of action will call for a different mind-set.

Just as unions organized many years ago before they became addicted to the election process, they will once again organize by signing-up employees for genuine union membership, which will create an authentic agency relationship.[10] Employees who join the union during that organizing stage will do so with a commitment to the payment of dues—however nominal—and they will thus be aware that their act of joining represents a serious commitment[11]—indeed, it will be a superior indication of voluntary intent than either signing

9 Which under *Linden Lumber Div.*, Summer & Co, v. NLRB, 190 NLRB 718 (1971), *rev'd & remanded sub nom.*, 487 F.2d 1099 (D.C. Cir. 1973) *rev'd*, 419 U.S. 301 (1974), is deemed insufficient to establish majority status; thus, absent an agreement from the employer, such cards are currently useful only to establish a 30% showing of interest to obtain an election. NLRB STATEMENT OF PROCEDURE, §101.17. *See* note 22 *infra*.

10 The basic agency relation is generally understood. Here is a common definition:

> A "fiduciary relationship between two parties in which one (the 'agent') is under the control of (is obligated to) the other (the 'principal'). The agent is authorized by the principal to perform certain acts, for and on behalf of the principal. The principal is bound by the acts of the agent, performed in carrying out entrusted duties and within the scope of agent's authority." www.businessdictionary.com/definition/agency.html .

11 "Payment of union dues, even though nominal in amount, will mean that pro-union workers will have 'put their money where their mouth is.'" CHARLES J. MORRIS, THE BLUE EAGLE AT WORK: RECLAIMING DEMOCRATIC RIGHTS IN THE AMERICAN WORKPLACE, 187 (2005) (hereinafter BLUE EAGLE). However, I don't consider dues payments to be absolutely essential at an early stage, and I also describe and recommend a multi-tiered dues structure that might be adopted for these new unions, such as a moderate fee on joining, followed by dues increases later tied to advanced stages in the bargaining process. *Id., at 186-87.*

a card or casting a vote. And these new union members will be expected to participate generously in many phases of union activity, such as organizing, electing officers, selecting union stewards, creating and working within committees, engaging in group decision making; and some members will probably meet and negotiate directly with representatives of management. They will thus be actively using old peer-driven tools, which, as previously noted, represent a channeling of peoples' increasing thirst to participate because of the so-called "IKEA effect, a tendency of people to place a higher value on self-made products [including] objects and experiences they are able to shape [that] reinforce the human instinct to cooperate rather than compete."[12] These are characteristics likely to be found in the NMCB process. Thus, from the beginning, their concerted cry can become "union now"—not "union maybe if we win an election."

Through this process, the *employee-rights* mandate in Section 7— the provision aptly called *labor's bill of rights* or "the heart of the Act."[13]—will be literally engaged, because that provision unambiguously specifies that:

> Employees shall have the right to self-organization, to form, join, or assist labor organizations, *to bargain collectively through representatives of their own choosing,* and to engage in other concerted activities for the purpose of collective bargaining or other mutual aid or protection. . . . [14]

Employees, thus acting concertedly, will be exercising their "fundamental"[15] and "guaranteed"[16] right to join unions and engage in collective bargaining regardless of their numbers. Therefore, as long as there are union members in a workplace, there will be a lawful union presence at that location. Although it's undoubtedly true that minority unions with only a few members will have little bargaining power, those few members will at least have the benefit of their *group presence* plus the Act's requirement that with respect to their "wages, hours,

12 Jeremy Heimans & Henry Timms, New Power 126 (2018). *See* chap. 1 *supra* at note 8.

13 Thomas C. Kohler, *National Labor Relations Act,* in 3 Major Acts of Congress 37 (Brian K. Landsberg, ed. 2004).

14 29 U.S.C. § 157. Emphasis added.

15 NLRB v. Jones & Laughlin Steel Corp., 301 U.S. 1, 33 (1937) ("the right of employees to self-organization and to select representatives of their own choosing for collective bargaining...is a *fundamental right.*" (Emphasis added).

16 § 8(a)(1), 29 U.S.C. §158(a)(1), which references § 7 rights as "guaranteed."

and other terms and condition of employment"[17] their employer must deal with them through their union rather than with them individually.[18] This will mean that employees, whether by themselves or with the assistance of union organizers, will be able to join unions when they perceive a need, instead of having to wait months or even years exhausting election procedures under Section 9(c).[19] And as their new union grows in membership and attains some success in representation and bargaining—even if in the beginning it only succeeds in becoming a collective voice for common grievances—it will have established the union's identity and legitimate right to maintain a visible presence in the workplace. When that occurs, the employer will either bargain collectively or become the subject of unfair labor practices (ULPs) and NLRB orders, even including, when appropriate, Section 10(j)[20] injunctions and other administrative and judicial actions.[21] And regardless of the time that may be required to complete an NLRB enforcement action against a recalcitrant employer, the charging union will have the right to be present in the workplace for representational purposes, and the employer's duty to bargain will continue. These projections assume a sufficiently funded NLRB, which may depend on a favorable political environment and more good will from the public and media. Regardless, however, because of the union's continued presence in the workplace and expectation that there will ultimately be greater acceptance of—or reconciliation with—the national policy favoring collective bargaining, the Board's enforcement role ought eventually to decrease as a result of this members-only minority-union bargaining concept—although that may be an overly sanguine expectation.

When such a minority union finally achieves majority status—which should be expected in most cases—there ought ordinarily to be no need for an election, for the objective procedure of counting employee-members to determine whether a

17 § 8(d), 29 U.S.C. § 158(d).

18 *See* NLRB v. Katz, 369 U.S. 736 (1962) (granting of non-automatic wage increases); Garment Workers Local 512 v. NLRB (Febrow, Inc.), 795 F.2d 705 (9th Cir. 1986) (unilateral economic layoffs). See also Oneita Knitting Mills, 205 NLRB 500 (1973) (unilateral grant of merit increases); Medo Photo Supply Corp. v. NLRB, 321 U.S. 678 (1944); General Elec. Co., 150 NLRB 192 (1964), *enforced*, 418 F.2d 736 (2nd Cir. 1969), *cert. denied*, 397 U.S. 965 (1970) (no direct dealing with union members' working conditions).

19 29 U.S.C. §159(c). (Election procedures.)

20 29 U.S.C. §160(j).

21 § 10. [29 U.S.C. § 160.]

unit-majority exists can be easily verified from union records.[22] Elections should therefore be conducted only for the purpose Congress intended, i.e., to resolve questions concerning representation when a union's claim of majority status in an appropriate bargaining unit is legitimately in doubt.[23] However, if and when an NLRB election is held with a union that has already engaged in successful members-only bargaining, in almost all such cases a positive election result should be a foregone conclusion.

This social phenomenon of members-only organizing and bargaining ought to produce unions in which their members are conscious of being integral parts of an employee-sensitive working organization. A worker's common question of "what can the union do for me?" may therefore be changed to "what can we do for ourselves, for we are the union." That realization should be especially important at the organizational stage, even when organizing relies on the participation of outside organizers. This new, yet old-fashioned, type of union—which organizes while simultaneously bargaining—should thus become a welcome means to achieve union representation for millions of American workers who want and need it, but for whom it has previously been rarely obtainable.

III. MEMBERS-ONLY BARGAINING IN OPERATION

In response to those who might question whether members-only bargaining is a "good idea," my answer is a definite "yes," especially when one recognizes that such bargaining will usually be preliminary to the establishment of majority-based exclusivity bargaining; but also even if the union remains a member-based non-majority union, that should be preferable to the alternative. And during its growing period before the union arrives at majority/exclusivity status, its very presence in the workplace should be a positive factor that contributes to improving the quality of working life. Even where the minority union never achieves majority status, or where its existence prompts the formation of new types of representation in response to changes in the nature of work, or where

22 *Linden Lumber Div.*, Summer & Co, v. NLRB, *supra* note 9, should thus not apply, for unlike the uncertainty that might attach to employees' intent based on authorization cards, there can be no such uncertainty when the employees' union commitment can be easily verified by their dues-paying status as union members. *Cf.* Charles J. Morris, *Undercutting Linden Lumber: How a Union Can Achieve Majority-Status Bargaining without an Election*, 35 HOFSTRA LAB. & EMPL. L. J. 1 2017).

23 *See* BLUE EAGLE, *supra* note 11 at 71.

several minority unions exist simultaneously in the same workplace, the resulting conditions should be superior to most nonunion alternatives. At the very least, the presence of a NMCB union provides a medium for productive interchange between groups of employees and management—something not legally possible in a nonunion setting under Section 8(a)(2).[24]

By way of preview, the following is a glimpse at the main features of what can be expected to occur after the validity of non-majority collective bargaining becomes widely recognized. When employees with shared interests join together and organize into an identifiable group that satisfies the broad definition of a "labor organization" under Section 2(5)[25] of the Act, they become a stronger presence for meeting with management to resolve common problems and grievances—much stronger than would be the case if they were each trying to act alone. In all but the smallest workplaces, or where a close-knit or family-type relationship exists between employer and employees, communication between management and workers concerning conditions of employment is likely to be more productive where there's a union.[26] And to achieve maximum benefit from the union's presence, that communication should be genuine dialogue, not merely unilateral announcements of chain-of-command instructions from management. A members-only union, even if small or informal with or without outside-union affiliation, can be ideal for this purpose because union employees—unlike nonunion at-will employees—have the legal benefits of job protection under Section 7 and its unfair-labor-practice safeguards. The employer's obligation to bargain with a members-only union—regardless of its size—provides union-member employees with a legal voice that must be heard and a response that must be forthcoming.

That response must be forthcoming because the Act requires the employer to respond to the employees' union representative rather than to each employee

24 *See* Electromation, Inc., 309 NLRB 990 (1992), *enforced*, 35 F.3d 1148 (7th Cir. 1994), *and* E.I. DuPont de Nemours, 311 NLRB 893 (1993), construing § 8(a)(2) [29 U.S.C. §158(a)(2)]..

25 29 U.S.C. § 152(5): "The term 'labor organization' means any organization of any kind, or any agency or employee representation committee or plan, in which employees participate and which exists for the purpose, in whole or in part, of dealing with employers concerning grievances, labor disputes, wages, rates of pay, hours of employment, or conditions of work."

26 "If management uses the collective bargaining process to learn about and improve the operation of the workplace and the production process, unionism can be a significant plus to enterprise efficiency." Richard B. Freeman & James L. Medoff, What Do Unions Do? 12 (1984). *See also* Aaron J. Sojourner et al, *Impacts of Unionization on Quality and Productivity: Regressive Evidence from Nursing Homes*, 68(4) ILR Review 771 (2015). And the reader will recall the description of union-management relations at Southwest Airlines in chap. 1, *supra* at notes 65-67.

individually and to negotiate with their union before any changes in their employment conditions can be affected. Fundamental to this legal concept of collective bargaining is that management has a duty to meet with the union "at reasonable times and confer in good faith"[27] regarding statutory subjects of collective bargaining, i.e., "wages, hours, and other terms and conditions of employment,"[28] which means there can be no further unilateral changes in the union members' working conditions[29] and any further direct dealing with them regarding those conditions.[30]

Although members-only bargaining in its earliest stages may appear to be no more than informal meet-and-confer sessions, even under that simplistic format workplace problems and grievances are more likely to be settled satisfactorily than under a hierarchical nonunion employment-at-will system. After it is generally accepted that employers are legally required to recognize and bargain with members-only unions, aggrieved employees should normally not need to resort to confrontational activity in order to focus management's attention on workplace matters requiring correction,[31] such as have occurred in many publicized walk-outs at various Wal-Mart, fast-food, and warehouse locations in recent years.[32] Furthermore, when a NMCB union does choose to resort to strikes, picketing, or consumer leafleting as a part of the collective-bargaining process, such concerted activity will have the defensive benefit of both the protective and bargaining provisions of the Act, which are designed to ultimately produce bilateral agreements; and employers by law will be required to engage in good-faith bargaining, unlike the employers involved in recent nonunion walkouts.

After the proposed re-validation becomes fully recognized—however reluctantly by some employers—and employees begin to organize and bargain through their members-only unions, what are some of the differences that might be expected? For employees who choose to join such unions, the resulting

27 § 8(d). [29 U.S.C. § 158(d).]

28 *Id.*

29 *See Katz* case *supra* at note 18.

30 *See* Medo Photo Supply. *Id.*

31 *See* NLRB v. Washington Aluminum, 370 U.S. 9 (1962) (strike by minority group of employees over work-related grievance is protected concerted activity under § 7).

32 *See, e.g.*, Steven Greenhouse, *Labor Union to Ease Walmart Picketing*, N.Y. TIMES Feb. 1, 2013; Steven Greenhouse, *Strike for Day Seeks to Raise Fast-Food Pay*, N.Y. TIMES Aug. 1, 2013; and chap. 2 *supra* at notes 23-29.

availability of collective bargaining should lead to noticeable improvements in their employment conditions—however slight. But when this new union grows in membership and authority, the benefits should likewise grow, for that's what collective bargaining is designed to produce—though often only after overcoming many employer-placed obstacles. When the union is still relatively new it might make its first move in the bargaining process by presenting the employer with a simple written notice advising that a group of employees are members of the union.[33] Whereupon, that union becomes their agent for all matters relating to their bargainable working-conditions pursuant to Section 8(d)[34] of the Act, and management should thereafter refrain from making any unilateral changes in those conditions, or negotiating directly with any of those union employees without first providing the union with a reasonable opportunity to participate in the process, thereby avoiding commission of ULPs.

The union might begin its efforts at more formal bargaining by seeking to negotiate about general problems or grievances that affect both union and non-union employees, although such bargaining would be on behalf of the union employees only and enforceable only by them. When agreement is reached on such an ad hoc matter, it should be recorded promptly and appropriately, with such possible labeling as "memo of agreement," thus distinguishing it from a formal Section 8(d) collective-bargain contract. Although any agreed-upon benefits as to such matters will be legally binding only as to union-member employees, management might unilaterally decide to extend some or all of those benefits to other employees. Even though this minority-union will have no authority to represent nonunion employees, an employer's extension of union benefits to other employees should reflect favorably on the new union's on-going efforts to recruit new members. A similar advantage might be achieved from the union's attempt to obtain a fair grievance procedure, especially one that includes third-party arbitration. If it is successful in that endeavor, it will have demonstrated a significant advantage in union membership because that procedure, being purely *representational,* will be available only to union members.[35] But even if

---

33 *See* BLUE EAGLE, *supra* note 11 at 192-193 regarding the pros and cons of early member-name identification. For test-case purposes before final legal validation is achieved, the union might choose to condition the revealing of members' names on when the employer indicates its recognition of the union for collective-bargaining purposes.

34 29 U.S.C. § 158(d). For bargainable "wages, hours, and other terms and conditions of employment," see chap. 16 in THE DEVELOPING LABOR LAW: THE BOARD, THE COURTS, AND THE NATIONAL LABOR RELATIONS ACT (John E. Higgins, Jr. ed., 7th ed. 2017) (hereinafter DLL7^{th}).

35 A grievance procedure applicable only to union members, where the union has no authority to

the union isn't successful in obtaining third-party arbitration, its effort will call attention to the likely absence of due process in the existing grievance procedure—if there is such a procedure—which might encourage more employees to join the union and thus help make a fair grievance procedure an ultimate reality.

The new union in all probability will not yet request bargaining for a comprehensive collective agreement—i.e., an agreement that resembles a Section 9(a) majority contract except that it covers only union members—until its membership has reached a size large enough to command serious attention. How large that membership should be and the timing of that request will depend on various factors, including the size of the union's membership, economic conditions, the nature and importance of the union members' jobs, the nature and extent of the employer's business, and of course sound judgment and good fortune.[36] Despite the likely preference of employers not to engage in any collective bargaining, a few pragmatic incentives might encourage some voluntary recognition of and bargaining with the minority union—however grudging. Inasmuch as that is what the law will require, any conduct that might constitute a ULP, such as unilateral changes in working conditions affecting union members, discriminatory grants of special benefits to nonunion employees to discourage their joining the union, employment discrimination against union members, granting preferential treatment to a company-favored union,[37] or actions that reveal an intent not to reach an agreement,[38] could invite the filing of unfair-labor-practice charges and their consequences. And, as previously noted, a NMCB union will ordinarily have the right to continue with its presence on the employer's property, however limited, regardless of the outcome of pending ULP charges. Employers will also be aware that a strike by a minority-union to achieve recognition or to protest a refusal to bargain will almost certainly be an unfair-labor-practice strike—thus entitling the striking employees to reinstatement at the conclusion of the

represent nonmembers, is a legally enforceable contract. *See* Retail Clerks v. Lion Dry Goods, Inc., 369 U.S. 17, 29 (1962).

36 This formal collective agreement—in contrast to an ad hoc "memo of agreement" (see text following note 34 *supra*) relating to individual subjects of bargaining, probably meets the requirements of §§ 8(d)(1-4) regarding various required notice regulations, whereupon such time-periods and notices should be complied with.

37 § 8(a)(2). 29 U.S.C. §158(a)(2).

38 *See* Atlas Mills, 3 NLRB 10 (1937); National Licorice Co. v. NLRB, 309 U.S. 350 (1940).

strike.[39] Minority unions might thus prove to be more successful in achieving first contracts than their present-day majority-union counterparts.

Under members-only bargaining, a union's bargaining strength will usually depend mostly on the extent of its membership. Notwithstanding that fact, all minority unions—including unions with small memberships in large companies—should be able to achieve some improvement in wages and working conditions, however minimal, when they utilize, or stand ready to utilize, lawful means of applying economic pressure toward the employer, even if they are unable to achieve Section 9(a) majority status. Those means might include traditional picketing and leafleting and/or using more modern social media programs such as Facebook, YouTube, or Twitter, and specially designed "apps" or other forms of high-tech media. Whatever the success of a minority union—whether great or small—it will constitute a visible and important presence in the workplace that can serve as a conspicuous medium for constructive dialogue between employees and management. As the walkouts at Wal-Marts, fast-food restaurants, warehouses, hotels and many other workplaces have demonstrated, in most nonunion companies there's an urgent need for such dialogue.

There is indeed a strong need for worker-representation at the lower tiers of the economic ladder, such as at the Beverly Enterprises nursing homes, which Cecile Richards described as "cheap as dirt." As she pointed out, those women simply wanted respect for the work they do, and organizing a union accomplishes that, for thereafter "their boss has to sit across the table from them as equals and talk about wages and working conditions,"[40] which otherwise never happens. Indeed, dignity is an important factor in all levels of union representation, and members-only bargaining will make organizing much easier.

Although working life for non-majority union employees will be expected to improve, what about the employer's business? What effect will members-only bargaining have on management? Although some adjustments in human-resource (HR) procedures will undoubtedly be necessary, considering the human benefits–such as improved morale and greater productivity–those adjustments should prove tolerable, at least in due time. Accommodation to this new bargaining method ought to be no more difficult than what presently transpires when an employer first begins to bargain in good faith with a traditional majority-based Section 9(a) union. Although it's true that almost every nonunion employer

39 *See* DLL7th, *supra* note 34 at 19-21 to 19-25 and cases cited therein.

40 Cecile Richards, Make Trouble 69 (2018)

would prefer to retain hierarchical control of a workforce that's answerable to no one but management, that's not what the law requires—and what democratic morality needs. Nevertheless, just as employers have traditionally adjusted to dealing with Section 9(a) majority unions, once they become fully familiar with members-only bargaining I believe that most of them will adjust to the process. Except for its more limited contractual coverage, dealing in members-only minority-union bargaining will in most respects not be substantially different from Section 9(a) bargaining. However, because newly granted economic benefits resulting from members-only negotiations will contractually apply only to union employees, management alone must decide whether all, part, or none of those benefits will be made available to similarly situated nonunion employees, because the employer is legally free to withhold all or part of those collectively bargained benefits from other employees. However, the NMCB union must be careful not to request or demand that any union-negotiated non-representational benefits be withheld from nonunion employees, because Section 8(b)(2)[41] prohibits a union from causing or attempting "to cause an employer to discriminate against an employee in violation of subsection 8(a)(3)," i.e., to discriminate as to any term or condition of employment "to encourage or discourage membership in any labor organization."[42]

IV. BUILDING-TRADES BARGAINING

Building-trades unions will especially benefit from members-only minority-union collective bargaining, for union representation in the construction industry has had a long and checkered history that's sorely in need of a new organizational approach. The persistent problems that construction unions face today began many years ago with the one-size-fits-all manner in which the NLRA developed. That Act and its administration has generally emphasized elections, with collective-bargaining occurring only after a union has established an employee-majority in an appropriate bargaining unit. In the early years of the Act those requirements didn't pose any insurmountable problems, for building-trades unions represented an overwhelming majority of workers

41 29 U.S.C. § 158(b)(2).

42 29 U.S.C. § 158(a)(3). For applicable legal considerations affecting both the minority union and the employer *see* app. *infra* at notes 143-177.

in their industry and "enjoyed formidable bargaining power, and unionized construction workers were among the highest paid blue collar workers in the world."[43] Furthermore, building contractors were generally satisfied with the unions' arrangements, which included apprenticeship programs and hiring halls as reliable sources of skilled labor, and uniform wages were standard in most areas. Unions thus "added a measure of stability to a wildly unstable business."[44] However, those conditions didn't last.

During the past several decades, the NLRB's rigid approach failed to find a good fit for changing conditions in the building industry. This occurred because of many factors, including the emergence of strong and combative nonunion employers, the emergence of powerful national and regional contractors, and the vastly different nature of the various employment practices that are peculiar to this industry, which include the inability or reluctance of building-trades unions to switch from unreliable top-down organizing to serious bottom-up organizing and their need for more flexibility regarding overlapping craft jurisdictions. Those differences are related to the inherently dissimilar characteristics of employment in this industry, which include the short duration of most jobs, the many employers for whom an employee typically works, the multiplicity of skills those jobs require, the changing geographical locations of those jobs, the cyclical nature of the industry, the influence of weather and seasonal swings, and of course the excessive number of individual building-trades unions, most representing crafts that often overlap with other union jurisdictions.

For a variety of reasons, nonunion construction has vastly increased and union membership has steadily declined. For the year 2017, only 14 per cent of construction employees were union members,[45] and in widespread areas of the country virtually all construction is now conducted nonunion. And just as this industry has become predominantly nonunion, wages have plummeted in most parts of the country. This race to the bottom has occurred notwithstanding that the construction industry hasn't suffered from globalized competition or from overwhelming technological changes.

It is a fact that the law and its changes have played a major role in shaping labor relations in this industry. A key building-trades' statutory change in

43 Jeff Grabelsky, *Building and Construction Trades Unions: Are They Built to Win?*, Social Policy 35, 35 (Winter 2004/2005) (hereinafter Grabelsky).

44 M. Erlich and J. Grabelsky, Standing at a Crossroads: The Building Trades in the Twenty-First Century 421, 424, 46(4) Labor History (2005).

45 Bureau of Labor Statistics, *Economic Release*, Jan. 19, 2018.

the NLRA occurred in 1959 with the addition of Section 8(f))[46] as part of the Landrum-Griffin amendments. That provision allowed unions and employers to negotiate union-shop contracts before the union had demonstrated majority support—in fact even before employees were hired—hence these agreements came to be known as "pre-hire" agreements. For several years, when unions were strong, they served their intended purpose, but that usage failed when employers refused to be parties to new 8(f) agreements. And after the Board's 1987 *Deklewa* decision,[47] which held that these pre-hire agreements could no longer be unilaterally renewed, employers who had signed such agreements were no longer obligated to sign successor agreements. Regardless, although Section 8(f) appears to be meaningless today, it isn't dead yet, for as will be noted below, when members-only bargaining is finally validated, that process can be effective again.

Except for Section 8(f) and a no-longer significant Landrum-Griffin hot-cargo concession in Section 8(e),[48] all other efforts by building-trade-unions to amend the NLRA have failed. However, better than focusing on unobtainable future legislation, under NMCB procedures these unions will be able to achieve significant gains with the aid of legalized members-only bargaining.

In addition, however—although outside the direct scope of this book—my examination of building-trade problems has convinced me that those unions need to be ready, not just to recognize the reality of changes in their industry, but also to make their own necessary internal changes and alter some of their traditional organizational structures and methods, all of which will aid them in coping with their many problems, including a major problem about which one commentator reports: "Many building trades leaders admit . . . that there are simply too many affiliates in the unionized sector of [this] industry."[49]

The nonunion share of this industry is now so large and powerful that a different organizational approach is called for. The extreme craft distinctions that used to prevail—and which are still important in a few well-organized areas—are no longer hard and fast concepts in most of the country, and they

46 29 U.S.C. § 158(f),

47 John Deklewa & Sons, 282 N.L.R.B. 1375 (1987), *enf'd sub nom*, Iron Workers Local 3 v.NLRB, 843 F.2d 770 (3rd Cir,) *cert. denied*,488 U.S. 889 (1988) ("upon the expiration of the agreement the union would enjoy no 'presumption'" of majority status, and either party [might] repudiate the 8(f) bargaining relationship." *Id.* at 1378.).

48 29 U.S.C. § 158(e).

49 Grabelsky, *supra* note 43 at 38.

hardly exist at all in nonunion sectors. Inasmuch as the nonunion part of this industry has substantially blurred the craft distinctions that used to be common, union organizing and bargaining needs to be appropriately adjusted. This isn't to say, however, that all traditional organizing, including the use of "salts"[50] can never work, but they can't work well under today's *Linden Lumber*[51] requirement of union-majorities established through employer-controlled NLRB elections. Salting could work, however, under a system that permits members-only minority-union collective bargaining. Pre-hire agreements under Section 8(f) could likewise be more successfully employed under a minority-union system. And even the problem of "double-breasting"[52] could be lessened, because a double-breasted employer's operations could henceforth be easier to disrupt with members-only picketing, which does not seek Section 9(a) majority recognition.

In other words, building-trades unions and the employees whom they represent will benefit greatly from members-only collective bargaining. In view of the numerous variables affecting employment in the construction industry, I won't hazard a precise description of how that process will function. Nevertheless, here are a few possible scenarios:

Inasmuch as no majority will be required for recognition and bargaining, a union's organizational drive might begin by approaching—with or without the help of "salts"—a small number of employees in an identifiable craft-group for whom nominal dues-payments[53] will be used to establish membership status. One must remember, the goal will now be union membership, not an election majority.[54] If conditions permit, those early joiners might be given the assurance of future employment with a union contractor should they be fired, though of course such a firing should be promptly followed by a Section 8(a)(3) charge with the Board. When this newly organized group is large enough to have an impact on a current building project should a strike occur, a request for recognition and bargaining might then be made, for majority-union status or an appropriate bargaining unit will no longer be a requirement. If the employer

50 In NLRB v. Town & Country Electric, 516 U.S. 85 (1995), the Supreme Court validated the employee status of paid union organizers, i.e.,"salts," who solicit coworkers into supporting a union.

51 *Linden Lumber Div.*, Summer & Co, v. NLRB, *supra* note 9 & 22.

52 Employer operating as two companies, one union and the other non-union. See DLL7th *supra* note 34 at 13-247 to 13-257.

53 *Supra* note 11.

54 *Supra* at notes 8-36.

grants recognition, the ensuing bargaining may require the union to make some adjustment in its usual bargaining objective. If the employer denies recognition and a strike follows, it would clearly be an unfair-labor-practice strike with a future prospect of job-return and/or a backpay awards if and when the time comes for an unconditional offer to return to work.[55] The obvious advantage of this scenario is that at no time would an election be required.

If, however, the members-only organizing is sufficiently successful so that it produces an employee-majority in an appropriate bargaining unit, what will then happen? This is where Section 8(f) comes into play, If and when the union achieves a legitimate majority that's provable without an election, a revived Section 8(f) will allow a union-shop agreement without a seven-day waiting period, plus other benefits of that provision. And even if the employer refuses to agree to a Section 8(f) agreement, the union will still have not only its full economic and picketing power to use toward reaching an agreement, it will also have a Section 8(a)(5)[56] bargaining order, because a Section 9(c) election certification would not be required by the employer in the face of proof of actual membership status, as distinguished from a representation-card majority that would be deemed insufficient under *Linden-Lumber*.[57]

The members-only bargaining process will allow organizing to follow the natural order—just like the old days—of first organizing the hard-to-replace key employees and then, if appropriate, applying economic pressure. And since bargaining will no longer require majority status as a prerequisite, this old-fashioned procedure could become an important route to successful building-trades organizing.

There are many other possible scenarios in which the legality of members-only minority-union bargaining could produce positive organizational results for building-trades unions. It suffices, however, to conclude this section simply with the obvious conclusion that while this process may not be the magic bullet those unions would like to acquire, it is a workable plan that will give individual construction employees who are "willing to put their money where their mouth is"[58] an opportunity to obtain union representation and collective-bargaining benefits—thus a viable way to move up on the middle-class ladder.

55 DLL7th *supra* note 34 at 1,686-91.

56 29 U.S.C. § 158(a)(5).

57 *Supra* note 9.

58 *Supra* notes 9-11.

V. BARGAINING IN "RIGHT-TO-WORK" STATES

Members-only collective bargaining will be particularly important for unions hoping to organize in "right-to-work" (RTW) states. This is so because under this bargaining concept it will be appreciably no more difficult for unions to organize in RTW states than in non-RTW states. As in non-RTW states, they will now be able to achieve bargaining rights without first running the gauntlet of seeking and campaigning in a difficult NLRB election. It will thus be much easier than organizing under the current system.

The intertwined approach of simultaneously organizing and bargaining—followed by further organizing—should be a welcome contrast to the existing situation in RTW states, where only unions that are willing and have the means to invest substantial time and money in the organizational and election process ever do so. Today, the odds are heavily stacked against a union successfully organizing and winning a hotly-contested election in an anti-union RTW state. For major examples of such obstacles, see references to the organizing drives at the Boeing, Volkswagen, and Kumho plants in Chapter 1.[59] And because required representation of nonmembers, i.e., "free-riders," means less income to cover the cost of representation, and because union members have to pay higher dues to cover those costs, there's presently diminished incentive for unions to organize extensively in most of the RTW states. Under members-only bargaining, however, there will be little difference between organizing in RTW and non-RTW states. Moreover, under the NMCB concept unions will have an obvious answer to the commonly-voiced RTW objection that employees ought not to be represented by a union against their will, because at the critical stage of organizing and bargaining a members-only union will be visibly proving that it doesn't represent anyone except voluntary dues-paying employees. Which also means that when a members-only union points to the benefits it has gained for its members, it will be demonstrating to the other employees what unionized employees can achieve through concerted action.

It's even conceivable that in some RTW workplaces of imprecise size there might be no hurry to determine whether and when a members-only union crosses the fifty-percent threshold into total unit representation required by Section 9(a), and if no one files an NLRB representation petition seeking that determination, a collective-bargaining contract applicable only to union

59 Chap. 1 *supra* at notes 75-78.

members might continue for an extended or indefinite period of time. More likely, however, in RTW workplaces where members-only representation has been successful, passage into majority status will be timely noted and the union will simply become a conventional Section 9(a) collective-bargaining representative for all employees in that unit, including free-riders.

Regarding that free-rider problem—which is indeed a moral problem in RTW states that's comparable to persons refusing to pay rent or taxes—there's credible anecdotal evidence that in workplaces where an established union pays vigorous attention to local problems and where its members are engaged in hands-on involvement in union activity, the number of free-riders can be kept to a tolerable minimum.[60] As one commentator reports: "Several powerful unions have hung on or even grown in that environment. Take the Culinary Union Local 226 in Las Vegas [in RTW Nevada], where about 90 percent of its 60,000 hotel and casino employee members pay dues."[61] Members-only unions might encounter a relatively low percentage of free-riders inasmuch as these unions will likely have a high level of membership-participation because of the necessary involvement of their members in the organizing and bargaining process.[62]

After members-only minority-union collective bargaining is validated and becomes effective generally, there could be a welcome—but nevertheless unlikely—happening: RTW states losing much of their appeal to companies seeking to locate in, or relocate to, those states; and in non-RTW states, anti-union political interests will have less of a desire to attempt to enact new RTW legislation. I wish that were a likely prediction, but it's obviously not on the visible horizon.

VI. NON-CONFORMING NMCB PROCESSES

The preceding parts of this chapter focused on the expected most-likely course of events following introduction of minority-union bargaining, to wit, that these new unions would usually organize and bargain for their employee-members and thereafter evolve into traditional Section 9(a) majority unions that would

60 E-mail reports from Texas and Florida and my own observations in Texas.

61 Lydia DePillis, *Laws That Decimate Unions May Be Inevitable. Here's How Labor Can Survive.* WASHINGTON POST, March 8, 2015.

62 *See* text following note 11 *supra.*

represent all employees in their respective bargaining units. That scenario was typical of the members-only bargaining process during the first decade following passage of the original NLRA[63] and could be typical again. However, because this renewed statutory interpretation, i.e., NMCB, will introduce a more readily available collective-bargaining concept, certain non-traditional bargaining arrangements might also develop. These less-likely scenarios are treated here. The *first part* addresses situations where minority-union bargaining simply continues as minority-union bargaining; the *second part* addresses situations where two or more members-only unions arise within the same potential bargaining unit; and the *third part* addresses the development of novel, non-conforming employee-representational structures and how they might function.

A. Minority-Union Bargaining that Never Evolves into Majority Bargaining

What will likely happen when a minority-union fails to achieve majority status? The answer might be "nothing," at least nothing that would automatically change the relationship between the parties. Such a non-event could mean that a majority of the employees will have continued to choose not to join the union, which is their right under Section 7 provided the employer has not induced that decision by an unlawful means. If the employer has committed no ULPs, however, the parties would likely carry on as they have in the past. The employer would be obligated to continue to bargain with the union regarding its employee members, the union would continue as bargaining agent for those members only, and the nonunion employees would remain as at-will employees for whom the employer need not,[64] but could, provide union negotiated economic benefits. However, the employer could not lawfully provide non-union employees with *discriminatory* preferred treatment—though it could, if it chooses, provide them with non-representational union-negotiated economic benefits, but the union

63 *See supra* at notes 45-48.

64 *See* Radio Officers Union v. NLRB, 347 U.S. 17 (1954), which declared:

> The language of § 8(a)(3) is not ambiguous. The unfair labor practice is for an employee to encourage or discourage membership by means of discrimination. Thus this section does not outlaw all encouragement or discouragement of membership in labor organizations; only such as is accomplished by discrimination is prohibited. Nor does this section outlaw discrimination in employment as such; only such discrimination as encourages or discourages membership in a labor organization is proscribed.... That Congress intended the employer's purpose in discriminating to be controlling is clear.

For more detailed discussion of this proposition, *see* app. *infra* at notes 145-177.

would have no obligation to provide them with representation as long as majority status has not been achieved in an appropriate bargaining unit.

B. Multiple-unions in the Same Potentially Appropriate Bargaining Unit

Although the presence of multiple unions in the same workplace is a situation that's likely to occur only rarely, if and when it does occur it will present the parties with several options. One that Professor Catherine Fisk has noted favorably is that the presence of multiple unions "might promote competition among unions to obtain the best possible employment conditions for their members,"[65] which could, indeed, be beneficial. Another possibility is *plurality* bargaining,[66] a procedure to which the Board gave its blessing long ago in *The Hoover Co.*[67] case. And there are several directions in which the latter procedures might move: The multiple unions might choose to bargain separately, they might agree to bargain jointly, or one or more of those unions or the employer might file a petition for an election under Section 9 to determine which, if any, will represent all the employees in the bargaining unit.[68] That last option could produce a traditional Section 9(a) single-union majority/exclusive bargaining outcome; however, should no union win a majority in such an election, the separate unions would simply return to square-one to begin or continue plurality bargaining, which could be conducted either separately[69] or jointly. There's both European and American precedent for joint bargaining.

---

65 Quoted by Lawrence E. Dubé, *Debate Continues on Rulemaking Proposal for NLRB to Back Members-Only Bargaining,* 41 DAL. LAB. REP. (BNA) C-1 (3/02/2011).

66 *See* Matthew W. Finkin, *The Road Not Taken: Some Thoughts on Nonmajority Employee Representation,* 69 CHI.-KENT L. REV. 195 (1993) (hereinafter Finkin), for a quasi-favorable treatment of plurality bargaining.

67 90 NLRB 1614 (1950), where the Board indicated that an employer faced with rival recognition demands from two unions "may, without violating the *Midwest Piping* doctrine, grant recognition to each of the claimants on a members-only basis." (Midwest Piping Co., 63 NLRB 1060 (1945), held that it is an unfair labor practice under § 8(2) for an employer to recognize one of two competing unions after a representation petition had been filed with the Board.)

68 The petitioning party, if a union, must comply with § 9(c)(1)(A) [29 U.S.C. § 159(c)(1)(A)], if an employer, with § 9(c)(1)(B) [29 U.S.C. § 159(c)(1)(B)].

69 In the event multiple members-only unions in America choose to bargain separately, the employer, because of the constraints of Section 8(a)(2), must deal with them equally, without discrimination. DLL 7th *supra* note 36 at 829-837. *And see* Finkin, *supra* note 66.

The European experience commonly occurs in countries where multiple unions usually exist in the same establishments, particularly in Belgium[70] and the Netherlands.[71] The late Professor Roger Blanpain provided the following description of joint-bargaining between Belgium's two principal unions, the Socialist Trade Union Movement (FGTB) and the Christian Trade Unions (CSC):

> There are no jurisdictional disputes between the parallel organizations of CSC and FGTB; rather they present a common front to the employers or employers' associations. This means that the unions will bargain with the employer on the basis of a "common" programme. Firstly the several unions will draft their separate programmes; they will meet together and formulate a "common" programme to be presented jointly to the employer(s). Both organizations are equally recognized by the employer side of the bargaining table, although of course each movement will be seeking to attract as many members as possible.[72]

The American experience is represented by a long and impressive history of joint bargaining within the construction industry. Several different building-trades craft unions typically join together to conduct such bargaining through a *council-type format* on behalf of their members who work at a particular geographic location or sometimes at a single job-site.[73] Under the minority-union concept presented here, similar joint-bargaining could be practiced where two or more unions possess separate authority to bargain with a single employer on behalf of their respective members.

Another multi-union possibility—though not one likely to occur often—would be the presence of an independent NMCB union in the same workplace, and at the same time, as another minority-union that's unlawfully favored by the employer. For such an event, a straight-forward Section 8(a)(2) company-union

---

70 Roger Blanpain, International Encyclopedia of Labour Law and Industrial Relations, *Belgium monograph* (1977) (hereinafter International Encyclopedia) at 114-117.

71 Thomas Kennedy, European Labor Relations 119 (1980).

72 International Encyclopedia, *supra* note 70 at 117.

73 The popularity of such bargaining is demonstrated, for example, by the BNA Labor and Employment Law data base, which listed 136 cases in which one of the named parties was a "Building and Construction Trades Council" (as of Sept. 15, 2009). Many of those cases can also be found in the case table of DLL 7th, *supra* note 36; *see e.g.*, under index heading of "Building Trades Council."

ULP proceeding would be appropriate and should be sufficient to address that problem.

C. Non-traditional Bargaining Phenomena

When employees become more familiar with the availability and practice of members-only bargaining, it's possible that some non-traditional forms of collective bargaining might be spawned. Some yet unknown, novel, different, unfamiliar, and/or non-conforming employee-representational groupings might seek recognition and bargaining on behalf of their employee members. Thus, in addition to the expected increase in traditional non-affiliated labor unions in organizationally active workplaces, some innovative union formats with quite different approaches to collective bargaining might also develop.

This newly available opportunity to devise or utilize diverse forms of representation should be especially attractive to professional and highly-skilled technical employees who want and/or need union representation but find it difficult or undesirable to meet the Section 9(a) representational requirements of both an employee-majority and an appropriate-bargaining unit. With the rapidly-changing nature of the global, technology-based, and demographic factors that are re-shaping the nature of work, including work that involves artificial intelligence (AI) and gig or part-time concepts, minority-union bargaining might spur creation of unique union structures that will facilitate new ways for employees to couple *employee-cooperation* and *shared common-interests* to the bargaining process and thereby develop different types of employee groupings which might bargain effectively with their employers. Some of these groupings might resemble employee caucuses that have already developed in a few American companies;[74] for these, the members-only concept might conceivably confer added legitimacy, enhanced legal status, and a better means to achieve work-related objectives. The prospect of an opportunity to try new employee grouping is indeed inviting.

---

74 See Alan Hyde, *Employee Caucus: A Key Institution in the Emerging System of Employment Law*, 69 Chi-Kent. L. Rev. 149 (1993).

CHAPTER 4.
The Legal Case for Members-Only Non-Majority Bargaining

This chapter presents the definitive legal proof that allows me to state, without any reservation, that—contrary to popular misunderstanding—the National Labor Relations Act (NLRB or Act) does not require majority-union representation as the prerequisite for all collective bargaining. The assumption that majority status is a *sine qua non* for such bargaining is based purely on custom that evolved from many years of habit and convenience, not from statutory text. It's only with regard to *exclusive* union representation of *all* employees in an appropriate bargaining unit that statutory text requires majority status, not with regard to the duty to bargain as such. And let it be said loud and clear, that the *text* of the Act that authorizes bargaining with a less-than-majority union is unambiguous. And now, at long last, we finally have an opinion from the National Labor Relations Board (NLRB or Board) which says exactly that. That conclusion, contained in Member Hirozawa's concurring opinion in *Oakland Children's Hospital and Research Center of Oakland,*[1] being a concurring opinion in a little-known case, occurred so quietly that it never received the publicity that it deserved.

This book provides the ideal opportunity to bring that important opinion to light, for that it confirms the validity of the members-only bargaining thesis that I've been asserting for several years and which this book advances. Hirozawa's finding and the thesis of this book rely on the same statutory text—which is clear, brief, precise, and spelled out in plain English. It is ordinary language that conveys its "unambiguous" status as *step-one Chevron* text,[2] thus indicating that it is the clearly articulated intent of Congress; therefore, in the Supreme Court's own words in that decision. "that is the end of the matter."[3] The finding

1 364 NLRB No. 114 (2016). *See infra* at notes 29-32.

2 Chevron U.S.A. v. Natural Resources Defense Council, Inc., 467 U.S. 837 (1984). *See* chap. 2 *supra* at notes 58-63.

3 *Id.*, at 843.

in *Oakland Children's Hospital* is treated below, following my analysis of the pertinent statutory text.[4]

Because members-only pre-majority collective-bargaining is an unfamiliar process, I'm willing to be charged with over-kill with my analysis, which spells out in considerable detail exactly what the pertinent text in the Act provides and what both legislative history and usage history strongly support.

I. UNAMBIGUOUS STATUTORY LAW

A. Statutory Construction According to Antonin Scalia

The Act's authorization of members-only minority-union collective bargaining is in accord with Justice Antonin Scalia's strictest standard of judicial textualism,[5] for it is contained in unambiguous statutory text. Although the logical place to begin the examination of that text might seem to be with Section 1 of the Act (with which I opened Chapter 3) in that it declares that the basic labor policy of the United States is "encouraging the practice and procedure of collective bargaining," it suffices here to simply note that non-majority collective bargaining (NMCB) will make it easier to realize that policy.[6] This examination will therefore concentrate on the controlling text, which begins with and relies heavily on Section 7,[7] which the late and great Professor Clyde Summers called "the tap-root and trunk of the statute."[8] Its pertinent language simply states, unequivocally and without any *majority* prerequisite or *majority* reference, that

> *Employees shall have the right* to self-organization, to form, join, or assist labor organizations, *to bargain collectively through representatives of their own*

4 *See supra note 1 and infra* at notes 27-32.

5 *See infra* at notes 35-37

6 29 U.S.C. § 151. *See* chap. 3 *infra* for an explanation of how the process works.

7 29 U.S.C. § 157. Emphasis added.

8 Clyde Summers, *The Kenneth M. Piper Lecture: Unions without Majority—A Black Hole?*, 66 CHI-KENT. L. REV. 531, 531 (1990) (hereinafter Summers).

> *choosing*, and to engage in other concerted activities for the purpose of collective bargaining or other mutual aid or protection . . . .[9]

That provision mandates in clear English that employees *shall* have the *right* to organize into unions of their own choosing and to bargain collectively. And *Section 8(a)(1)*, the general enforcer of that provision, specifies that "it is an unfair labor practice for an employer . . . to interfere with . . . employees in the exercise of the rights *guaranteed* in section 7."[10] This is straight-forward language that uses the mandatory word "shall"[11] and the fundamental word "right,"[12] all of which is "guaranteed"[13] by Section 8(a)(1). It thus ensures in the strongest statutory terms that "employees"—i.e., *all employees* covered by the Act, not just majority-union employees—shall have the "right . . . to bargain collectively." And because collective bargaining is a two-party process, which was widely understood at the time of enactment, the employer's participation as a bargaining party is essential to that process. Accordingly, an employer's refusal to bargain represents a patent "interference" with this Section 7 right, hence a violation of Section 8(a)(1).[14]

Section 8(a)(5)[15] supplements the broad language of Section 7 with a separate and specific provision that states that it is an unfair labor practice for an employer

> to refuse to bargain collectively with the representatives of his employees, subject to the provisions of section 9(a).

---

9 29 U.S.C. § 157. Emphasis added.

10 29 U.S.C. § 158(a)(1). Emphasis added.

11 *See* Mallard v. U.S. Dist. Ct. for So. Dist. of Iowa, 490 U.S. 296, 302 (1989) ("shall" confirmed as a word of requirement).

12 *Cf.* NLRB v. Gissel, 395 U.S. 575, 617 (1969).

13 In its first case that reviewed the NLRA, the Supreme Court characterized that guarantee as "a fundamental" right. NLRB v. Jones & Laughlin Steel Corp., 301 U.S. 1, 33 (1937).

14 This conclusion was fully recognized and expressed by the Act's sponsors prior to passage. 1 LEGISLATIVE HISTORY OF THE NATIONAL LABOR RELATIONS ACT OF 1935 (1949) (hereinafter 1 LEGIS. HIST.) at 1419. Several weeks later Senator Wagner confirmed that position. 2 LEGISLATIVE HISTORY OF THE NATIONAL LABOR RELATIONS ACT OF 1935 (1949) (hereinafter 2 LEGIS. HIST.) at 2102.

15 29 U.S.C. § 158(a)(5).

This too is unambiguous text. It was inserted late in the enactment process as an after-thought amendment in order to emphasize and reinforce the duty to bargain that was already contained in Sections 7 and 8(a)(1).[16] Notwithstanding the transparent meaning of Section 8(a)(5), in order to avoid any careless or erroneous reading of its language the following discussion explains in detail what this text says.

First, an examination of Section 9(a), to which Section 8(a)(5) refers: The original text is shown in ordinary type; the text added by the Taft-Hartley Act (which is not here relevant) is shown in italic type:

> Representatives designated or selected for the purposes of collective bargaining by the majority of the employees in a unit appropriate for such purposes, shall be the exclusive representatives of all the employees in such unit for the purposes of collective bargaining in respect to rates of pay, wages, hours of employment, or other conditions of employment: Provided, That any individual employee or a group of employees shall have the right at any time to present grievances to their employer *and to have such grievances adjusted, without the intervention of the bargaining representative, as long as the adjustment is not inconsistent with the terms of a collective-bargaining contract or agreement then in effect: Provided further, That the bargaining representative has been given opportunity to be present at such adjustment.*[17]

Clearly, the use of the word "majority" in Section 9(a) above is purely *conditional* with a meaning that is readily apparent. Only a union that represents a majority of the employees in an appropriate unit's can be the exclusive representative of all the employees in that unit. That means that this clause, with its *exclusivity* feature, applies only if, when, and after the representative, i.e. the union, has been "*designated or selected'* by a majority of the employees in an "*appropriate*" bargaining unit. Its application is thus unequivocally *conditional*—it has no relevancy whatever unless and until a union achieves majority status. It doesn't in any way limit bargaining only to majority unions, or restrict non-majority unions from bargaining collectively.

The *majority* concept under the Act is nevertheless highly important, for it relates to the ultimate scheme of the Act, for which it was expected that most

16 *See infra* at notes 71-75.

17 29 U.S.C. § 159(a).

collective bargaining would typically be conducted by majority unions—a concept that will continue after the NMCB process is restored. Indeed, *majoritarianism* defines what Congress intended to be the future of *mature* collective bargaining, i.e., majority-exclusivity bargaining.[18] For present purposes, however, Section 9(a)'s significance lies primarily in the identification of its *provisions* to which Section 8(a)(5) refers.

Section 8(a)(5) expressly requires an employer to bargain collectively with the "*representatives* of his [i.e. its] *employees*." But inasmuch as this subsection applies to only one *specific* unfair labor practice—in contrast to the broad and comprehensive unfair labor practices covered by Sections 7 and 8(a)(1)—it appropriately recognizes and accounts for the Section 9(a) deviation from the Section 7 "right" of *all* employees "to bargain collectively through *representatives of their own choosing*," because when a union achieves 9(a) majority and exclusive representational status there will usually be some employees—albeit a minority—who will thereafter not be represented by a union "of their own choosing." That's the inevitable consequence of the majority-exclusivity choice that Congress intended for collective bargaining to function ultimately at its most effective level,[19] i.e., as mature and established collective bargaining. It thus justified this necessary exception for *non-choosers* by relying on the democratic principle of majority rule. The reference to Section 9(a) "provisions" accommodates this exception to the employees' own right to choose, for it adds the requirement that where there's a *majority representative* in an *appropriate bargaining unit* within the meaning of Section 9(a), the "provisions" of that subsection must apply. Those "provisions" include not only the *majority* and *exclusivity* requirements, but also the subjects of collective bargaining—i.e., "rates of pay, wages, hours of employment, or other conditions of employment"—and the additional right of an "individual or a group of employees" to present "grievances.[20] However, as the statutory language alone literally indicates—as does legislative history[21]—and as a related provision of the Act, Section 8(a)(3),[22] unequivocally

18 *See* note 86 *infra* and accompanying text.

19 § 9(a) "was expressly designed to establish what Congress deemed to be the ideal form of mature collective bargaining, to wit: majority and exclusive representation and bargaining covering all employees in an appropriate bargaining unit." CHARLES J. MORRIS, THE BLUE EAGLE AT WORK: RECLAIMING DEMOCRATIC RIGHTS IN THE AMERICAN WORKPLACE 102 (2005) (hereinafter BLUE EAGLE).

20 *See text* at note 17 *supra.*

21 *See infra* at notes 64-99

22 *See infra* at notes 28-32.

confirms, neither Section 8(a)(5) nor Section 9(a) confines the employer's obligation to bargaining with majority-representatives only.

Accordingly, where there's no majority representative, the unfettered duty-to-bargain *spelled out* in Sections 7, 8(a)(1), and 8(a)(5) also applies to employees who are represented by a minority union—but obviously only on a *non-exclusive* basis. Congress thus recognized and protected the process of pre-majority collective bargaining as a *stepping-stone* precursor that was expected to lead normally to mature majority/exclusive bargaining—just as organizing and bargaining commonly occurred immediately before and after passage of the Act in 1935.[23]

Furthermore, although Congress included a comma in Section 8(a)(5), it is clear that even without the comma—which will be discussed separately below—it is the obligation "to bargain collectively," not the "representative of the employees," that is "subject to the *provisions* of section 9(a)." No other conclusion makes grammatical sense because those "provisions" include not only the *majority* and *appropriate bargaining unit* provisions that are prerequisite to a representative becoming the "*exclusive*" representative of "*all the employees*" in such a unit, but also the *subjects* of collective bargaining and the additional exception to the exclusivity provision, that "*any individual employee or group of employees shall have the right at any time to present grievances to their employer.*"[24] Had Congress intended to confine that bargaining obligation only to unions that had already achieved employee-majority and appropriate-unit status, it would have so specified.[25] All of those identified provisions are matters which the Act properly addresses with regard to the employer's duty to bargain under Section 8(a)(5). Clearly, it's the "*bargain[ing] collectively*" obligation, not the "*representatives of his employees,*" that is "subject to the provisions of Section 9(a)." Therefore, with or without the comma, that is the only intelligible reading possible.

By inclusion of the *comma*, however, Congress made it absolutely clear that any other reading is impossible. This is so because the defined unfair labor practice, as previously noted, is not the employer's "refusal to bargain collectively with the *representatives of his employees [who are] subject to the provisions of section 9(a)*;" but rather—as the punctuated language makes doubly clear—it's

23 *See* notes 50 & 102-120 *infra* and chap.2 *supra* at notes 46-49.

24 Emphasis added. The additional phrase added by the Taft-Hartley Act (note 17 *supra*) was further indication of its application as an *exclusivity* provision.

25 As the full legislative-history record shows. *See* text accompanying notes 28-32 & 79-82 *infra.*

the unfair labor practice of the employer's "*refus[ing] to bargain collectively* with the representatives of his employees" that is "*subject to the provisions of section 9(a)*." The comma unequivocally indicates that it's the *bargaining process*, not the *representatives*, that is qualified by the requirements of section 9(a).[26]

Accordingly, Section 8(a)(5) cannot be read, as some opponents of the process grasping at straws have proposed to read it, as a limitation that would confine the duty to bargain with only representatives "*chosen as provided in section 9(a)*"—text that was specifically considered in the drafting process and expressly rejected.[27] Furthermore, language in another provision of the Act likewise confirms—now with the agreement of Board Member Hirozawa's concurring opinion—what the text of Section 8(a)(5) does not mean.

That other provision is Section 8(a)(3).[28] As Member Hirozawa pointed out in 2016 in his concurring opinion in *Oakland Children's Hospital*,[29] the phrase "*subject to the provisions of section 9(a)*" in Section 8(a)(5) "does not mean that for an employer to have a duty to bargain with a union on behalf of its employees, the union must be a Section 9(a) exclusive representative "He stressed that" [c]learly the Wagner Act Congress, which drafted the language of *Section 8(a)(5)*, knew how to impose such a requirement if it so intended," for it "imposed precisely that requirement, using precisely that language" in Section 8(a)(3), which is "a strong indication that no such requirement was intended by Congress." He thus recognized that "there is no requirement that the representatives through which employees exercise their right to bargain have attained Section 9(a) status or otherwise demonstrated majority support."[30]

---

26 *See* United States v. Ron Pair Enterprises, Inc., 489 U.S. 235, 241-42, n. 4 (1989), and its reliance on Best Repair Co., v. United States, 789 F.2d 1080 (4th Cir. 1986), for the significance of comma placement in comparable statutory language.

27 *See infra* at notes 79-82.

28 29 U.S.C. § 158(a)(3).

29 *Supra* note 1. The unfair-labor-practice issue in the case was whether the employer's bargaining obligation included a requirement to proceed with arbitration of three grievances at a time when the contracting union had been replaced by a newly certified majority-union. The grievances originated under an expired contract before it had expired. The three-member Board panel agreed unanimously that this was a violation because requiring such arbitrations "serves important statutory policies." The panel consisted of Member (later Chairman) Philip A. Miscimarra and Members Kent Y. Hirozawa and Lauren McFerran. Although there was no objection raised as to the Hirozawa Concurring Opinion, footnote 30 recorded that Members Miscimara and McFarran "express no views on the additional rationale articulated" in that Opinion.

30 Emphasis in original.

Furthermore, even standing alone, Section *8(a)(3)* represents statutory evidence of Congressional *recognition* and *expectation* of the commonplace existence of minority-union bargaining, for it expressly denies minority labor organizations the right to enter into compulsory union agreements, specifying that such agreements are permitted only, as emphasized by Member Hirozawa, "if such labor organization is the representative of the employees as provided in section 9(a)," i.e., a majority union. This was a requirement that Congress first stipulated with regard to *closed-shop* agreements in the original 1935 Act and reconfirmed with reference to *union-shop* agreements in the 1947 Taft-Hartley Act. [31] It was in fact that express majority-union requirement in Section 8(a)(3) that the Wagner Act proponents used to justify not outlawing the closed shop. As the Senate committee's report on this provision specifically stated:

> the proviso [to Section 8(3)] actually narrows the now extant law regarding closed-shop agreements. While today an employer may negotiate such an agreement *even with a minority union*, the bill provides that an employer shall be allowed to make a closed-shop contract only with a [majority] labor organization. . . .[32]

Section 8(a)(3) thus represents unequivocal statutory recognition by both the Wagner-Act Congress and the Taft-Hartley Congress of the expectation, presence, and acceptance of non-majority unions and their right to bargain collectively concerning all subjects of bargaining except compulsory-union membership. In fact, Section 8(a)(3) is the only place in Section 8, the sole unfair-labor-practice section, where the word "majority" appears, and that appearance further confirms the conditional nature of Section 9(a).

The bottom line to the foregoing statutory analysis is that in workplaces where the Section 9(a) majority-bargaining-unit condition isn't activated, the unambiguous text of the Act *guarantees* that employees *shall* have the enforceable *right to bargain collectively* through a less-than-majority union of their own choosing on a nonexclusive, i.e., members-only, basis. Thus, an employer who refuses to bargain collectively with that union commits an unfair labor practice

31 61 Stat. 136 (1947). Emphasis added.

32 Emphasis added. 2 LEGIS. HIST., *supra* note 14 at 2311. This feature was also noted promptly by E. G. Latham, *Legislative Purpose and Administrative Policy under the National Labor Relations Act,* 4 GEO. WASH. L. REV. 433, (1936) (hereinafter Latham) ("A minority organization could not, therefore, conclude a closed shop agreement."). See notes 97-98 *infra.*

in violation of Sections 8(a)(1) and 8(a)(5). This statutory text isn't Humpty-Dumpty language that naysayers might like to say means whatever they "choose it to mean."[33] Rather, it is plain, explicit language that means exactly what it says. It thus means that collective bargaining is available for *all employees*, not just majority employees, which scope and intent was explicitly confirmed by the specific explanation of the meaning of section 8(5) in the Senate and House reports and by Senator Wagner.[34]

Accordingly, as we've seen, the aforesaid reading of the plain meaning of the relevant NLRA provisions passes Justice Scalia's most severe test of statutory construction. He insisted that "[t]he text is the law, and it is the text which must be observed,"[35] and "[o]nce Congress floats that text out there, it has its own life. It means what it means. It means what it says."[36] Indeed, he actually applied that principle to an NLRB case where the issue was similar to the minority-union bargaining issue herein. In *NLRB v. Kentucky River Community Care, Inc.*,[37] he read the statutory definition of "supervisor," that included authority that "requires the use of independent judgment,"[38] to mean just what those words say—notwithstanding that those words were "indisputably ambiguous."[39] Thus, the natural reading of the duty-to-bargain provisions herein, which does not depend on any ambiguity, provides an even stronger example, for it is where the *Chevron* Court emphasized that "the agency must give effect to the unambiguously expressed intent of Congress."[40] To illustrate, for example, "employees" in Section 7 are given the right "to bargain collectively through representatives of

33 Lewis Carroll, Alice Through the Looking Glass, chap. 6.

34 *See infra* at note 75.

35 Antonin Scalia, A Matter of Interpretation 22 (1997). *See also* the Supreme Court's decision in Nielsen v. Preap, 2019 U.S. LEXIS 2088, 2019 WL 1245517 (decided Oct. 10, 2018), (*citing* A. Scalia & B. Garner, Reading Law: The Interpretation of Legal Texts, 140 (2012): "Words are to be given the meaning that proper grammar and usage would assign them.")

36 Adam Liptak, *On the Bench and Off, the Eminently Quotable Justice Scalia,* N.Y. Times, May 12, 2009, at A13 & A16. And as Justice Rehnquist wrote in Griffin v. Oceanic Contractors, Inc., 458 U.S. 564, 570 (1982), "The words chosen by Congress, given their plain meaning, leave no room for the exercise of discretion. . . . Our task is to give effect to the will of Congress, and when its will has been expressed in reasonably plain terms, 'that language must ordinarily be regarded as conclusive.'" (quoting from Consumer Products Safety Comm'n. v. GTE Sylvania, Inc., 447 U.S. 102, 1108 (1980)).

37 532 U.S. 706 (2001).

38 *Id.*, at 720.

39 In Justice Stevens' dissent, *id.*, at 725.

40 *Chevron U.S.A., supra* note 2 at 843.

their own choosing," which unquestionably means *all employees* covered by the Act, not just majority-employees in an appropriate bargaining unit.

With reference to the same kind of broad and sweeping language that's involved here, Chief Justice John G. Roberts, when he was a judge on the District of Columbia Circuit Court of Appeals, observed in two separate decisions that "[t]he Supreme Court has consistently instructed that statutes written in broad, sweeping language should be given broad, sweeping application."[41]

Although the cases are legion that declare such plain language to be a paramount factor in statutory construction, one case on which Judge Roberts particularly relied, *New York v. Federal Energy Regulatory Commission (FERC),*[42] is especially relevant here because its facts and the Court's statutory construction parallel the rediscovered reading of the NLRA statutory language here being construed.

The statutory language in issue in *New York v. FERC*, like the NLRA language here under review, was broad language that Congress enacted in the Federal Power Act (FPA) as part of President Roosevelt's "New Deal" legislation in 1935. Sixty years later, FERC, the administrative agency charged with enforcement of the FPA, issued a regulatory order that affected the "unbundling" of electric power transmission, which it based on original language in the FPA.[43] Notwithstanding the Supreme Court's recognition that "the landscape of the electric industry has changed since the enactment of the FPA," it ruled that the original "statutory text . . . unambiguously authorizes" the regulation in issue and therefore rejected New York's effort to "discredit this straightforward analysis of the statutory language."[44] That same straightforward analysis of statutory language is appropriate here, for notwithstanding that the landscape of American labor relations has also changed since enactment of the NLRA, its statutory text still unambiguously means exactly what it says, which is what this book says it means.

---

41 In re England, Secretary of the Navy, 375 F.3d 1159, 1179 (D.C. Cir. 2004); Consumers Electronics Ass'n v. Federal Communications Commission, 347 F.3d 291, 298 (D.C. Cir. 2003).

42 535 U.S. 1 (2002).

43 Regarding this language: "the transmission of electric energy in interstate commerce . . . ." Jurisdiction was based on § 201(b) of the FPA, 16 U.S.C. § 824(b) on which its jurisdiction was based. 535 U.S. at 7. "Unbundling" was the separation of transmission costs from energy costs in retail billing.

44 *Id.*, at 16, 19, & 20.

B. Section 8(a)(1) Construction Alone—An Alternative

Although the above analysis conclusively demonstrates the applicable meaning of Sections 1, 7, 8(a)(1), 8(a)(3), and 8(a)(5) confirming the validity of enforceable collective bargaining conducted by pre-majority unions on behalf of their members only, it should also be noted that the same conclusion is reached by applying an alternative and more limited interpretation of the Act based only on Sections 7 and 8(a)(1).

In the unlikely event that Section 8(a)(5) and/or Section 9(a) were to be interpreted as requiring bargaining *only* with representatives that have achieved majority status under Section 9(a)—an interpretation that seems inconceivable in view of the clarity of the contrary statutory language and the strength of its legislative history—such a construction would nevertheless have no effect on an employer's duty to bargain with a non-majority collective bargaining (NMCB) union in workplaces where there is not currently a designated Section 9(a) majority representative. This is so because even if the unfair labor practice defined in Section 8(a)(5) were thus narrowly construed to compel employers to bargain only with unions that satisfy the majority conditions of Section 9(a), a separate right to engage in minority-union bargaining for union members only would still remain and be enforceable as an *independent violation of Sections 7 and 8(a)(1)*—which is what Senator Wagner originally intended.[45] This would be a type of coverage that is commonly and regularly applied to many other types of protected concerted activity. For example, although Section 8(a)(3) is the provision that specifically prohibits employment discrimination relating to tenure of employment, such as discharges, only Section 8(a)(1), standing alone, provides protection to employees who are discharged for pre-union concerted activity.[46] Thus, in the unlikely event that Section 8(a)(5) were deemed applicable only to majority-based collective bargaining covered by Section 9(a), non-majority collective bargaining would still be guaranteed to employees under the broad language of Section 7, denial of which would be enforceable as an independent violation of Section 8(a)(1)—which is what the original NLRA bill intended, as history will show.[47]

---

45 *See infra* at notes 71-74.

46 For a description of independent § 8(a)(1) violations, *see* John E. Higgins, Jr. ed., THE DEVELOPING LABOR LAW: THE BOARD, THE COURTS, AND THE NATIONAL LABOR RELATIONS ACT (7th ed. 2017) at 6-14 & 15.

47 *See infra* at notes 71-74..

II. CONSISTENT AND SUPPORTING LEGISLATIVE HISTORY

Although legislative history fully supports the above textual reading, it is a basic tenet of statutory construction that where the text is clear—as it is here—legislative history is not a consideration.[48] Nevertheless, because over the years inaccurate conventional wisdom has so blurred recognition of the plain meaning of the text, and because opponents of minority-union bargaining have asserted many false examples of legislative history,[49] I believe it important to clarify the historical record, for that record unequivocally reinforces the legal validity of the NMCB process that's inherent in the text of the Act.

A. The Enactment Period: The Great Depression and Senator Wagner

Before clarifying the historical record, it will be useful to take a brief but important glance at the time period when the legislative stage was being set. An examination of the traditional means by which unions were organized before and during the Great Depression—the period in which the NLRA was conceived and enacted—is therefore in order. Unions almost always organized and bargained based on their unity and strength, not on the basis of formal majority selection, and organizing and bargaining were conducted as an overlapping process. Despite strong and often violent employer-opposition, groups of workers with common grievances made commitments–usually with the active encouragement and assistance of outside union organizers–to become union members, after which they could confront their employers from positions of combined strength rather than individual weakness. As these fledgling unions increased their visibility and appeal, they typically grew in membership and authority. One contemporary union observer described that process as follows:

> [U]nions were free to organize in whatever manner they found most effective. Frequently, a union would build its membership in a shop by first organizing a small group of workers who had the fortitude to stand strong for the union. Upon the organization of such group, certain job improvements would be

48 "We do not inquire what the legislature meant; we ask only what the statute means." Oliver Wendell Holmes, *The Theory of Legal Interpretation*, 12 HARV. L. REV. 419 (1899). *See also* Ratzlaf v. U.S., 510 U.S. 135, 147-48 (1994) ("[w]e do not resort to legislative history to cloud a statutory text that is clear.").

49 *See infra* at chap. 6 notes 34-36 and app. notes 106-110.

> obtained for them from management. And this working example of the gains to be achieved through organization frequently formed the most potent organizational appeal to other workers in the shop, and they too would join to improve their conditions.[50]

Now to a specific review of pertinent NLRA history. The leading, indeed the towering, figure in the legislative action that produced the Act that bears his name, was Senator Robert F. Wagner. He envisioned this statute to be the means by which *industrial democracy*, which was to be achieved through the medium of collective bargaining, would become a reality in America. He considered this "democratic method" to be the preferred method for coordinating industry, for "it places the primary responsibility where it belongs and asks industry and labor to solve their mutual problems through self-government." It was his view that the "right to bargain collectively is at the bottom of social justice for the worker, as well as the sensible conduct of business affairs." Wagner deemed collective bargaining to be a partnership that presupposes "some equality of bargaining power,"[51] hence the ideal format for workplace democracy— which fits well as an integral part of a democratic capitalist system.

Those concise remarks tell us what Wagner intended for his bill to accomplish, and that intent was the intent of Congress, for unlike most other major legislation, this statute was the product of a single legislator. Although Wagner received assistance from various sources, he was fully in control of all the bill's contents from introduction to final passage.[52] The Wagner Act was assuredly his Act. The core provisions of that Act, including all of the provisions in issue herein, are still in the law, not having been altered by the subsequent

---

50 Paul R. Hutchings, *Effect on the Trade Union*, in THE WAGNER ACT: AFTER TEN YEARS 73 (Louis G. Silverberg ed. 1945)..

51 The three foregoing quotations are from Address at National Democratic Club Forum, May 8, 1937, quoted in Leon H. Keyserling, *Why the Wagner Act?*, in Silverberg, *id.*, at 13.

52 Although Leon H. Keyserling, Wagner's legislative assistant, was the primary draftsman of both the bill and all of Wagner's public statements and materials—including his speeches and key committee reports—Wagner was kept fully advised at all stages of the work and was in total agreement with the final product. Kenneth M. Casebeer, *Holder of the Pen: An Interview with Leon Keyserling on Drafting the Wagner Act*, 42 U. MIAMI L. REV. 295, 302-03, 341-43, 361 (1987) (hereinafter Casebeer, *Holder of the Pen*); Kenneth M. Casebeer, *Drafting Wagner's Act: Leon Keyserling and the Precommittee Drafts of the Labor Disputes Act and the National Labor Relations Act* , 11 INDUS. REL. L. J. 73, 76 (1989) (hereinafter Casebeer, *Keyserling Drafts*); IRVING BERNSTEIN, TURBULENT YEARS, A HISTORY OF THE AMERICAN WORKER 1933-1941 (1969), at 340; *see also* Leon H. Keyserling, *The Wagner Act: Its Origin and Current Significance*, 29 GEO. WASH. L. REV. 199, 215 (1960).

Taft-Hartley[53] and Landrum-Griffin[54] amendments,[55] both of which carefully preserved those basic features.

B. Prelude to the Wagner Bill

In order to better understand the genesis of the provisions of this Act that protect the right of non-majority employees to engage in members-only bargaining, the place to begin is with the fourteen-word statutory phrase in Section 7 which states that "[e]mployees shall have the right to . . . bargain collectively through representatives of their own choosing," for that text had been contained in Section 7(a) of the National Industrial Recovery Act (NIRA),[56] the 1933 flagship statute in President Franklin Roosevelt's "New Deal" administration; that phrasing was based on similar language in the Norris-LaGuardia Act.[57] Section 7(a) of the NIRA thus contained the essence of what was later to emerge as the substantive law of the Wagner Act. Employers who conformed to the *codes of fair competition* referenced in Section 7(a) were entitled to display a "Blue Eagle" poster or banner signifying their compliance.[58] That specific Section 7(a) text is thus important here because its wording is the same as the current language in Section 7 of the NLRA. Having knowingly borrowed this text verbatim, Congress thereby reenacted the same basic substantive labor law that had

53 29 U.S.C. §§ 141-187 (1947).

54 *Id.*, §§ 401-531 (1959).

55 *See generally* Charles J. Morris, *How the National Labor Relations Act was Stolen and How it Can Be Recovered: Taft-Hartley Revisionism and the National Labor Relations Board's Appointment Process*, 33 BERKELEY J. EMP. & LAB. L. 1, 15-19 (2012).

56 Ch. 90, § 7(a), 48 Stat. 195 (1933) The text of § 7(a) reads as follows:

> Every code of fair competition, agreement, and license approved, prescribed, or issued under this title shall contain the following conditions: (1) ***That employees shall have the right to*** *organize and* ***bargain collectively through representatives of their own choosing****, and shall be free from the interference, restraint, or coercion of employers of labor, or their agents, in the designation of such representatives or in self-organization or in other concerted activities for the purposes of collective bargaining or other mutual aid or protection*; (2) that no employee and no one seeking employment shall be required as a condition of employment to join any company union or to refrain from joining, organizing, or assisting a labor organization of his own choosing; and (3) that employees shall comply with the maximum hours of labor, minimum rates of pay, and other conditions of employment, approved or prescribed by the President.
>
> Ch. 90, § 7(a), 48 Stat. 195 (1933). Italic emphasis added for comparison with §7 of the Wagner Act, and the basic fourteen-word phrase is highlighted in **bold** face.

57 *Compare* § 7(a) of the NIRA with 29 U.S.C. § 102 of the Norris-LaGuardia Act.

58 Lloyd K. Garrison, *The National Labor Boards*, 184 ANNALS AM. ACAD. POL. & SOC. SCI. 138, 145 (1936) (hereinafter Garrison).

previously existed under the NIRA. The familiar "borrowed statute" rule of construction is applicable. As Professor William Eskridge has pointed out, "when Congress borrows a statute, it adopts by implication interpretation placed on that statute, absent express statement to the contrary."[59]

To oversee the operation of Section 7(a), President Roosevelt created two rudimentary labor boards.[60] Both boards accorded the fourteen-word phrase its literal meaning, including recognition of the right of less-than-majority union employees to engage in collective bargaining and the corresponding duty of employers to bargain with those minority unions. Even after those boards had adopted the practice of granting exclusive representation to unions that had won majority status through governmentally supervised elections, they continued to rule that employers had a duty to bargain with non-majority unions in workplaces where there hadn't been a majority determination through an election.[61] However, because there was no effective means to enforce Section 7(a), Senator Wagner and his supporters recognized the need to replace it with a new statute—one that would retain the basic substantive provisions of Section 7(a) and also provide an effective means to require compliance from recalcitrant employers. As the chairman of the former National Labor Relations Board (old NLRB) described the enforcement weakness of Section 7(a),

> There were only two means of enforcement, and neither was satisfactory. The first was, upon noncompliance by an employer, to refer the case to the NRA[62] for removal of his Blue Eagle . . . . But in most cases, it meant nothing, and then the only recourse was to refer the matter to the Department of Justice for prosecution in the courts, which would have been too slow and cumbersome to accomplish anything, and it was not attempted by the Department except in a few ill-starred cases.[63]

---

59 William N. Eskridge, Jr., Dynamic Statutory Interpretation, Appendix 3, *The Rehnquist Court's Canons of Statutory Construction,* 323, 324, (1994), *citing* Molzof v. United States, 502 U.S. 301 (1992); Metropolitan Life Ins. Co. v. Taylor, 481 U.S. 58 (1987).

60 National Labor Board (NLB) and the National Labor Relations Board (old NLRB). *See* Blue Eagle, *supra* note 19 at 31-40 & 46-52).

61 *See* notes 69-70 *infra.*

62 The "NRA" reference is to the National Recovery Administration, the agency created by the NIRA and charged with its enforcement.

63 Garrison, *supra* note 58 at 145.

C. The Key Provisions of the Wagner Bill and its Late Amendment

Wagner's 1935 bill clarified and strengthened the substantive rights that were contained in the earlier statute and codified, as the new Section 9(a), the majority-exclusivity principle that had been generated by decision and practice under the old NLRB[64] and its predecessor the National Labor Board (NLB).[65] It also added an administrative mechanism with remedial authority, to wit, the National Labor Relations Board (the present NLRB). It should therefore be emphasized that the Wagner Act wasn't intended to create new law but rather to reestablish old law with clarity and teeth.[66] Its legislative history is replete with declarations to that effect. For example, on the very day the bill was introduced, Wagner told his Senate colleagues that "[t]he national labor relations bill which I now propose is novel neither in philosophy nor in content. It creates no new substantive rights."[67]

A review of the status of minority-union bargaining under Section 7(a) of the NIRA sheds revealing light on the intent of Congress. Majority status wasn't a prerequisite for bargaining, nor was an election. The NLB, the first board that President Roosevelt created to implement that provision, routinely found breaches of the duty to bargain with less-than-majority unions, and it ordered elections for only three reasons: (1) when a dispute existed between two unions claiming representation (one of which was usually a company union),[68] (2) when an employer questioned a union's claim of majority representation, or (3) when a substantial number of employees made the request. In all other cases majority

64 Established by executive order in 1934. *See* Blue Eagle, *supra note 19* at 48.

65 Established by President Roosevelt's announcement and later executive order in 1933. See Blue Eagle, *supra* note 19 at 25 & 34.

66 This perception is widely recognized and accepted. See, e.g., Melvyn Dubofsky, The State and Labor in Modern America 127 (1994) (confirming that the bill was "designed to clarify § 7(a) and create a permanent NLRB with enforcement powers.")

67 1 Legis. Hist., *supra* note 14 at 1312. *See also* Senate committee testimony of Milton Handler, of the Columbia University Law School faculty and former general counsel of the NLB: "[The bill] codifies the administrative experience of the National Labor and National Labor Relations Boards and succinctly summarizes their many rulings and decisions. In so doing, it makes no departure from the underlying policy of 7(a)." *Id.* at 1611.

68 *See* Emily Clark Brown, *Selection of Employees' Representatives*, 40 Monthly Lab. Rev. 1, 4-6, Tables 1-4 (1935).

status was deemed irrelevant to the duty to bargain.[69] These practices and interpretations were reconfirmed by the NLB's successor, the old NLRB.[70]

It is historically significant—but probably a surprise to most of the labor-law community—that the original Wagner bill didn't contain a separate duty-to-bargain unfair-labor-practice provision; and when such a provision, Section 8(5),[71] was belatedly added as an after-thought amendment, it was never the subject of separate Congressional discussion or debate. Wagner and his legislative assistant Leon Keyserling, the primary draftsman of the bill, had been of the opinion that such a specific clause was unnecessary because the employer's duty to bargain was adequately covered by the broad collective-bargaining requirement contained in the familiar fourteen-word clause in Section 7. Under that clause, a refusal to bargain represented an *interference* with the employees' right to bargain collectively, hence the employer's duty to bargain was fully enforceable under Section 8(1),[72] just as it had been under Section 7(a) of the NIRA. This construction had been emphasized in *Houde Engineering Corporation*,[73] a leading case under the old NLRB that Wagner cited when he testified before the Senate Committee on Education and Labor, stating that

---

69 Illustrative of this construction of § 7(a) were National Lock Co., 1 NLB (Part 2) 15 (1934); Bee Line Bus Co., 1 NLB (Part 2) 24 (1934); and Eagle Rubber Co., 1 NLB (Part 2) 31 (1934)—-all of which were decided subsequent to Denver Tramway, 1 NLB 64 (1934), the key decision in which the NLB established the principle of majority-exclusivity applicable to a union that had demonstrated its majority in a Board-ordered election. *See* BLUE EAGLE, *supra* note 19 at 39. *See also* Minier Sargent, *Majority Rule in Collective Bargaining Under Section 7(a)*, ILLINOIS L. REV. 275 (1934) ("The concept of a representative selected merely by a majority of the employees in a plant being the representative of all, with power to make a contract for all covering terms and conditions of employment for a specified period of time was foreign to the labor relations field in general industry prior to the NIRA. The only principle of majority rule known prior to the statute was the principle of rule by a majority within an organization voluntarily chosen by the employee, from which organization the employee was free to withdraw without losing his employment if he so desired." *Id.*, at 278, with n. 5: "The case of the closed shop must, of course, be excepted from this statement."). For other contemporaneous appraisals of practices relating to plurality and majority bargaining under § 7(a), *see* Emmett B. McNatt, *Organized Labor and the Recovery Act*, 32 MICHIGAN L. REV. 807 (1934), and Raymond S. Smithhurst, *Effect of Administrative Interpretation on the Powers of the National Labor Relations Board*, 3 GEO. WASH. L. REV. 141 (1935).

70 *See* Houde Engineering Corp., 1 NLRB (old) 35 (1934). *See also* BLUE EAGLE, *supra* note 19 at 48-52.

71 The present § 8(a)(5).

72 § 8(1) [the present § 8(a)(1)] declares that it is an unfair labor practice for an employer "to interfere with, restrain, or coerce employees in the exercise of the rights guaranteed in section 7. . . ."

73 *Supra* note 70.

> The right of employees to bargain collectively implies a duty on the part of the employer to bargain with their representatives. [T]he incontestably sound principle is that the employer is obligated by the statute to negotiate in good faith with his employees' representatives; to match their proposals, if unacceptable with counter proposals; and to make every reasonable effort to reach an agreement.[74]

The 1935 bill's only limitation on that Section 7 bargaining requirement was contained in the *conditional language in* Section 9(a), the previously emphasized part of which reads as follows:

> Representatives designated or selected for the purposes of collective bargaining by the majority of the employees in a unit appropriate for such purposes, shall be the exclusive representatives of all the employees in such unit for the purposes of collective bargaining . . . .

As previously observed, that text indicates that Section 9(a) was entirely conditional, to be activated only *if, when,* and *after* a majority of the employees in an appropriate bargaining unit designate a single union as their representative.

Section 8(5) wasn't added until the half-way point in the life of the bill—ten weeks after its introduction—and, as we have seen, it is undisputed in the legislative record that it wasn't intended to change the substantive bargaining requirements of the original bill. The reason it was added was that Francis Biddle, chairman of the old NLRB, had lobbied long and hard for its inclusion, and although Wagner finally consented to Biddle's proposed amendment, he and the Senate and House committees made it expressly clear that the new Section 8(5), together with the other three subject-specific unfair labor practices, were "*designed not to impose limitations or restrictions upon the general guaranties of the first* [Section 8(1)], but rather to spell out with particularity some of the practices that have been most prevalent and most troublesome."[75] The four separate unfair labor practices were therefore meant to reinforce their respective prohibitions, not to diminish them. It's significant that there was virtually no

---

74 *See* 1 LEGIS. HIST., *supra* note 14 at 1,419. Several weeks later Wagner reaffirmed that position. 2 LEGIS. HIST., *supra* note 14 at 2,102. For the same view reconfirmed by Keyserling in an interview in March, 1986, *see also* Casebeer, *Holder of the Pen, supra* note 51 at 330.

75 Senate Committee Report, 2 LEGIS. HIST., *supra* note 14 at 2,309. Emphasis added. *See also* comparable Wagner statement and House Committee Report, id., at 2,333 and 2,971 respectively.

discussion of the new Section 8(5) amendment in the Senate committee[76] where the amendment had originated,[77] and both the Senate and House adopted it pro forma without debate.[78]

Regarding the meaning of that Section 8(5) amendment, its legislative history shows that it was deliberately worded so as not to confine the employer's obligation to bargaining with majority unions only, thereby ensuring applicability of the bargaining requirement with minority unions in workplaces where Section 9(a) majority-unions had not yet been selected. This revealing fact was expressly contained in a post-introduction draft of the Wagner bill that included various proposed amendments.[79] After the original bill had been introduced and referred to the Senate Committee on February 21, 1935, Biddle presented for the committee's consideration—as indicated by the typewritten insert onto this draft—alternative texts of his proposed new Section 8(5) unfair-labor-practice amendment. Here are his two versions, verbatim from that insert:

76 "[T]here was little discussion of the bargaining concept at the committee hearings. Even the suggestion of Chairman Biddle of the old NLRB that an express duty to bargain be inserted in the bill failed to stimulate discussion, though the suggestion was adopted." Russell A. Smith, *The Evolution of the "Duty to Bargain" Concept in American Labor Law*, 39 MICH. L. REV. 1065, 1085 (1941).

77 *Id.*

78 2 LEGIS. HIST., *supra* note 14 at 2,348 & 3,216.

79 Casebeer, *Keyserling Drafts, supra* note 52, at 131. *See also* BLUE EAGLE, *supra* note 19 at 62-63 & 241. For an explanation of the proper designation of this draft, see BLUE EAGLE, *id.*, at 299, n. 19. This draft had been in the possession of Leon Keyserling and was published in 1989 by Professor Kenneth Casebeer. The original of the draft is in the collection of the Leon Keyserling papers in the Lauinger Library of Georgetown University, of which a photocopy was provided to Professor Morris as part of his research for the BLUE EAGLE, *supra note* 19. This draft shows proposed revisions superimposed on an officially printed version of the original bill that was introduced on February 21, 1935. All of the changes on the document appear either in handwriting or as typed copy on inserted flaps—the latter being how the two versions of § 8(5), noted below, appear, with the handwritten identification of "Biddle." There are also other handwritten marginal designations elsewhere in the document which show the sources or sponsors of the various proposed changes, except—presumably—where Keyserling was himself the source or sponsor. *See also*, for comparative purposes, the proposed changes inserted in this draft with their identification of sources and the proposed changes with their sources as announced by the Senate Committee on March 11, 1935, in its Comparison of S. 2926 and S.1958, 1 LEGIS. HIST., *supra* note 14 at 1,319-71, especially at 1331, which shows Biddle's final proposal for § 8. *See also* the changes that were later incorporated in the final bill as reported by the committee on May 2, 1935, *id.*, at 2,285, which shows that this draft was a preliminary committee mark-up of Senator Wagner's original bill, i.e., a working draft composed during committee consideration between February 21 and March 11, 1935. Such comparison indicates that most but not all of the inserted changes were incorporated into the final bill as reported, thus demonstrating the preliminary nature of the draft's mark-up status, and—more important for present purposes—that every change or proposed change included in this draft of § 8(5) occurred within the Senate committee and thus received the consideration of that committee.

> (5) To refuse to bargain collectively with the representatives of his employees, subject to the provisions of Section 9(a).
>
> or, (5) To refuse to bargain collectively with employees through their representatives, *chosen as provided in Section 9(a).* [80]

What happened to that alternative dual presentation absolutely confirms that the addition of Section 8(5) wasn't meant to confine an employer's bargaining duty to majority unions only. By adopting the first version—which is the text now contained in the statute—Biddle, Keyserling, Wagner, and the Senate committee consciously chose language that would ensure that the duty to bargain with a majority union wouldn't exclude the duty to bargain with a minority union prior to establishment of its Section 9(a) majority status. Patently, had the drafters intended to exclude such minority bargaining they would have selected either that second alternative version–the version spelled out immediately above–or the previously noted qualifying language used in Section 8(3), i.e. "if such labor organization is the representative of the employees as provided in section 9(a)."[81] Either would have limited the bargaining obligation under Section 8(5) to Section 9(a) majority/exclusivity unions. Here then were the "*smoking guns*" that reinforce the plain and literal reading of Section 8(a)(5), which conclusively confirm that it contains no such limitation and was not intended to be so limited.

As the Supreme Court has emphasized, "[f]ew principles of statutory construction are more compelling than the proposition that Congress does not intend *sub silentio* to enact statutory language that it has earlier discarded in favor of other language."[82] Accordingly, as verified by legislative history, Congress consciously intended that the only limitation on the duty to bargain contained in Section 7 and the combined texts of Sections 8(a)(5) and 9(a) was the condi-

80 Emphasis added. *See also* text accompanying notes 27-32 *supra.*

81 *Id.*

82 INS v. Cardoza-Fonseca, 480 U.S. 421, 442-43 (1987) (internal quotation marks omitted). *See also* United States v. Riverside Bayview Homes, Inc., 474 U.S. 121, 137 (1985) (holding that Congress's rejection of legislation curbing an agency's jurisdiction was evidence that Congress did not intend to overrule the agency's interpretation); Albemarle Paper Co. v. Moody, 422 U.S. 405, 414 n.8 (1975) (holding that Congress's rejection of a House amendment to Title VII (42 U.S.C. §§ 2,000e ff) that would have barred back pay to persons who had not filed EEOC charges showed Congress did not intend such a rule); Bradley v. Sch. Bd. of City of Richmond, 416 U.S. 696, 716 (1974) (holding that Congress's explicit rejection of House amendment limiting ability to recover attorneys' fees was evidence that Congress did not intend such limitation).

tional *exclusivity* requirement that would occur only *if* and *after* the employees in an appropriate bargaining unit designate or select a majority representative. Congress thus mandated that until that event occurs, nonexclusive—i.e., less-than-majority—members-only collective bargaining would be fully protected for those employees who choose a union to represent them for that purpose.

D. The Congressional Debates

The subject of minority-union collective bargaining prior to designation of majority representation was not even an issue in the Congressional debates. At that time the prevalence of less-than-majority members-only bargaining was common knowledge,[83] and Wagner and Keyserling were well-aware of the need to protect such bargaining,[84] and that intention was clearly demonstrated in the drafting process.[85] When the bill was being actively considered, pre-majority bargaining wasn't viewed as controversial. There was, however, considerable controversy concerning the ultimate configuration of mature post-majority bargaining. Proponents of the bill explained that majority/exclusivity bargaining—the bill's solution to the problems of plural unionism—would mean more effective bargaining, and this was the goal sought by Wagner and his supporters.[86] That concept of majority bargaining, however, was indeed the *ultimate objective* of the statute and its framers. It was recognized and frequently announced by the bill's proponents that for collective bargaining to have its maximum impact it should be representative of all the affected employees. It was thus intended that once a majority union had been designated there should

---

83 *See* National Industrial Conference Board, INDIVIDUAL AND COLLECTIVE BARGAINING UNDER THE N.I.R.A.--A STATISTICAL STUDY OF PRESENT PRACTICE (1933), Tables 1 & 2 at p. 16; *see also* BLUE EAGLE, *supra* note 19 at 26-31.

84 *See* BLUE EAGLE, *supra* note 19 at 26-30, 31 n. 87, 42-46, 56-64, & 69.

85 The drafts of both the 1934 and 1935 bills show the development of provisions that were tentatively designed to protect minority-union bargaining. See BLUE EAGLE, *supra* note 19 at chaps. 2 & 3, at 41-64 and their appendices of pertinent early drafts of the 1934 and 1935 bills, at 231-242. See also app. *infra* at notes 42-46 & 106-109, which show how opponents of the process have dishonestly portrayed those irrelevant portions of legislative history.

86 *See* 1 LEGIS. HIST., *supra* note 14 at 1419; BLUE EAGLE, *supra* note 19 at 103 ("It was Wagner's view and that of others who supported his 1935 bill . . . that if plural representation were allowed following the selection of a majority union an employer could play off one group against the other, thereby reducing substantially the bargaining power of the majority union."); Summers, *supra* note 8 at 539 ("The history of the majority rule principle shows that its purpose was not to limit the ability of a non-majority union to represent its own members, but to protect a majority union's ability to bargain collectively.").

be no recognition of or dealing with any minority union, and there's abundant legislative history regarding that final bargaining stage.

On the other side of that debate, the employers' lobby opposed majority/ exclusivity bargaining as a denial of the rights of minorities, for they favored pluralism in collective bargaining and the continued inclusion of company unions;[87] they also argued that the Board's authority to determine a bargaining unit would lead to a closed shop.[88] Thus, in the context of post-majority bargaining, employers favored the right of minority unions to engage in collective bargaining even after majority status had been determined—which they did not achieve—but *they never voiced any objection to the role of minority-union bargaining prior to the designation of a majority representative.*[89]

The view of the proponents of the 1935 bill favoring exclusivity in mature majority-based collective bargaining was the legacy of both the NLB and the old NLRB under the NIRA.[90] It shouldn't be confused, however–as it wasn't confused by Congress–with the collective bargaining in which minority unions often engaged during preliminary organizational stages, i.e., before they attained majority-status. That early *stepping-stone stage* of minority-union bargaining was deemed a normal and frequently necessary part of a union's natural maturation process, and it continued to be protected by the 1935 Act. It was the expected norm that unions, like business enterprises, would often begin small but eventually grow larger and become more effective.

That was certainly the expectation when the Act was passed, for a union's bargaining status at that time was commonly based on actual membership, not on authorization cards or elections.[91] Thus, like its precursor Section 7(a) under the NIRA, the collective-bargaining requirements of the NLRA were written so that employees could begin the bargaining process on a limited basis through less-than-majority unions on behalf of their employee-members only.

The Congressional debates concentrated on bargaining rights *after* a majority union had been chosen, particularly whether minority unions should have any presence at that mature bargaining stage. Although there was no debate

87 IRVING BERNSTEIN, THE NEW DEAL COLLECTIVE BARGAINING POLICY *108-109* (1950).

88 *Id.*

89 *See* BLUE EAGLE, *supra* note 19 at 69-70.

90 Exemplified by the *Denver Tramway* (*supra* note 69) and *Houde Engineering Corp.*, (*supra* note 70) cases.

91 *See* BLUE EAGLE, *supra* note 19, at 17-40.

about minority-union bargaining *prior to* establishment of majority representation, numerous statements by the bill's proponents showed full recognition that the *exclusivity* principle in Section 9(a) —generally referred to simply as "majority rule"—would apply only *after* employees had selected their majority representative. There was never a question voiced about the non-applicability of that restriction prior to majority selection. And although elections were looked upon as one of the best means for settling disputes over union representation, the elections that were anticipated concerned the choice of *which union* would represent the employees, not *whether* the employees would be represented by a union. [92] Minority-union bargaining prior to the selection of a majority representative was a nonissue. Although the fanfare that surrounded the collective-bargaining process during the Congressional debates was focused on the majority-exclusivity rule and on representation elections, the validity of members-only minority-union bargaining emerged intact from that same legislative process, quietly and without fanfare.

E. The Committee Reports

What I have just recorded was recognized and noted in the Senate and House committee reports on the final Wagner bill, and as might be expected, the reports concentrated on descriptions and explanations concerning the mature majority-union bargaining process. However, even though pre-majority members-only bargaining—not being controversial—was not a subject of Congressional debate like post-majority bargaining, which was hotly contested, the continuing role of minority unions was nevertheless recognized in the committee reports, just as it was clearly recognized in the text of the Act. Thus, for example, as the following excerpt confirms, the final Senate report carefully recorded that the limitations of Section 9(a) did not apply until after the employees had selected a majority representative:

> Majority rule carries the clear implication that employers shall not interfere with the practical application of the right of employees to bargain collectively through chosen representatives by bargaining with individuals or minority

92 *Id.*, at 71.

> groups in their own behalf, *after* representatives have been picked by the majority to represent all.[93]

The House report contained a similar statement, that it is only "*after* [a Section 9(a)] representative has been so designated" that the employer is barred from negotiating "with individuals or minority groups in their own behalf on the basic subjects of collective bargaining."[94]

And regarding recognition of the limits of minority-bargaining concerning closed-shop contracts, the Senate committee, as previously noted,[95] reported further that

> *While today an employer may negotiate such an agreement even with a minority union*, the bill provides that an employer shall be allowed to make a closed shop contract only with a labor organization that represents the majority of employees in the appropriate collective-bargaining unit covered by such agreement when made.[96]

My final reference to what little the Congressional committees had to say about pre-majority union bargaining—"little" because this was not a contested issue—concerns a statement in the Senate report that was noted by E. G. Latham in the first law-review article that reviewed the NLRA,[97] That committee statement was the following:

> Another protection for minorities is that the right of a majority group through its representatives to bargain for all is confined by the bill to cases where the majority is actually organized "for the purposes of collective bargaining in respect to rates of pay, wages, hours of employment, or other conditions of employment."[98]

About which Latham wrote:

---

93 2 Legis. Hist., *supra* note 14 at 2,313. Emphasis added.

94 *Id.*, at 2,974. Emphasis added.

95 *Supra* note 32.

96 2 Legis. Hist., *supra* note 14 at 2,311.

97 Latham, *supra* note 32.

98 2 Legis. Hist., *supra* note 14 at 2,313.

> Presumably where a majority is not actually organized for such purposes, the right of minorities to bargain for themselves is reserved. It is reasonable to suppose that *where there is no majority organization at all, such minority rights are similarly reserved.*[99]

This is clearly the case. Here was clear scholarly recognition immediately after passage of the Act that minority-union collective bargaining was protected. In fact, regardless of how the minority-union is organized, inasmuch as it is a labor organization under Section 2(a)[100] it would have the right to bargain, which is what soon occurred abundantly, as will be described in the following discussion .

F. Post-Enactment Legal History

In its first case reviewing the NLRA, the Supreme Court stressed that Section 7's expression of the "right of employees to self-organization and to select representatives of their own choosing for collective bargaining . . . is a *fundamental* right.[101] And during the years immediately following passage of the Act minority-union bargaining was a fundamental right that was much in evidence. It wasn't qualified by any majority requirement. Members-only minority-union collective-bargaining contracts were then as prevalent as majority-exclusivity contracts, and their coverage of employees may have been even more extensive.[102] These agreements were recognized as part of an ordinary organizational practice engaged in by many unions.[103] That's how the newly created Steelworkers Union and the United Automobile Workers (UAW) union first bargained with their corporate counterparts in the late nineteen-thirties and early

99 Latham, *supra* note 32 at 454. Emphasis added.

100 29 U.S.C. § 152(a).

101 NLRB v. Jones & Laughlin Steel Corp., *supra* note 13. Emphasis added.

102 *Union Recognition as Shown in Contracts,* 1A L.R.R.M. (BNA) 781 (1938). For details, *see* Blue Eagle, *supra* note 19 *at* 82-85.

103 "[U]nions looked upon these membership-based agreements as merely a temporary means to an end, for they were convinced—as had been Senator Wagner and the Congress—that for collective bargaining to achieve maximum effectiveness, exclusive representation, hence majority status, was necessary. Accordingly, during the early Wagner Act years unions sought exclusive recognition by a variety of means. . . ." Members-only agreements were one of those means. . . ." *Id.,* at 85.

nineteen-forties.[104] NMCB agreements were also popular in many other industries. Almost all of these unions grew in membership and became recognized as Section 9(a) majority/exclusive unions.[105]

It was with reference to several such agreements with an electric utility company during that period that the Supreme Court declared in *Consolidated Edison Co. v. NLRB*[106] that

> [t]he Act contemplates the making of contracts with labor organizations. That is the manifest objective in providing for collective bargaining . . . . [I]n the absence of . . . an exclusive agency the employees represented by the Brotherhood *even if they were a minority*, clearly had the right to make their own choice.[107]

The Court there confirmed, as it later reiterated in two other cases,[108] that members-only non-majority contracts are authorized by and do not violate

104 *See* THE TWENTIETH CENTURY FUND, HOW COLLECTIVE BARGAINING WORKS: A SURVEY OF EXPERIENCE IN LEADING AMERICAN INDUSTRIES 24 (Harry A. Millis, Research Director, 1942) ("many agreements in the 1930's with new industrial unions in the mass production industries stated that the union was to bargain for members only. However, as collective bargaining gained more general acceptance and as unions won National Labor Relations Board elections, these 'membership' agreements were generally replaced by contracts designating the union as exclusive representative of all employees . . . ."). *And see* chap.2 *supra* at notes 45-46 regarding the role of Myron Taylor and John L. Lewis.

105 The automobile industry was a stellar example of that process. Upon the conclusion of the members-only UAW contracts that had been executed in the late thirties, the NLRB in 1940 conducted *elections* that resulted in certification of the UAW as exclusive bargaining representative for 130,000 employees at General Motors and 50,000 employees at Chrysler. 5 NLRB ANN. REP. 18-19, 141, 151 (1941). *See also* SIDNEY FINE, SIT-DOWN: THE GENERAL MOTORS STRIKE OF 1936-1937, 266-312 & 328 (1969).

106 305 U.S. 197 (1938).

107 *Id.*, at 236-237. Emphasis added. In its original *Consolidated Edison* decision, the Board expressly held that the involved companies "have not engaged in unfair labor practices within the meaning of Section 8(2) [presently § 8(a)(2)] of the Act." Therefore, the Supreme Court ruled only that the execution of a members-only collective bargaining agreements does not violate §§ 8(1) and) 8(3), the present §§ 8(a)(1) & 8(a)(3), respectively; without a § 8(a)(3) violation there can be no § 8(b)(2) violation, which requires union forcing of an employer to violate § 8(a)(3).

108 International Ladies Garment Workers v. NLRB (Bernhard-Altmann Tex. Corp.), 366 U.S. 731, 736, 742-43 (1961); Retail Clerks v. Lion Dry Goods, Inc., 369 U.S. 17, 29 (1962).

the NLRA. And in *The Solvay Process Co.*,[109] *The Hoover Co.*,[110] and *Consolidated Builders, Inc.*,[111] the NLRB likewise approved less-than-majority members-only recognition and bargaining and the members-only contracts that resulted from such bargaining. In so confirming the legality of that bargaining and resulting contracts, those Supreme Court and Board decisions also established that such conduct doesn't constitute unlawful *per se* discrimination against non-union employees under Sections 8(a)(1), 8(a)(3), or in effect 8(b)(2) or Section 8(a)(2)—the company-union provision of the Act.[112] Although there have been no cases where the Board has ever had to rule on the issue of an employer's duty to bargain with a minority union for its members only, the law is clear that such a duty exists, as the preceding statutory analysis, legislative history, and voluntary compliance demonstrate, and now the concurring opinion in *Oakland Children's Hospital*[113] further confirms.

Despite widespread early usage of members-only agreements, such contracts haven't been commonly used for many years. As noted in Chapter 1,[114] that practice was abandoned because unions discovered during that early period that NLRB representation procedures generally provided an easier, faster, and less expensive way to achieve Section 9(a) majority/exclusivity representation and bargaining—in other words, it was just a matter of convenience.[115] Consequently, institutional memory eventually faded and that slower members-only route to organizing and bargaining was effectively forgotten. As a result, through force of habit that grew into accepted custom, most of the labor-management

109 5 NLRB 330 (1938), where the Board reaffirmed its prior *Consolidated Edison* dismissal of the § 8(2) charge, expressly holding that an employer's recognition of a minority union "as the sole bargaining agency for its members only" was not a violation of § 8(2).

110 90 NLRB 1614 (1950), where the Board indicated that an employer faced with rival recognition demands from two unions "may, without violating the *Midwest Piping* doctrine, grant recognition to each of the claimants on a members-only basis." (Midwest Piping Co., 63 NLRB 1060 (1945), held that it is an unfair labor practice under § 8(2) for an employer to recognize one of two competing unions after a representation petition had been filed with the Board).

111 99 NLRB 972 (1952), where the Board again held that recognition of, and a collective agreement with, a members-only minority union does not violate § 8(a)(2) and likewise does not violate § 8(a)(1).

112 For a more detailed discussion of these post-enactment cases and their aftermath *see* app. *infra* at notes 125-145.

113 *Supra* notes 1 & 29-32.

114 Chap. 2 *supra* at note 50.

115 See BLUE EAGLE, *supra note* 19, at 85-88 and nn. 35-44 (analyzing NLRB contemporary election results).

community came to believe that only Section 9(a) majority unions have the right to bargain. That misperceived belief evolved into latter-day conventional wisdom, which the Board must now confront, with or without judicial input.[116]

What of the fact that for so many decades most NLRB users believed that majority-employee status was a *sine qua non* for the duty to bargain? Belief alone does not pose a serious legal obstacle. A common belief and practice that never received judicial confirmation doesn't override unambiguous statutory language and consistent legislative history. A position premised only on a long-held popular misunderstanding is no more valid today under the NLRA than was a comparable misunderstanding under the Civil Rights Act of 1866[117] when, more than a century later, that Act's previously misperceived clear and unambiguous statutory language was finally read correctly in *Jones v. Alfred W. Meyer Co.*[118] The Supreme Court there observed that the fact that the "statute lay partially dormant for many years does not diminish its force today."[119] By the same token, the fact that a right within the NLRA has lain dormant for many years does not preclude restoration and enforcement of that right today. Like the circumstances at the time of the *Meyer* case, in order to benefit the population for whom the statute was passed, there is today a pressing need to re-validate the correct application of the statutory right described in this book.

The Board's most recent occasion to examine the pre-majority stage of the collective-bargaining process occurred in the *Dana Corp.*[120] case, where it inserted the following favorable pre-majority collective-bargaining dictum:

> The Board and courts have long recognized that various types of agreements and understandings between employers and unrecognized unions fall within the framework of permissible cooperation. Notably, employers and unions may enter *into "members-only" agreements, which establish terms and conditions of employment only for those employees who are members of the union.* [citing

116 *See* chap. 6 *infra* at notes 44-109.

117 42 U.S.C. §1982.

118 392 U.S. 409 (1968).

119 *Id.* at 412. *See also* Smiley v. City Bank, 517 U.S. 735, 740 (1996), where Justice Scalia, on behalf of a unanimous court, wrote that although the challenged regulation was issued more than 100 years after the enactment of the applicable statutory provision, "[t]he 100 year delay makes no difference. [N]either antiquity nor contemporaneity with the statute is a condition of validity."

120 356 N.L.R.B. 256, 259 (2010), *enforced sub nom* Montague v. NLRB, 2012 U.S. App l, LEXIS 31950 (6th Cir. 2012).

> *Consolidated Edison* [121]]. In that decision, the Supreme Court reasoned that such agreements could be beneficial to interstate and foreign commerce by protecting against disruptions caused by industrial strife.

There is now an acute need for employees to be permitted to organize and bargain through unions that represent their members only, just as employees and their unions organized and bargained during the first decade of the NLRA as that statute guarantees. I hope this chapter and this book will help to achieve that objective.

121 *Supra* note 106.

Chapter 5. Worker Rights as Human Rights: How the United States Can Comply with its International Obligations Under Existing Law

I. INTRODUCTION

One of the best kept secrets in American labor law is that key elements of the statutory law relating to the rights of employees to join and organize into labor unions and to engage in collective bargaining are affected by two international compacts to which the United States is a party, to wit, the *International Covenant on Civil and Political Rights* (ICCPR or *Covenant*)[1] and the *International Labor Organization's (ILO's) 1998 Declaration on Fundamental Principles and Rights at Work* (ILO Declaration).[2] This Chapter will explain how those two instruments apply to the most important features of the National Labor Relations Act (NLRA or Act)[3]—features as to which the United States is not presently in full compliance[4]—and how the essence of those features can now be achieved through proper interpretation and application of long dormant but still viable statutory text—text that frames the NMCB proposal that's the subject of this book)[5]

As the reader is now aware, the basic question addressed by the NMCB proposition—i.e. minority-union collective-bargaining for members only where the union doesn't represent an employee majority in an appropriate bargaining

1 International Covenant on Civil and Political Rights, S. Exec. Doc. E, 95-2 (1978), 999 U.N.T.S. 171 (adopted in 1966, entered into force in 1976, ratified by U.S. in 1992); 42 U.S.C. §1983 (1994).

2 INTERNATIONAL LABOUR ORGANIZATION DECLARATION ON FUNDAMENTAL PRINCIPLES AND RIGHTS AT WORK, International Labour Conf., 86th Sess. (June 1998); reprinted in 144 CONG. REC. S6909-10 (daily ed. June 23, 1998) (with statement of Sen. Moynihan); available at http://www.ilo.org/public/english/standards/decl/declaration/text (hereinafter Declaration).

3 49 Stat. 449 (1935) as amended, 29 U.S.C. §§ 151-69.

4 Spokespersons for American management strongly contend that the U.S. is in compliance. For a brief view of the various contentions, *see* Lance Compa, *Workers' Freedom of Association under International Human Rights Law* in WORKERS' RIGHTS AS HUMAN RIGHTS (James Gross ed., 2003) (hereinafter Compa) at 28-30.

5 *See* CHARLES J. MORRIS, THE BLUE EAGLE AT WORK: RECLAIMING DEMOCRATIC RIGHTS IN THE AMERICAN WORKPLACE (2005) (hereinafter BLUE EAGLE), chap. 8, which contains an earlier version of parts of this chapter.

unit—is one that's been virtually ignored since the end of the first decade following passage of the Act in 1935. As we've seen, during the late nineteen-thirties and early forties such bargaining was as prevalent as majority-exclusivity bargaining, and the resulting minority-union contracts, which were especially instrumental in organizing the steel and automobile industries, served as stepping-stones that almost always led to full-fledged majority-based exclusivity bargaining. This chapter contends that this minority-union bargaining process, which flourished so abundantly during those early years,[6] can now help to bring the United States into compliance with its obligations under the aforesaid international labor-law compacts and thus provide meaningful recognition that worker rights are human rights.

As many in the American labor relations community are well aware, the United States has assiduously refrained from directly ratifying two specific international compacts, ILO Convention 87, which concerns the *freedom of association and protection of the right to organize*,[7] and ILO Convention 98,[8] which concerns the *right to bargain collectively*.[9] Nevertheless, by virtue of the aforesaid ICCPR and ILO *Declaration*, the key principles of both non-ratified conventions have been indirectly incorporated into the international labor-law obligations of the United States. It is widely recognized, however, that many of the most basic features of those principles that affect the rights of employees to engage in labor-union activity are not being complied with or have not been effectively implemented by the National Labor Relations Board (NLRB) and the courts. Professor James Gross perceptively sums up the cause and result of that condition with his assertion that it derives from

6 *See* chap. 2 *supra* at notes 46-49.

7 *International Labour Organization*, 31st Sess. (1948), INTERNATIONAL LABOUR CONVENTIONS & RECOMMENDATIONS 435 (1992).

8 International *Labour Organization*, 32nd Sess. (1949), INTERNATIONAL LABOUR CONVENTIONS & RECOMMENDATIONS 524 (1992).

9 Organized management and organized labor in America have long engaged in a bitter and polarized debate over whether the U.S. should ratify these conventions. For the supporting view, *see* Richard McIntyre & Matthew M. Bodah, *The United States and ILO Conventions 87 and 98: The Freedom of Association and Right to Bargain Collectively*, *in* JUSTICE ON THE JOB: PERSPECTIVES ON THE EROSION OF COLLECTIVE BARGAINING IN THE UNITED STATES 231, 232 (Richard N. Block et al eds., 2006 (hereinafter McIntyre & Bodah). For the opposing view, *see* Edward E. Potter, FREEDOM OF ASSOCIATION, THE RIGHT TO ORGANIZE AND COLLECTIVE BARGAINING: THE IMPACT ON U.S. LAW AND PRACTICE OF RATIFICATION OF ILO CONVENTIONS No. 87 & No. 98 (1984). *See also* Compa, *supra* note 4.

> the management rights value judgment [that] has dominated U.S. labor relations and law [and is] a major block to the realization of workers' rights as human rights in this country. The right of workers to participate in the decisions affecting their workplace lives is most consistent not only with the principles of human rights but also with democratic principles.[10]

The essence of those principles, the right to join trade unions and engage in collective bargaining, are now recognized to be fundamental *human rights*, the origins of which are deeply rooted in diverse historical sources, including traditional trade union movements in industrial democracies,[11] the American "progressive movement" of the early twentieth century,[12] and competing doctrines from both the Catholic Church[13] and the socialist movement.[14] Those principles, derived from such widely divergent sources, coalesced and found expression in several carriers of international law. Although I shall note the major documentary locations and textual configurations of those expressions—particularly within the two featured compacts to which the United States has agreed—I emphasize that many of these same features are presently contained in domestic American labor law. Thus, their U.S. legitimacy is derived primarily from statutory text enacted by

10 JAMES A. GROSS, A SHAMEFUL BUSINESS: THE CASE FOR HUMAN RIGHTS IN THE AMERICAN WORKPLACE 210 (2010).

11 *See generally* Allan Flanders, *Great Britain, in* COMPARATIVE LABOR MOVEMENTS 1, (Walter Galenson ed., 1952); Walter Galenson, *Scandinavia, in* COMPARATIVE LABOR MOVEMENTS 1, (Walter Galenson ed., 1952); Philip Taft, *Germany, in* COMPARATIVE LABOR MOVEMENTS 1, (Walter Galenson ed., 1952); Walter Galenson, *Scandinavia, in* COMPARATIVE LABOR MOVEMENTS 1, (Walter Galenson ed., 1952); Everett M. Kassalow, TRADE UNIONS AND INDUSTRIAL RELATIONS: AN INTERNATIONAL COMPARISON, 5-82 (1969); FOSTER RHEA DULLES, LABOR IN AMERICA, 1-241 (3rd ed. 1966); NORMAN J. WARE, THE LABOR MOVEMENT IN THE UNITED STATES 1860-1890: A STUDY IN DEMOCRACY (1929, reprinted 1964).

12 *See generally*, Daniel Rogers, ATLANTIC CROSSINGS: SOCIAL POLITICS IN A PROGRESSIVE AGE (1998); Harry W. Arthurs, Where Have You Gone, John R. Comons, Now that We Need You So, 21 Comp. Lab. L. & Pol. J. 373, 386 (2000); THE PROGRESSIVE MOVEMENT 1900-1915, Richard Hofstadter ed. 1963), and *The Progressive Party Platform of 1912, id.* at 128, 130-31 ("The supreme duty of the nation is the conservation of human resources through an enlightened measure of social and industrial justice....We favor the organization of the workers, men and women, as a means of protecting their interest and of promoting their progress....")

13 David L. Gregory, *The Right to Unionize as a Fundamental Human and Civil Right*, 9 MISS. COL. L. REV. 135, 151-53 (1988) ("The right to unionize is expressly regarded as a human right in Catholic social teaching."); Pope Leo III, *Rerum Novarum (On the Condition of Labor)* (1891) in SEVEN GREAT ENCYCLICALS 1 (W. Gibbons ed. 1963); In 1981 Pope John Paul II issued *Laborem Exercens* (On the Nature of Work) in which he reiterated the right of workers to unionize; again, in 1987, in his major social encyclical *Sollicitudo Rei Socialis* (On Social Concern) he "expressly reminded the world that the rights of workers and unions are fundamental human rights."

14 *See generally* WRITINGS AND SPEECHES OF EUGENE V. DEBS (1948).

the United States Congress rather than from their presence in international law, or indeed from the First Amendment of the United States Constitution, which also guarantees the same basic protections.[15]

The ICCPR and the 1998 ILO Declaration were preceded by several decades of international developments for which the United States, despite its unquestioned status as a democratic role-model, acted chiefly as a bystander. The first major event in this developmental history was the creation of the International Labor Organization (ILO) pursuant to the 1919 Treaty of Versailles. Although the ILO concept had been strongly supported by the U.S. delegation—in fact Samuel Gompers, president of the American Federation of Labor, was elected president of the commission that established the ILO—isolationist sentiment at home blocked United States acceptance of the Versailles treaty, membership in the League of Nation, and membership in the ILO.[16] Indeed, the United States didn't join the ILO until 1934.[17]

The next historical highlight was the ground-breaking conference the ILO held in Philadelphia in 1944, during World War II, when it adopted the major statement of policy and purpose known as the *Declaration of Philadelphia.* That declaration, which was subsequently incorporated into the ILO constitution,[18] reaffirmed that "labour is not a commodity [and that] freedom of expression and of association are essential to sustained progress. . . ."[19] Among that declaration's several objectives was recognition of "the solemn obligation of the International Labour Organization *to* further among the nations of the world programs which will achieve. . . . *the effective recognition of the right of collective bargaining.*"[20] That document also affirmed "that the principles set forth in this

15 *See* Blue Eagle, *supra* note 5 at chap. 6.

16 *See* Edward C. Lorenz, Defining Global Justice: The History of U.S. International Labor Standards Policy, 69-74 (2002); McIntyre & Bodah, *supra* note 9.

17 *Id.*; John E. Lawyer, *The International Labor Organization and Freedom of Association*, 15 J. Bar Ass'n D.C. 141, 150 (1948) (hereinafter Lawyer). In the fall of 1946 the ILO entered into an agreement with the United Nations in which it was recognized as a specialized agency with the responsibility of performing functions entrusted to it by the governments of its member states pursuant to its constitution. *Id.* at 148. In 1977 the U.S. withdrew from the ILO because of that organization's alleged sympathy with Soviet-block nations, but two years later it rejoined. McIntyre & Bodah, *supra* note 9. *See also* Lorenz, *supra* note 16 at 123-29.

18 *See* Lawyer, *supra note* 17 at 146; ILO Constitution, Annex, available at http://www.ilo.org/public/english/about/iloconst.htm.

19 ILO Constitution, Art. I.

20 *Id.*, Art. III. Emphasis added.

Declaration are fully applicable to all peoples everywhere . . . ."[21] Membership in the ILO therefore committed the member states to an affirmative obligation to further these objectives, a conclusion that was later reconfirmed by the 1998 ILO Declaration.[22]

In 1948 the General Assembly of the United Nations adopted and proclaimed the Universal Declaration of Human Rights,[23] key provisions of which characterized the "right of peaceful assembly and association" and the "right to form and join trade unions for the protections of [one's] interests" as "human rights."[24] As will be noted below, the United States agreed to those key provisions when it ratified the ICCPR in 1992.

II. INTERNATIONAL COVENANT ON CIVIL AND POLITICAL RIGHTS

Now to an examination of the legal implications of the two compacts to which the United States has agreed. I shall begin with the ICCPR, the *International Covenant on Civil and Political Rights.*[25] Although this Covenant contains the potential for contributing to an improved application of American labor law, it has thus far received only passing judicial recognition and has yet to be applied to any subject of its coverage.[26] The Covenant was adopted by the United Nations General Assembly in 1966, signed by President Carter in 1978, and ratified by President George H.W. Bush with the concurrence of the Senate in 1992 with five "Reservations," five "Understandings," four "Declarations" and one "Proviso."[27] It is thus now a United States treaty, hence part of the "supreme Law of the Land."[28]

21 *Id.*, Art V.

22 *See infra* at note 71.

23 G.A. Res. 217A, U.N. GAOR, 3d Sess., Supp. No. 1, at 135, U.N. Doc. A/810 (1948).

24 *Id.* Arts. 20(1) & 23(4) respectively.

25 Note 1 *supra.*

26 *See* Roper v. Simmons, 543 U.S. 551, 567, 622 (2005), and Sosa v. Alvarez-Machain, 542 U.S. 692, 734-35 (2004), discussed *infra* in note 45.

27 For a summary of these conditions, *see* Kristen D. A. Carpenter, *The International Covenant on Civil and Political Rights: A Toothless Tiger?* n. 17, 26 N.C. J. INT'L L. & COM. REG. 1 (2000) (hereinafter Carpenter).

28 U.S. Const., art. VI, §2 ("This Constitution, and the Laws of the United States, which shall be made in Pursuance hereof; and all "Treaties made, or which shall be made, under the authority of the United

When the ICCPR was presented to the Senate for approval, the Senate Foreign Relations Committee provided the following explanation of its function and purpose and what would be required of the United States as a ratifying party:

> The Covenant guarantees a broad spectrum of civil and political rights, rooted in basic democratic values and freedoms [and] *obligates each State Party to respect and ensure these rights,* to adopt legislative or other necessary measures to give effect to these rights, and to provide an effective remedy to those whose rights are violated.[29]
>
> The Covenant is part of the international community's early efforts to give the full force of international law to the principles of human rights embodied in the Universal Declaration of Human Rights and the United Nations Charter. The Civil and Political Rights Covenant is rooted in western legal and ethical values. The rights guaranteed by the Covenant are similar to those guaranteed by the U.S. Constitution and the Bill of Rights.[30]

The provisions of the ICCPR that have a material bearing on union-organizing and collective-bargaining include the following:

> *Preamble*—which identifies the rights protected in the Covenant as "human rights"—recognizes
>
> that these rights derive from the inherent dignity of the human person [and] that, in accordance with the Universal Declaration of Human Rights, the ideal of free human beings enjoying civil and political freedom and freedom from fear and want can only be achieved if conditions are created whereby everyone may enjoy his civil and political rights, as well as his economic, social and cultural rights . . . .

States shall be the supreme Law of the Land...."). A treaty, duly ratified by the Senate, must thus "be regarded in courts of justice as equivalent to an act of the legislature. . . ." Foster v. Neilson, 27 U.S. (2 Pet.) 253, 315 (1829) (Marshall, C.J.). *See also* notes 44-46 *infra.*

29 Senate Comm. on Foreign Relations, Report on the Int'l Covenant on Civil and Political Rights, S. Exec. Rep. No. 102-23, at 1-2 (1992), 31 I.L.M. 645, 648 (hereinafter Senate Report). Emphasis added.

30 *Id.* at 2.

Article 2—concerning implementation—provides that

> 1. Each State Party undertakes to respect and *to ensure to all individuals* within its territory and subject to its jurisdiction the rights recognized in the present Covenant....
>
> 3. Each State Party to the present Covenant undertakes:
>
> (a) *To ensure* that any person whose rights or freedoms are herein recognized are violated shall have *an effective remedy....;*
>
> (b) *To ensure* that any person claiming such a remedy shall have his right thereto determined by competent *judicial, administrative*, or *legislative* authorities, or by any other competent authority provided for by the legal system of the State, and to develop the possibilities of *judicial remedy....;*
>
> (c) *To ensure* that the *competent authorities shall enforce such remedies when granted....*[31]

Article 22—concerning right of association and trade unions—provides that

> 1. Everyone shall have the freedom of association with others, including *the right to form and join trade unions for the protection of his interests.*
>
> 2. *No restrictions may be placed on the exercise of this right other than those which are prescribed by law and which are necessary in a democratic society in the interests of national security or public safety, public order* (ordre public), the protection of public health or morals or the protection of the rights and freedoms of others....[32]

None of the above provisions was the subject of any reservation by the United States, which, however, did attach specific reservations to several other provisions of the Covenant, for example Article 20 relating to war propaganda and

31 Emphasis added.

32 Emphasis added.

incitement to discrimination,[33] and Articles 6 and 7 relating to capital punishment and cruel and unusual punishment.[34] Those reservations have been the subjects of much scholarly attention[35] and some litigation,[36] but they are not relevant here.

Although none of the *reservations* specified by the United States are pertinent to the focus of this article, one *understanding* and two *declarations* attached by the U.S. are relevant to the trade-union provisions quoted above.

Understanding No. (5) provides

> That the United States understands that this Covenant shall be implemented by the Federal Government to the extent that it exercises jurisdiction over the matters covered therein....[37]

Declarations (1) and (2) provide:

> (1) That the United States declares that the provisions of *articles 1 through 27* of the Covenant are *not self-executing.*
>
> (2) That it is the view of the United States that States Party to the Covenant should wherever possible *refrain from imposing any restrictions or limitations on the exercise of the rights recognized and protected by the Covenant....*[38]

I shall first address the "not self-executing" (NSE) declaration, which has aroused considerable academic attention and comment.[39] Although the matter

33 *See Reservation (1)* specifying that Art. 20 "does not authorize or require . . . action . . . that would restrict the right of free speech and association protected by the Constitution and laws of the United States."

34 *See Reservations (2)* and *(3),* which refer to constitutional restrains relating to capital punishment and to cruel and unusual treatment and punishments.

35 *E.g., see generally* citations in notes 44-46 *infra.*

36 *E.g.,* Roper v. Simmons, *supra* note 26; Maria v. McElroy, 68 F. Supp. 2d 206 (E.D.N.Y. 1999), *aff'd sub nom.* Pottinger v. Reno, 242 F.3d 367 (2nd Cir. 2000); Beharry v. Reno, 183 F. Supp. 2d 584 (E.D.N.Y. 2002), *rev'd & remanded sub nom.* Beharry v. Ashcroft, 329 F.3d 51 (2nd Cir. 2003) (without decision on ICCPR issue).

37 Emphasis added.

38 Emphasis added.

39 See notes 44-46 *infra.*

has yet to be tested, this NSE feature should pose no bar to enforcement of the labor-related provisions in Article 22 of the Covenant, for according to the text of the NSE *Declaration* and its justification as asserted by the Senate Foreign Relations Committee, the "not self-executing" limitation affects only the initial procedural aspects of applying Article 22 and not application of its substantive provisions. When the Senate committee presented the Covenant for ratification on behalf of the George. H.W. Bush administration, it stated without qualification that "[t]he intent is to clarify that the Covenant will not create a *private cause of action* in U.S. courts."[40] Thus an administrative agency—e.g., the NLRB—as to a matter in issue under the National Labor Relations Act (NLRA), is obligated to enforce the appropriate treaty provisions. That conclusion comports with the comprehensive observation which the late Frank C. Newman voiced shortly after the ICCPR was ratified. He wrote that the implication of the Bush administration's statement, that as a non-self-executing (NSE) treaty, Article 22 of the Covenant would not become *directly* enforceable as United States law in U.S. courts, was that "the Covenant's commands are to be promoted and respected by U.S. officials *otherwise than 'in U.S. courts,'*"[41] for which he provided this specific illustration: "[I]f (via either rule-making or adjudication) federal or state officials jeopardize the right prescribed in Article 22 to 'freedom of association with others,' an individual or group may appeal administratively, via whatever channels are available,"[42] which would most likely be the NLRB. He also reminded that "[a]dministrative law deals with rule-making as well as adjudicating,"[43] thereby underscoring the appropriateness of the rulemaking format for the minority-union bargaining concept. The substantive mandates of the ICCPR are thus fully enforceable, either by adjudication or rulemaking regarding the obligation of the United States to ensure that all workers, including those under the jurisdiction of the NLRA, have a *meaningful* right to join trade unions for their "protection," which necessarily incorporates a relatively unrestricted right to engage in collective bargaining.

40 Senate Report, *supra* note 29, 31 I.L.M. at 657. Emphasis added. *See* John Quigley, *The Rule Of Non-Inquiry And Human Rights Treaties,* 45 CATH. U.L. REV. 1213, 1230, n. 118 (1996).

41 Frank C. Newman, *United Nations Human Rights Covenants and the United States Government: Diluted Promises, Foreseeable Futures,* 42 DEPAUL L. REV. 1241, 1246 (1993). (Hereinafter Newman.) Emphasis added.

42 *Id.*

43 *Id.* at 1247.

Although much scholarly writing has addressed various implications of the NSE feature[44] and the Supreme Court has noted its presence with reference to the ICCPR,[45] there should be no question about what the U.S. Senate intended by the inclusion of the NSE declaration regarding judicial enforcement of the Covenant's provisions relevant to the labor law concerns of this book. As Carlos Manuel Vazquez summed up the state of the law, "a treaty that does not itself confer a right of action.... is not for that reason unenforceable in the courts.... If the treaty expressly entitles the individual to a remedy, he is entitled to that remedy by virtue of the Supremacy Clause."[46] Indeed, in response to specific labor-related questions raised by Senator Moynihan, the Senate Foreign

---

44 *E.g., see* David Sloss, *Using International Law to Enhance Democracy*, 47 VA. J. INT'L L. 1 (2006); JOHN J. PAUST, INTERNATIONAL LAW AS LAW OF THE UNITED STATES, 67-98, 361-93 (2nd ed. 2003) (hereinafter PAUST); David Sloss, *Non-Self-Executing Treaties: Exposing a Constitutional Fallacy*, 37 U.C. DAVIS L. REV. 1 (2002); John Henry Stone, *The International Covenant on Civil and Political Rights and the United States Reservations: The American Conception of International Human Rights*, 7 U.C. DAVIS J. INT'L L. & POL'Y 1 (2001); Carpenter, *supra* note 28; Curtis A. Bradley & Jack L. Goldsmith, *Treaties, Human Rights, and Conditional Consent*, 149 U. PA. L. REV. 399 (2000); David Sloss, *The Domestication of International Human Rights: Non-Self-Executing Declarations and Human Rights Treaties*, 24 YALE J. INT'L L. 129 (1999) (hereinafter Sloss 1999); John Quigley, *The International Covenant on Civil and Political Rights and the Supremacy Clause*, 42 DEPAUL L. REV. 1287 (1993) (hereinafter Quigley); M. Cherif Bassiouni, *Reflections on the Ratification of the International Covenant on Civil and Political Rights by the United States Senate*, 42 DEPAUL L. REV. 1169 (1993); Newman, *supra* note 41; John H. Jackson, *Status Of Treaties In Domestic Legal Systems: A Policy Analysis*, 86 AM. J. INT'L L. 310 (1992); Jordan J. Paust, *Self-Executing Treaties*, 82 AM. J. INT'L L. 760 (1988) (herinafter Paust); Yuji Iwasawa, *The Doctrine Of Self-Executing Treaties In The United States: A Critical Analysis*, 26 VA. J. INT'L L. 627, 645 (1986) (hereinafter Iwasawa) ("U.S. courts have consistently recognized that provisions of constitutions and statutes are the law of the land, whether or not they are self-executing. Non-self-executing treaty provisions should not be treated any differently.") Stefan A. Riesenfeld, *The Doctrine Of Self-Executing Treaties And U.S. V. Postal: Win At Any Price?*, 74 AM. J. INT'L L. 892 (1980).

45 In Sosa v. Alvarez-Machain, *supra* note 26, the Supreme Court noted that "although the Covenant *does bind the United States as a matter of international law*, the United States ratified the Covenant on the express understanding that it was not self-executing and so did not *itself* create obligations enforceable in the federal courts." *Id.* at 735 (emphasis added). In view of the Court's recognition that the treaty "does bind the United States," the only rational meaning of the "not itself" limitation is that although the Covenant creates no independent private cause of action in the federal courts, implicitly its substantive provisions must be invoked through the medium of existing domestic law.

46 Carlos Manuel Vazquez, *Treaty-Based Rights and Remedies of Individuals*, 92 COLUM. L. REV. 1082, 1143 (1992). *See also* Paust, *supra* note 44 at 78-79 ("Although [NSE] treaties cannot operate directly as domestic law to create a cause of action [they] are still law of the United States and can be used . . . indirectly as a means of interpreting relevant constitutional, statutory, common law or other legal provisions"); Sloss 1999, *supra* note 44 at 152 ("the fact that a treaty provision is not self-executing, in the sense that it does not create a private cause of action, does not preclude direct judicial application of the provision in all cases."), and *id.* at 146, n. 97 ("subject to a few narrow exceptions, non-self-executing treaty provisions are the "Law of the Land" under the Supremacy Clause, even if courts cannot apply them directly."), *citing, inter alia,* Louis Henkin, FOREIGN AFFAIRS AND THE UNITED STATES CONSTITUTION 203 (2nd ed. 1996) ("Whether a treaty is self-executing or not . . . it is supreme law of the land."); Iwasawa, *supra* note 44.

Relations Committee noted the absence of "explicit provisions" in Article 22 and called attention to the NSE feature, reminding Senator Moynihan that the treaty, therefore, "would not. . . .become *directly* enforceable as United States law in U.S. courts"[47]—which is unquestionably true, for enforcement is left to *indirect*—but no less valid—procedures of the NLRB and the courts. The absence of explicit procedures in the treaty doesn't prevent the enforceability of Article 22.[48]

Although no separate or independent cause of action may be brought in a court under the ICCPR, its substantive provisions may be raised and fully relied upon in an action based on existing domestic law, such as in an unfair labor practice case,[49] and courts and administrative agencies are obligated to enforce the treaty provisions appropriate to the matter in issue. Except for the Covenant's provisions for which reservations were appended, the *substantive* mandates are not diminished by the NSE feature.[50] It's thus my view that the NSE feature poses no real problem regarding the enforcement of trade-union-related rights, for they can be raised under the NLRA either through an unfair-labor-practice charge arising under Sections 7 and 8 or by substantive rulemaking. With these means, the United States has a duty to enforce the provisions to which it attached no reservations, especially those noted above, i.e., the Preamble, Articles 2 and 3, and especially paragraphs (1) and (2) of Article 22.

Accordingly, pursuant to the ICCPR the U.S. is required to exercise its "judicial jurisdiction"[51] "to ensure to all individuals [their] rights recognized in the present Covenant,"[52] "[t]o ensure that [they] have an *effective* remedy,"[53] and

---

47 *See* Senate Report, *supra* note 29, at 1.

48 The committee's response also noted the Administration's opinion that the covenant "does not, and will not, require any alteration or amendment to existing Federal and State labor law." *Id.* Regarding the issue here under consideration (without reference to other unrelated issues), I am fully in agreement that no such amendment is required.

49 *Id. See also* Carpenter, *supra* note 27, at 12 ("[the NSE declaration] should not. . . preclude a party raising the covenant either defensively or *through an existing enabling law*." (Emphasis added.).

50 Following ratification of the ICCPR, the United States assured the U.N Human Rights Committee that "[n]otwithstanding the non-self-executing declaration of the United States, American courts are not prevented from seeking guidance from the Covenant in interpreting American law." CONCLUDING OBSERVATIONS OF THE HUMAN RIGHTS COMMITTEE: UNITED STATES OF AMERICA, U.N. GAOR Hum. Rts. Comm., 53d Sess., 1413th mtg. at ¶ 276, U.N. Doc. CCPR/C/79/Add.50 (1995).

51 *Understanding No. (5), supra* at note 37.

52 Art. 2, ¶ 1.

53 Art. 2, ¶ 3(a). Emphasis added.

"that the competent authorities shall enforce such remedies when granted."[54] This means that the NLRB and the federal courts have an obligation to interpret and enforce the National Labor Relations Act in conformance with Article 22 of the Covenant. In so doing, they will be complying with what Chief Justice Rehnquist in *Weinberger v. Rossi* emphasized "has been a maxim of statutory construction"[55] since Chief Justice Marshall's 1804 postulated in *The Charming Betsy*, that "an act of congress ought never to be construed to violate the law of nations, if any other possible construction remains . . . ."[56] This is the criterion the Supreme Court applied when it construed the NLRA to conform to standards of international law in interpreting the Act to exclude employees of foreign flag-of-convenience ships from the Act's coverage—again relying on *The Charming Betsy*.[57] This approach to the construction of a domestic statute vis-à-vis an issue of international law is essentially the same as that which the Supreme Court applies to statutory construction that raises a serious question of constitutionality: "[w]here an otherwise acceptable construction of a statute would raise serious constitutional problems, the Court will construe the statute to avoid such problems unless such construction is plainly contrary to the intent of Congress."[58] Courts and administrative agencies are expected to treat statutory issues, whether arising under the Constitution or under international law, according to the same basic standard, i.e., to make every reasonable effort to construe the statute consistent with and not in violation of either the Constitution or the treaty.

There is another principle of construction germane to this issue, which is the canon the Supreme Court enunciated in *Asakura v. City of Seattle*,[59] that "treaties are to be construed in a broad and liberal spirit, and, when two constructions

54 Art. 2, ¶3(c).

55 456 U.S. 25, 32 (1982).

56 *Murray v. The Charming Betsy*, 2 Cranch 64, 118 (1804).

57 McCulloch v. Sociedad Nacional de Marineros, 372 U.S. 10 (1962). For application of this same principle to the ICCPR, *see* Maria v. McElroy, *supra* note 36 ("An act of Congress should be construed in accordance with international law where it is possible to do so without distorting the statute . . . .The retroactive deprivation [of plaintiff's] statutory right to humanitarian relief from deportation would arguable be contrary to both the International Covenant on Civil and Political Rights ('ICCPR') and customary international human rights law." 68 F. Supp. 2d at 231).

58 DeBartolo Corp. v. Florida Gulf Coast Bldg. & Constr. Trades Council, 485 U.S. 568 (1988). *See also* Crowell v. Benson, 285 U.S. 22 (1932); NLRB v. Catholic Bishop of Chicago, 440 U.S. 490 (1979).

59 265 U.S. 332 (1924) (holding a city ordinance to be in violation of a treaty that mandated equality between American citizens and Japanese citizens residing in the U.S.).

are possible, one restrictive of rights that may be claimed under it and the other favorable to them, the latter is to be preferred."[60] This guideline is especially appropriate for the construction and enforcement of a human-rights treaty.

In summation, Article 22 of the ICCPR commits the United States to ensuring that all workers have an unrestricted right "to form and join trade unions for the protection [of their] interests," and that "no restrictions may be placed on the exercise of this right [unless] "necessary.... in the interests of national security or public safety, public order.... protection of public health or morals.... or rights and freedoms of others...." This commitment is further reinforced by the *U.S. Declaration (2)* that a state party to the Covenant "should wherever possible refrain from imposing any restrictions or limitations" on such rights.

Applying the foregoing standards of construction to the reconciliation of the NLRA and the ICCPR, it follows that there cannot be any justification for misconstruing the former in a manner that would effectively place restrictions on the right of an employee "to form and join trade unions for the protection of his interests."[61] If the only employees who have the right to engage in collective bargaining are union members who already comprise an established majority within an appropriate bargaining unit, then the only unions that most American employees can safely join are those that have been previously recognized or certified as majority representatives. This Catch-22 restriction makes creation of new bargaining units difficult almost everywhere and impossible in most places. This is so because in the typical nonunion workplace, where retaliation and threatened retaliation against pro-union employees commonly occur, fierce employer opposition to unions produces a chilling effect that severely limits the right of employees to form or join unions.[62] This restriction of the right to form or join is built into the American collective-bargaining system to the extent that bargaining is confined exclusively to majority-based unions, for employees dare not—and do not—join a union until after that union has achieved majority status, which usually follows a hotly contested election. This is a restriction not remotely related to "national security" or any other exception named in the Covenant, and if it is required by law it would violate Article 22. Accordingly, in addition to their domestic statutory responsibilities under the NLRA, the NLRB and the federal courts are now mandated by international

60 *Id.* at 342,

61 ICCPR, Art 22 (1).

62 See *infra* at notes 76-80 and chap.1*supra* at note 71.

law to secure to workers their unrestricted right to "form and join trade unions" for the "protection" of their interests, which includes the right to join unions that can and will bargain on their behalf both *before* and *after* establishment of exclusive majority representation. As this book establishes, this is actually what the bargaining provisions of the NLRA already require. Thus administrative and judicial recognition of that requirement, albeit belated, would avoid "violat[ing] the law of nations" and thereby prevent Article 22 from becoming a Catch-22. The *Charming Betsy* would then sail on.

There is yet another aspect of the ICCPR that has a direct and positive bearing on the subject of the availability of collective bargaining, and that's the relationship between the right of association under this treaty and the right of association under the First Amendment to the U.S. Constitution and the combined effect of those relationships on the interpretation of the NLRA. Reference to these relationships can to be found in another response of the Senate Foreign Relations Committee to a question posed by Senator Moynihan. He had asked: "Does Article 22 of the Covenant alter or amend existing legal requirements under the National Labor Relations Act...?" The committee's response, as follows, was unequivocal:

> *No.* Article 22 only provides for a general right of freedom of association, including the right to form and join trade unions for the protection of his (sic) interests. These rights are fully contemplated by the First Amendment to the U.S. Constitution with respect to free speech, petition and assembly.[63]

That answer tied together three sources of legal rights for American workers: The NLRA, the First Amendment, and the Covenant. The Senate committee, which was also speaking on behalf of the George H.W. Bush Administration, thus expressly confirmed for the record the applicability of the First Amendment's protection of the right-of-association to *private sector* employees under the NLRA, for which *state action*[64] was not perceived to be a problem. Such protection was conceded to apply to "a general right" to form and join trade unions, which was thus considered to be "fully contemplated" by both the First Amendment and the Covenant. This was a reiteration of that position by the first Bush Administration expressed at the beginning of the Senate report,

63 Senate Report, *supra* note 29 at 26. Emphasis added.

64 *See* BLUE EAGLE *supra* note 5 at chap. 6.

that the "Administration has concluded that the rights of association embodied in Article 22 of the Covenant are general rights of association contained in the First Amendment. . . ."[65] And to underscore that this was not merely an allusion to a non-labor-specific right of association but was explicitly intended to be a right precisely applicable to employees, the committee thrice reiterated its mantra tying together Article 22 of the Covenant, federal labor law, and the First Amendment to the Constitution.[66]

III. THE 1998 ILO DECLARATION ON FUNDAMENTAL PRINCIPLES AND RIGHTS AT WORK

Now to a review of the other international compact that affects this country's labor-law obligations: the *1998 ILO Declaration on Fundamental Principles and Rights at Work*, the "ILO Declaration."[67] Although the ICCPR broadly concerns the right of workers to form and join trade unions for protection of their interests, the extent of that protection is reinforced and refined by this 1998 Declaration, which expressly spells out that such protection includes "*the right to collective bargaining*."

I begin this examination by returning to the Senate Foreign Relations Committee's response to Senator Moynihan as to the meaning of Article 22 of the ICCPR, for that committee made an effort to distinguish that provision from

65 Senate Report, *supra* note 29 at 5. This reliance on the First Amendment as support for the right of private-sector workers to join trade unions and engage in collective bargaining was not unique to the Bush Administration in 1992. The Truman and Carter administrations had expressed the same position. When President Truman submitted ILO Convention No. 87 in 1949 to the Senate for approval, it was accompanied by a letter from Secretary of State Dean Acheson noting "that the Convention affirms the guaranties provided under the first, fifth, tenth, and fourteenth Amendments to the Constitution of the United States." *The United States and the International Labor Organization: Hearing on Examination of the Relationship Between the United States and the International Labor Organization Before the Senate Committee on Labor and Human Resources,* 99th Cong., 1st Sess. 49, 53 (Sept. 11, 1985) (U.S. Dept. of Labor Briefing Paper, ILO Convention Concerning Freedom of Association, Oct. 1980). This represented early recognition that the rights of workers to join labor unions, contained in Section 7, were also protected by the Constitution. That same position was repeated in a 1976 *memorandum of law* submitted by the Solicitor of the U.S. Department of Labor in the Carter Administration, which asserted that the rights spelled out in Convention No. 87 "are inherent in the First, Fifth, and Fourteenth Amendments to the Constitution...." *Id.* at 62-63. For a detailed discussion of the First Amendment's application to union organization and collective bargaining, *see* BLUE EAGLE, *supra* note 5 at chap. 6.

66 Senate report, *supra* note 29 at 26-27.

67 Declaration, *supra* note 2.

ILO Convention 87, asserting that the latter sets out "*specific* protections of trade union rights that are not contemplated by Article 22 [which] does not make any *explicit* provision for the series of safeguards laid down in ILO Convention 87."[68] Indeed, Convention 87 does contains a number of explicit safeguards regarding the internal operation of trade unions and their legal personalities. Likewise, ILO Convention 98 contains several reasonably definite provisions concerning organizational and collective-bargaining procedures and protections. Although the lack of specificity in Article 22 may have seemed significant to the George H.W. Bush Administration in 1992—a concern that was not well-founded, as demonstrated in the above review—with the adoption of the 1998 ILO Declaration such concern is now of lesser importance, for that document expressly incorporates the basic requirements of Conventions 87 and 98.

When that Declaration was adopted at the International Labor Conference in Geneva in 1998, it was "hailed as a landmark achievement by the U.S. delegates."[69] It "committed the 174 countries belonging to the ILO to respect four principles embodied by seven ILO core conventions [including 87 and 98] and to promote application of the principles by all members. . . ."[70] Here are its directly relevant provisions:

The 1998 Declaration "*Recalls*"

> that in freely joining the ILO, all Members have endorsed the principles and rights set out in its Constitution and in the Declaration of Philadelphia,[71] and have undertaken to work towards attaining the overall objectives of the Organization *to the best of their resources* and fully in line with their specific circumstances....[72]

and "*Declares*"

68 *Id.* Emphasis added. The *citation* is to the 1969 *Comparative Analysis of the International Covenants on Human Rights and International Labor Conventions and Recommendations* in the Official Bulletin of the International Labor Office, referring to identical original-source language in the 1948 Universal Declaration of Human Rights, Art. 23(4). *See* text at notes 23-24 and text following note *28 supra.*

69 *Workplace Human Rights Focus of '98 Int'l Labor Conference,* ILO Focus (published by the Washington branch office of the ILO), Vol. 11, No. 2 (1998), at 1.

70 *ILO Meets Trade Challenge with New Message on Core Labor Standards, id.* at 1 & 6.

71 *See* text at note 18 *supra.*

72 Declaration, *supra* note 2 at ¶1(a). Emphasis added.

> that all Members, even if they have not ratified the Conventions in question, have an obligation, arising from the very fact of membership in the Organization, *to respect, to promote, and to realize in good faith,* and in accordance with the Constitution, the principles concerning *the fundamental rights which are the subject of those conventions,* namely:
>
> (a) freedom of association and the *effective* recognition of the right to collective bargaining....[73]

Abraham Katz, president of the U.S. Council for International Business, who was officially representing U.S. business interests at the ILO, confirmed that "[f]or the first time, the ILO has articulated a set of basic principles for workers' rights *to which every member country of the ILO must adhere by virtue of membership.*"[74] Although enforcement of the Declaration is the responsibility of each member state,[75] the United States is required by the Declaration to comply with the "principles concerning the fundamental rights" contained in Conventions 87 and 98, a duty which for present purposes is spelled out in consolidated phrases from the text as an "*obligation . . . to promote . . . the effective recognition of the right of collective bargaining.*"

The 1998 ILO Declaration thus provides the United States with additional international support for administrative and judicial recognition of the right of *all* employees covered by the NLRA—not just majority employees—to have "*effective*" access to union representation and collective bargaining. It's obvious, however, that the U.S. government has not in recent years promoted the *effective* recognition of that right. Indeed, in its official *Follow-Up Report* to the ILO in 1999[76] the Clinton Administration acknowledged such failure, reporting that

---

73 *Id.* at ¶2 & 2(a). Emphasis added. (The other included principles concern "(b)" elimination of forced or compulsory labor, "(c)" abolition of child labor, and "(d)" elimination of discrimination in employment and occupation.)

74 *USCIB Applauds ILO's Breakthrough in Campaign to Respect Workers' Rights,* PR NEWSWIRE ASSOCIATION, INC. June 19, 1998. Emphasis added.

75 The ILO's enforcement responsibility is confined to publicity, for which a *Follow-Up Annex* to the Declaration makes provision for the preparation and filing of annual reports that are designed to publicize the extent of member states' compliance with the Declaration. *E.g., see infra* at notes 77-80.

76 *Id.*

> The United States has an elaborate system of substantive labor law and procedures.... Nonetheless, the United States acknowledges that there are aspects of this system that *fail to fully protect the rights to organize and bargain collectively* of all employees in all circumstances. The United States is concerned about these limitations....[77]

Aside from that candid acknowledgement, it is well known and fully documented that the United States does not comply with ILO standards regarding the right of workers to engage in collective bargaining. As the Dunlop Commission[78] concluded in 1994, "[t]he evidence reviewed by the Commission demonstrated conclusively that current labor law is not achieving its stated intent of "encouraging" collective bargaining and protecting workers' right to choose whether or not to be represented in their workplace."[79] And *Human Rights Watch* has observed and reported that elements of U.S. labor law and practice "frustrate rather than promote workers' freedom of association."[80] Furthermore, notwithstanding minor corrective efforts by the NLRB during President Obama's administration, and efforts by the Trump NLRB to reverse those minor improvements, it's no surprise that the conventional assumption that certification or recognition of employee majority-status is still a precondition for union bargaining. Accordingly, cumbersome election-verification is still required as a perquisite for union recognition.[81] Needless to say, this provides

77 ANNUAL REPORTS UNDER THE FOLLOW-UP TO THE ILO DECLARATION ON THE FUNDAMENTAL PRINCIPLES AND RIGHTS AT WORK (2000) available at http://www.ilo.org/dyn; declaris/Show_ARHTML. Emphasis added. This admission elicited acclaim from the ILO Panel of Experts "for its open recognition of difficulties still to be overcome...relevant to achieving full respect for the principles and rights in the Declaration." REVIEW OF 1999 ANNUAL REPORTS BY ILO EXPERT-ADVISORS REGARDING COMPLIANCE WITH THE *DECLARATION*, ¶ 44, id. That the above 1999 U.S. statement was later deleted, without explanation, from the 2002 U.S. report submitted by the George H,W. Bush Administration, id., does not detract from its original honesty and significance.

78 *U.S. Department of Labor and U.S. Department of Commerce, Commission on the Future of Worker-Management Relations,* REPORT AND RECOMMENDATIONS (Dec. 1994).

79 *Id.* at xviii.

80 Lance Compa, UNFAIR ADVANTAGE: WORKERS' FREEDOM OF ASSOCIATION IN THE UNITED STATES UNDER INTERNATIONAL HUMAN RIGHTS STANDARDS, Human Rights Watch 17 (2000). ("Many workers who try to form and join trade unions to bargain with their employers are spied on, harassed, pressured, threatened, suspended, fired, deported or otherwise victimized in reprisal for their exercise of the right to freedom of association." *Id.* at 9).

81 Linden Lumber Div. v. NLRB, 419 U.S. 301 (1974). For analysis and proposal regarding effect of this decision, *see* Charles J. Morris, *Undercutting Linden Lumber: How a Union can Achieve Majority-Status Bargaining without an Election,* 35 HOFSTRA LAB. & EMP'L L. J. (2017).

employers with both the incentive and the means to deprive employees of their guaranteed right to engage in collective bargaining....

IV. THE NLRA COMPELS THE SAME BROAD CONSTRUCTION OF THE RIGHT TO BARGAIN COLLECTIVELY AS THE COVENANT AND 1998 ILO DECLARATION

The foregoing discussion has demonstrated that the United States has a duty to comply with its international labor-law commitments, including the duty to construe the NLRA's collective-bargaining provisions in conformance with those compacts. Employing the intertwined texts of the Covenant and the 1998 ILO Declaration, international law mandates a broad construction of NLRA bargaining provisions that will expressly ensure in good faith that all workers have the right to form and join trade unions for the protection of their interests and to respect and promote the effective recognition of collective bargaining. I have no illusion, however, as to the likelihood of U.S. courts applying such international law if there is perceived to be an absence of comparable domestic law; but—as this book demonstrates—that should not pose an insoluble problem for the foregoing international-law objectives are attainable under the NLRA, provided that this Act is interpreted correctly in accordance with its plain language, as Congress intended and as this book confirms.

This comparison of domestic labor law with its international counterparts is appropriately highlighted with the statement of policy contained in the NLRA, which is to "encourag[e] the practice and procedure of collective bargaining and... protect... the exercise by workers of full freedom of association, self-organization, and designation of representatives of their own choosing."[82] That's basically the same policy espoused by the aforesaid international compacts. Consequently, under international law the NLRB and the courts have an obligation to provide "effective" enforcement of the comparable text of Section 7 of the NLRA, which provides that "[e]mployees shall have the right to self-organization, to form, join, or assist labor organizations [and] to bargain collectively through representatives of their own choosing...." This includes the right to bargain even where there is no exclusive majority representative; denial of

82 §1 of the Act.

that right not only violates the NLRA, it also—as *The Charming Betsy* reminded us—"violate[s] the law of nations."

V. CONCLUSION

When American labor law finally recognizes that employees have the right to engage in collective bargaining regardless of whether they are members of a majority-union, the United States will be making common cause with other democratic industrialized countries and will be complying with major obligations under the ICCPR and the 1998 ILO Declaration. In every other advanced industrial democracy, trade-union representation and collective bargaining, conducted through diverse procedures, routinely thrive as the accepted norm, and labor-relations practices in those countries tend to conform to international standards.[83] Notwithstanding our diversity of procedures, it's now time for this nation to join with other highly developed countries and guarantee that the democratic values expressed in both domestic and international law become a reality in the American workplace, thereby treating union rights as truly human rights. But needless to say, when it's finally confirmed that employees have the right to bargain collectively through non-majority unions where there's not presently a majority-unit representative, it's not likely that unionization will occur without opposition. But union organizing will be easier, collective bargaining will be more widespread, and the original Congressional intent of bringing industrial democracy to the American workplace will become closer to realization.

83 *See generally* Hoyt N. Wheeler, The Future of the American Labor Movement 21-22 & 159-71 (2002).

Chapter 6. The Validation Process: Where Do We Go from Here?

I. Recent History and Its Obstacles

For the perplexed reader who wants to know why it's taken so long to resolve the issue of members-only minority-union collective bargaining, the short answer is that efforts to bring this matter to a decisional stage at the National Labor Relations Board (NLRB or Board)—*where direct-access is not allowed*[1]—were stymied by several internal agency problems and a series of political and oppositional obstacles which were apparently prompted by anti-union employers' and their powerful lobby, the United States Chamber of Commerce (hereinafter U.S. Chamber or Chamber). The following review of that experience reveals the nature of those obstructions and highlights the extensive support this concept has received from unions and university-based labor-law scholars, all of which set the stage for the upcoming task of making non-majority members-only collective bargaining a reality.

A. The *Dick's Sporting Goods* Case

The first effort to bring this issue to the Board was initiated in 2005 by the Steel Workers (USWA)[2] in the case of *Dick's Sporting Goods, Inc.*[3] This was an action begun on behalf of a small non-majority union of workers at a sporting-goods warehouse near Pittsburg, Pennsylvania, where the employer had refused to recognize or bargain with that union. Notwithstanding that it's the Board's exclusive function to interpret the National Labor Relations Act (NLRA or Act),[4] not the General Counsel's, Republican General Counsel Ronald Meisberg, who

---

1 *See infra* at notes 4 and 7.

2 United Steel, Paper and Forestry, Rubber, Manufacturing, Energy, Allied Industrial and Service Workers International Union, AFL-CIO/CLC (Steel Workers or USWA).

3 NLRB Case No. 6-CA-34821 (2005). *See* app. Part IA *infra* for refutation of the alleged reasons for dismissal of this case.

4 *See* § 10(a) [29 U.S.C. § 160(a)].

had been a management-side labor lawyer for twenty-three years prior to his appointment as a temporary Board Member and later as General Counsel,[5] chose in the *Dick's* case to interpret the Act on his own and thereby prevent consideration and determination by the Board. After holding the charge for almost a year, he concluded in a final *Advice Memorandum,* which was based entirely on demonstrably false historical readings and not on statutory text or actual legislative history, that the Act does not allow enforceable minority-union collective bargaining.[6] Accordingly, because of the generally accepted unreviewability of a General Counsel's refusal to issue a complaint,[7] that refusal prevented the minority-bargaining issue from reaching the Board; but despite popular misconception it has absolutely no valid legal authority. It is not *res judicata* because only the Board has statutory authority to interpret the Act. Nevertheless, the 18-page Advice Memorandum in *Dick's* "looks like" a decision and to a considerable—but erroneous—extent may have been treated like a decision.

Meisberg's principal conclusions were (1) that the minority-bargaining issue was already settled—which is palpably untrue, for there has never been a single case raising that non-majority collective bargaining (NMCB) issue; and (2) that statutory language and legislative history barred such bargaining—also untrue, as shown by his Memorandum's acknowledgement, without refutation, of the Charging Party's readings of the actual text of the NLRA.[8] There was also one other erroneous assertion that created long-term damage for which special attention is here appropriate.

That offending assertion, which was emphasized in the Advice Memorandum, falsely stated—even with self-contained proof of its inaccuracy—that the enacting "Congress *considered* and *rejected* a proviso to Section 9(a)[9] that would have protected the status of minority-supported unions,"[10] which was then quoted. Even the title of its source, however, signaled that the item was neither *considered* nor *rejected* by Congress. That title was: *Drafting Wagner's Act: Leon*

5 Apps.americanbar.org/labor/lel-annualcle/09/materials.

6 From Barry J. Kearney, Associate General Counsel, to Gerald Kobell, Regional Director, Region 6, June 22, 2006, in *Dick's Sporting Goods, Inc.* NLRB case 6-CA-3482. *See* app. *infra* at notes 3-102.

7 § 3(d). [29 U.S.C. § 153(d)]. *See* NLRB v. United Food & Commercial Wk'rs, 484 U.S. 112, 125-26 (1987); NLRB v. Sears, Roebuck & Co., 421 U.S. 132, 138-39 (1975); Vaca v. Sipes, 386 U.S. 171, 182 (1967). *But also see infra* at notes 53-80.

8 *Supra* note 6.

9 29 U.S.C. § 159(a). *Id.*

10 Advice Memorandum. *supra* note 6, at page 8. Emphasis added.

Keyserling and the ***Precommittee*** *Drafts of the Labor Disputes Act and the National Labor Relations Act.*[11] The word "*precommittee*" indicates accurately that these were only *preliminary* drafts that *never reached Congress*; and Professor Casebeer, in the text of the source, made it clear that the targeted proviso was only a tentative draft that preceded the definitive drafting of Section 7,[12] which was— among other things—a *replacement* rather than a rejection.[13] In fact, the cited proviso was actually drafted at least three months before the actual NLRA bill—which contained the broadly worded Section 7—was filed in Congress.[14] The touted proviso was thus never presented to Congress, hence never "*considered*" by or "*rejected*" by Congress.

B. Section 6 Rulemaking Petitions

The next effort to obtain Board consideration was begun again by the Steel Workers Union, this time as the *primary petitioner* in the filing of a Section 6[15] "rulemaking" petition[16] in which it was joined by six other major labor unions as *co-petitioners*, to wit (by their familiar acronyms): the IBEW,[17] the CWA,[18] the UAW,[19] the IAM,[20] the CNA,[21] and the UE.[22] That petition, which bore the signatures of all their respective general counsels, requested validation of

11 By Kenneth Casebeer in 11 Indus. Rel. L.J. at 73, 124 (hereinafter Casebeer). Emphasis and bold type added.

12 29 U.S.C. § 157. Casebeer, *supra* note 11 at 123.

13 *See* app. *infra* at notes 40-49.

14 Casebeer, *supra* note 11 at 130 and 1 Legislative History of the National Labor Relations Act of 1935 (1949) at 1,295.

15 29 U.S.C. § 156 and pursuant to Rule124 of NLRB Rules and Regulations, 29 C.F.R. § 102.124.

16 Entitled: Petition for Rulemaking Regarding Members-Only Minority-Union Collective Bargaining, filed Aug. 14, 2007.

17 International Brotherhood of Electrical Workers, AFL-CIO, CLC (IBEW).

18 Communications Workers of America, AFL-CIO, CLC (CWA).

19 United Automobile, Aerospace and Agricultural Implement Workers of America, AFL-CIO-CLC (UAW).

20 International Association of Machinists and Aerospace Workers, AFL-CIO-CLC (IAM).

21 California Nurses Association, AFL-CIO (CAN).

22 United Electrical, Radio and Machine Workers of America (UE).

members-only non-majority collective bargaining (NMCB) by promulgation of the following rule:

> Pursuant to Sections 7, 8(a)(1), and 8(a)(5) of the Act, in workplaces where employees are not currently represented by a certified or recognized Section 9(a) majority/exclusive collective-bargaining representative in an appropriate bargaining unit, the employer, upon request, has a duty to bargain collectively with a labor organization that represents less than an employee-majority with regard to the employees who are its members, but not for any other employees.

That petition was also supported by an extensive *amici brief* filed by forty-six university professors of labor law, all of whom are listed below.[23] And shortly

---

23 **James B. Atleson**, Distinguished Teaching Professor Emeritus, University of Buffalo, SUNY, School of Law

Richard Bales, Professor of Law, Northern Kentucky University, Salmon P. Chase College of Law

Mark Barenberg, Professor of Law, Columbia University School of Law

Janice R. Bellace, Samuel Blank Professor of Legal Studies, University of Pennsylvania, The Wharton School,

Susan Bisom-Rapp, Professor of Law Thomas Jefferson School of Law

Alfred W. Blumrosen, Thomas A. Cowan Professor Emeritus of Law, Rutgers University School of Law—Newark

Kenneth Casebeer, Professor of Law, University of Miami School of Law

Lance Compa, Senior Lecturer, Cornell University, New York State School of Industrial & Labor Relations

William R. Corbett, Frank L. Maraist Professor of Law, Louisiana State University, Paul M. Hebert Law Center

Angela Cornell, Associate Clinical Professor of Law, Cornell University School of Law

Roberto Corrada, Professor of Law, University of Denver, Sturm College of Law

Marion G. Crain, Wiley B. Rutledge Professor of Law, Director, Center for Interdisciplinary Study of Work and Social Capital, Washington University (St. Louis) School of Law

Charles B. Craver, Freda H. Alverson Professor of Law, George Washington University School of Law

Kenneth G. Dau-Schmidt, Willard & Margaret Carr Professor of Labor & Employment Law, Indiana University—Bloomington, Maurer School of Law

Henry Drummonds, Professor of Law, Lewis and Clark School of Law

Cynthia Estlund, Catherine A. Rein Professor of Law, New York University School of Law

Janice Fine, Assistant Professor, Rutgers University School of Management & Labor Relations

Michael Fischl, Professor of Law, University of Connecticut School of Law

Catherine Fisk, Chancellor's Professor of Law, University of California, Irvine, School of Law

William E. Forbath, Lloyd M. Bensen Professor of Law, University of Texas School of Law

Ruben J. Garcia, Associate Professor of Law, California Western School of Law

Michael Evan Gold, Associate Professor, Cornell University, New York State School of Industrial & Labor Relations

Michael Goldberg, Professor of Law, Widener University School of Law

thereafter,[24] Change to Win, an alliance of seven other major unions, then consisting of Teamsters,[25] LIUNA,[26] SEIU,[27] Carpenters Union,[28] Farm Workers,[29] UFCW,[30] and UNITE -HERE,[31] joined with the Steel Workers and its co-petitioning unions by filing a second rulemaking petition that also requested the Board

---

Jennifer L. Gordon, Associate Professor of Law, Fordham University School of Law

Joseph R. Grodin, John F. Digardi Distinguished Professor of Law, University of California, Hastings College of Law

James A. Gross, Professor, Cornell University, New York State School of Industrial & Labor Relations

Ann C. Hodges, Professor of Law, University of Richmond School of Law

Karl E. Klare, George J. & Kathleen Waters Matthews Distinguished University Professor, Northeastern University School of Law

D. Aaron Lacy, Associate Professor of Law, Southern Methodist University, Dedman School of Law

Ariana Levinson, Assistant Professor of Law, University of Louisville, Brandeis School of Law

Anne Marie Lofaso, Associate Professor of Law, West Virginia University College of Law

Charles J. Morris, Professor Emeritus of Law, Southern Methodist University, Dedman School of Law

Maria L. Ontiveros, Professor of Law, University of San Francisco School of Law

Joel Rogers, Professor of Law, Political Science, & Sociology, University of Wisconsin School of Law

George Schatzki, Professor of Law, Arizona State University, Sandra Day O'Connor College of Law

Paul M. Secunda, Associate Professor of Law, Marquette University School of Law

Calvin William Sharpe, Galen J. Roush Professor of Business Law & Regulation, Case Western Reserve University School of Law

Benjamin M. Shieber, Professor Emeritus of Law, Louisiana State University School of Law

Eileen Silverstein, Zephania Swift Professor Emerita of Law, University of Connecticut School of Law

Peggie R. Smith, Murray Family Professor of Law, University of Iowa College of Law

Katherine Van Wezel Stone, Professor of Law, University of California, Los Angeles, School of Law

Michael J. Wishnie, Clinical Professor of Law, Yale University School of Law

Donald H. Wollett, Professor Emeritus of Law, University of the Pacific, McGeorge School of Law

Donna Young, Professor of Law, Albany Law School

Kimberly A. Yuracko, Professor of Law, Northwestern University School of Law

Noah D. Zatz, Professor of Law, University of California, Los Angeles, School of Law

24 On January 4, 2008.

25 International Brotherhood of Teamsters (Teamsters).

26 Laborers' International Union of North America (LIUNA).

27 Service Employees International Union (SEIU).

28 United Brotherhood of Carpenters and Joiners of America.

29 United Farm Workers

30 United Food and Commercial Workers International Union (UFCW).

31 Formerly several different unions, including Amalgamated Clothing Workers of America (ACWA), International Ladies Garment Workers Union (ILGWU), Textile Workers Union of America (TWUA), Culinary Workers Union, Local 226 chartered, and New York City Hotel Trades Council (UNITE-HERE).

to adopt the aforesaid rule which the Steel Workers and its co-petitioner unions had proposed.

During the next several years, those two Section-6 petitions lay dormant at the Board while that agency was undergoing and responding to serious internal problems concerning membership vacancies, recess appointments, and actions related to judicial interventions regarding its functions when there was either an absence of a quorum or when cases were being determined without a proper quorum,[32] all of which contributed to no attention being given to the two aforesaid rulemaking petitions.

As a consequence of those problems and the NLRB's simultaneous involvement with two other major rulemaking cases and additional matters deemed highly important, the Board majority felt that it was unable to provide a timely response to the NMCB petitions relating to members-only bargaining prior to the forthcoming national election, whereupon, to avoid this important issue being determined later by what might have been an anti-union Republican-dominated agency, the Board dismissed these Steel Worker and Change-to-Win petitions without prejudice.[33]

C. U.S. Chamber of Commerce Report

The next significant event in this saga was publication by the U.S. Chamber of Commerce in 2014 of a lengthy propaganda report[34] that contained, as a central theme, several dishonest assertions directed at the NMCB concept. It asserted, falsely, that the 1935 Congress that enacted the NLRA had before it a proviso to Section 9(a) that would have granted representation rights for "minority, or members-only, unionism," and that "Congress *considered* such a system during its *debates* over passage of the NLRA" and "*expressly rejected*" that proviso. Those statements, as shown by the actual historical record recited in the Appendix *infra*,[35] were totally false and grossly misleading. Such a proviso was neither

32 *See* NLRB v. Noel Canning, 573 U.S.513 (2014), regarding unconstitutional recess appointments of several NLRB members.

33 NLRB Order dated Aug. 26, 2011, which stated that the dismissal was "without passing on the merits of the arguments set out therein." Former Board Chairperson Wilma Liebman, in retirement, confirmed to the author that the timing of that dismissal without prejudice was for the reason stated above.

34 *See* app. *infra* at notes 104-107.

35 *Id.*, at notes 40-49.

contained in the bill that Senator introduced, nor in any amended bill. It was thus never "debated," "considered," or "rejected" by the Congress.

That Chamber's report, and the critical role played by its participating attorneys[36] who supplied those historical falsehoods, might have been a causal factor that discouraged issuance of a complaint in another test case that followed. And this may have again prevented the Board from considering the minority-bargaining issue.

D. The SCA Tissue Case

That next potential opportunity for Board consideration occurred shortly after the Chamber had issued and circulated its report. This would have been in a new case, *SCA Tissue North America, LLC*,[37] in which the Steel Workers had once again filed a charge raising the same issue. But this too was met with disappointment, for General Counsel Richard Griffin—following the example set by former General Counsel Meisburg in the *Dick's* case—refused to issue a complaint, which of course again prevented the Board from considering the issue. Although in his dismissal letter[38] Griffin indicated that one reason for his refusal was the prior dismissal in the *Dick's* case,[39] that may not have been his dispositive reason because res judicata is not applicable to an NLRB General Counsel's refusal to issue a complaint.[40] His actual or primary reason may have been derived—either directly or indirectly—from the Chamber's previously noted untrue legislative-history allegation, for according to his *asserted* reason,

36 *Id.*, at notes 106-110.

37 NLRB case No. 03-CA-132930 filed July 24, 2014

38 Issued on June 5, 2015.

39 As asserted by the Regional Director in her original dismissal of August 25, 2014, from which the union appealed to the General Counsel.

40 For example, in *Epilepsy Foundation of Northeast Ohio*, 331 NLRB 676 (2000), *enforced in part*, 268 F.3d 1095 (D.C. Cir. 2001, *cert. denied*, 536 U.S. 904 (2002), the General Counsel issued a complaint that specifically contradicted the prevailing construction of the Act that limited the applicability of *NLRB v. Weingarten, Inc.*, 420 U.S. 251 (1975), to employees in unionized workplaces. As the Administrative Law Judge there wrote, "The General Counsel recognizes this but seeks to have the Board reconsider the matter." 1998 NLRB LEXIS 850, at pp. 32-33. The Board accordingly did reconsider. Furthermore, Griffin himself has urged the Board to reverse a prior ruling that was deemed erroneous (*see* Purple Communications, Inc., 361 N.L.R.B. No. 126 (2014), regarding reversal of the precedent in Guard Publishing Co. d/b/a Register Guard, 351 NLRB 1110 (2007), concerning an employer's limitations on employees' personal use of its computers and electronic communication systems).

"*Congress considered and rejected a proviso to Section 9(a) that would have protected the status of minority-supported unions.*" Here again *was* the Chamber's familiar falsehood on which Griffin was apparently relying. But, notwithstanding the apparent inconsistency, Griffin conceded, as noted above in Chapters 1[41] and 2,[42] that the charging parties' reading of "the language of Sections 7, 8(a)(1) and 8(a)(5)" was "plausible."

The U.S. Chamber and the contributors to its report may thus have caused substantial damage to the development of important law under the NLRA. I have no way of knowing whether anyone from the Chamber or from the Mittler Mendelson law firm personally appeared or otherwise contacted Griffin with reference to the *SCA* case, which may not have been improper at that pre-complaint stage. Regardless, however, the Chamber's report evidently—whether directly or indirectly—had its intended pernicious effect, for the untruthful "*considered-and-rejected*" characterization, which *had* not been mentioned by Griffin or his staff when I appeared for an oral presentation that Griffin had requested, reemerged as Griffin's dispositive issue for dismissal of the SCA charge.

II. CONVENTIONAL AND ALTERNATIVE PROCEDURES FOR NLRB AND JUDICIAL VALIDATION OF MEMBERS-ONLY COLLECTIVE BARGAINING

With all of the foregoing efforts now relegated to the irrelevant past, the time has come to take the necessary legal steps to bring this issue conclusively to the Board—and to the courts if necessary. The following procedures are directed to that endeavor.[43]

Regardless of the political make-up of the current NLRB, there should be no delay in proceeding with the necessary steps required for validation of members-only non-majority collective-bargaining. Unlike *Chevron* step-two confirmations, as I pointed out in Chapter 4,[44] legal authentication is here governed by the *clear text* of the Act rather than by what might be merely a *permissibly*

41 Chap. 1 at note 7.

42 Chap. 2 at note 34.

43 The following should command the special attention of the active reader who wishes to help move this project toward its ultimate conclusion.

44 Chevron U.S.A. v. Natural Resources Defense Council, Inc., 467 U.S.837 (1984). *See* chap. 2 *supra* at notes 71-74.

appropriate interpretation if Congress had not been unambiguously specific regarding the right of "employees . . . to bargain collectively through representatives of their own choosing,"[45] regardless of their minority or majority status.

Now to the task of spelling out how NLRB and judicial ratification of that objective can be accomplished. To begin with, the organizational and filing process that the Steel Workers instituted in the *Dick's* and *SCA* cases ought to be repeated. This members-only organizational process,[46] which calls for organizing employees into a viable and functioning labor union from the very beginning—even where the employer is actively engaged in anti-union conduct—should be easier than the traditional method of campaigning for authorization cards and election votes.[47] Thus, if a union were to begin an organizational drive where one of its objectives is to establish a factual basis to test the NMCB thesis, it would be in no worse position—and probably better—should it later choose to switch to a more traditional election-based campaign if its members-only effort is initially unsuccessful or inordinately delayed. Therefore, ideally, more than one test-case effort should be undertaken—although one is all that would be required.

For such a test case, a minority-union—even if small—should request recognition and collective-bargaining, and after the employer denies such request, the union should file a refusal-to-bargain unfair-labor-practice (ULP) charge with the NLRB Regional Office alleging a *violation of Sections 7, 8(a)(1).* With this filing, the charging union will now have a new and more powerful factor to cite then was available in the *Dick's* and *SCA* cases, which should make it easier for the General Counsel to authorize a complaint—that factor being the well-reasoned concurring opinion that Member Hirozawa issued in *Children's Hospital and Research Center of Oakland.*[48] As former General Counsel Arthur F. Rosenfeld emphasized in his testimony before a Congressional committee, "[I]t has always been the policy of the Office of the NLRB General Counsel to . . . *place unresolved legal issues before the Board for decision,.*"[49] and regarding directional changes, "[I]f there is a *signal* given . . . then there may be ways in which to get a complaint

45 § 7. *See* chap. 4 *supra* at notes 9-22.

46 *See* chap. 3 *supra* at notes 3-22 and with reference to name-identification of union-member employees *see* note 33.

47 *Id.*

48 *See* chap. 4 *supra* at notes 29-30.

49 Testimony and statement of Arthur F. Rosenfeld at Hearing before House Subcomm. on Workforce Protections of Comm. on Education and the Workforce, *Beck Rights 2001: Are Workers' Rights Being Adequately Enforced?* Nov. 14, 2001, Serial No. 107-39, at p. 126.

on these charges so that the Board can revisit it, because ultimately the Board and the courts have the final say on these matters."[50] The concurring opinion in *Children's Hospital*—which was issued *after* the denials of complaints in both the *Dick's*[51] *and SCA*[52] cases—was such a signal. Indeed, it's a strong sign that ought to mean that when this issue reaches the General Counsel again, a complaint should issue forthwith—but if it's to a pro-employer-majority Board and General Council, that may not happen.

Regardless of the immediate outcome, widespread and highly visible attempts by minority-union employees to achieve collective bargaining with recalcitrant employers could help foster awareness by the public and the media of the need and nature of this unfamiliar process. Efforts should therefore be made to disseminate information and education about those efforts and their expectations regarding administrative and/or judicial relief. Creating a critical mass of favorable public opinion will thus be important to attain the ultimate objective; widespread discussion and debate will help to create a sympathetic atmosphere conducive to eventual NLRB and judicial articulation of what might otherwise be deemed a strange outcome. Erroneous conventional wisdom can thereby be discredited, and democratic free-speech can aid in the restoration of a significant labor-union presence in the American economy.

A. Implementation Through Normal NLRB Procedures[53]

Because of the absence of a right of an aggrieved party to independently file suit for violation of the NLRA—a missing feature in the NLRA of which the public is generally unaware—and because the NLRB General Counsel has exclusive jurisdiction to issue complaints and bring cases before the Board for final orders,[54]—as demonstrated by the several years of trying described hereinabove—obtaining

50 *Id.* at 42.

51 *See* notes 2-5 *supra.*

52 *See* notes 37-38 *supra.*

53 Because of the logical and necessary connection between the essence of the NMCB concept and the remainder of this chapter, which describes the implementation of that concept, I have borrowed heavily for such material, including some verbatim portions, from chapter 10 (especially pages 175-183), of my earlier book, THE BLUE EAGLE AT WORK: RECLAIMING DEMOCRATIC RIGHTS IN THE AMERICAN WORKPLACE (2005), with permission of Cornell University Press.

54 §3(d), 29 U.S.C. §153(d).

an NLRB decision on this book's central question will be difficult—or at least delayed—unless the General Counsel is supportive of the legal objective

It will of course be preferable if the General Counsel issues a complaint, whereupon the Board will consider the case and render its decision in due course without judicial intervention prior to the Board's decision, for deciding cases is the Board's principal responsibility.

What if, however, the General Counsel refuses to issue a complaint, as happened in the *Dick's* and *SCA* cases? Should that occur, four other approaches would be available to achieve litigation of this issue. Proponents could thus pursue judicial intervention either by (1) direct court-action or by (2) picketing, or proceeding through (3) a piggy-back amendment to a complaint in a hearing being conducted by an Administrative Law judge (ALJ) or by a (4) petition to the Board for substantive rulemaking. The essential features of each of these judicial courses of action are contained in the following explanatory materials:

B. Implementation Through Direct Judicial Intervention

Either or both of the following scenarios describe appropriate direct judicial actions that could–or should–produce the desired result. The *first* involves a suit in federal district court to mandate that the General Counsel issue a complaint. The *second* involves picketing for members-only recognition, which would likely cause the employer to file an unfair-labor-practice charge alleging violation of Section 8(b)(7),[55] whereupon the Regional Director—assuming she or he determines that there is reasonable cause to believe the charge to be true—would petition a federal district court for a Section 10(l)[56] injunction.

1. Direct Legal Action Against the General Counsel

This scenario concerns a role that the judiciary must occasionally perform in the area of administrative law, either by direct district-court action or by extraordinary appellate action. Such judicial intervention, though rare, becomes possible when an administrative agency patently misconstrues key statutory language as to which the statute is silent regarding judicial review and there's no factual issue to be resolved. Notwithstanding past history regarding the *Dick's*

55 29 U.S.C. §158(b)(7).

56 29 U.S.C. §160(l).

and *SCA* cases, where the charging union didn't choose to pursue this remedial approach, such intervention would be appropriate if the NLRB General Counsel should refuse to issue a complaint to enforce the proposed minority-union bargaining requirement, for—as I have briefly noted previously—such a refusal denies the Board an opportunity to exercise its assigned function of interpreting and rendering a final order that would be subject to ordinary judicial review.[57] Notwithstanding popular perception about the unreviewable discretion of the NLRB's General Counsel to issue a complaint, there are indeed limits to such discretion, much of which, however, is yet to be defined. Although the Supreme Court has never ruled directly on the issue of General-Counsel unreviewability, it has on several occasions indicated in dicta that a general rule to that effect exists, and I note that proposition.[58] That Court, however, has also recognized several exceptions applicable to this concept. Five cases in particular define the principal areas of exception: *American Federation of Labor v. NLRB,*[59] *Leedom V. Kyne,*[60] *Boire v. Greyhound Corp.,*[61] *Heckler v. Chaney;*[62] and *Citizens to Preserve Overton Park. Inc. v. Volpe.*[63]

In *American Federation of Labor* the Supreme Court posed the basic question of whether a claimant is "precluded . . . from maintaining an independent suit in a district court to set aside the Board's action because it is contrary to the statute."[64] It later addressed that question in *Leedom v. Kyne. Kyne* involved a direct action in federal district court by a union of professional employees seeking to vacate an NLRB certification that violated the statutory provision prohibiting the grouping of professional and nonprofessionals in the same bargaining unit without affording the professionals an election to determine their consent to such inclusion. In allowing that suit, the Court said that

57 §10(f), 29 U.S.C. §160(f), provides in pertinent part: "Any person aggrieved by a final order of the Board granting or denying in whole or in part the relief sought may obtain a review of such order in [an appropriate United States Court of Appeals]."

58 *See* NLRB v. United Food & Commercial Wk'rs, Local 23, *supra* note 7 at 112 & 125-26; NLRB v. Sears, Roebuck & Co., *supra* note 7 at 138-39; Vaca v. Sipes, *supra* note 7 at 182.

59 308 U.S. 401 (1940).

60 358 U.S. 184 (1958).

61 376 U.S. 473 (1964).

62 470 U.S. 821 (1985).

63 401 U.S. 402 (1971).

64 308 U.S. at 412.

> "absence of jurisdiction of the federal courts" would mean "a sacrifice or obliteration of a right which Congress" has given professional employees, for there is no other means within their control . . . to protect and enforce that right. . . . This Court cannot lightly infer that Congress does not intend judicial protection of rights it confers against agency action taken in excess of delegated powers.[65]

Later, in *Boire v. Greyhound*, the Court stressed that the *Kyne* exception was a narrow one, applicable only where the Board had patently misconstrued the Act, and it wouldn't be applied where there was a question of fact to be reviewed.

Although *Kyne* involved the Board's violation of a negative statutory provision, "its rationale has been held to be equally applicable when . . . the Board or its agents act in disregard of an affirmative or mandatory command,"[66] and its rationale has likewise been applied to actions or inactions of the Board's General Counsel and Regional Director.[67] Although the Supreme Court hasn't specifically ruled on the reviewability of the NLRB General Counsel's authority to issue a complaint, its decisions involving other administrative agencies subject to the same provisions of the Administrative Procedure Act (APA)[68] are here applicable. Recognized judicial exceptions to the doctrine of unreviewability of discretionary administrative action indicate that such authority is directly reviewable where the issue is one of *pure statutory construction* and the matter hasn't been committed to the agency's sole discretion or a right under the Constitution is involved, provided no other adequate remedy is available.[69]

In *Heckler v. Chaney* the Court addressed the central issue that defines the limits on the NLRB General Counsel's discretionary authority regarding judicial review of agency action allegedly "committed to agency discretion by law" within the meaning of Section 701(a)(2) of the APA.[70] The Court spelled out

65 358 U.S. at 190, quoting from Switchmen's Union v. National Mediation Board, 320 U.S. 297 (1943).

66 Terminal Freight Handling Co. v. Solien, 444 F.2d 699, 703 (8th Cir. 1971), *cert. denied*, 405 U.S. 996 (1972) (holding that the district court had subject-matter jurisdiction in a mandamus type action against a Regional Director for failure to file a secondary-boycott §10(l) injunction petition). *See also* Templeton v. Dixie Color Printing Co., 444 F.2d 1064 (5th Cir. 1971); Miami Newspaper Printing Pressmen's Union Local 46 v. McCulloch, 322 F.2d 993 (D.C. Cir. 1963).

67 Terminal Freight Handling Co. v. Solien, *Id.*

68 5 U.S.C. §§701-706.

69 Inasmuch as no Constitutional issue is here being claimed, that exception will not be reviewed here.

70 5 U.S.C. §§701(a)(2). The Court's opinion addressed the relevant review provisions of the APA,

specific guidelines for determining when a refusal of an agency to initiate action is subject to judicial review.[71] In an opinion by Justice Rehnquist, the Court indicated that "an agency's decision not to take enforcement action should be *presumed* immune from judicial review under §701(a)(2),"[72] but in so stating, the Court declared that

> we emphasize that the decision is *only presumptively unreviewable;* the presumption may be rebutted where the substantive statute has provided guidelines for the agency to follow in exercising its enforcement powers. Thus, in establishing this presumption in the APA, *Congress did not set agencies free to disregard legislative direction in the statutory scheme that the agency administers.*[73]

The *Heckler* opinion pointed with approval to *Citizens to Preserve Overton Park. Inc. v. Volpe* regarding the "threshold question"[74] of whether the agency's action was at all reviewable and quoted the following excerpt from the opinion in that case, the essence of which applies to the issue here under consideration:[75]

> In this case, there is no indication that Congress sought to prohibit judicial review and there is most certainly no 'showing of "clear and convincing evidence" of a . . . legislative intent' to restrict access to judicial review.[76] Similarly, the Secretary's decision here does not fall within the exception for action 'committed to agency discretion.' This is a very narrow exception. . . . The legislative

which it succinctly framed as follows: "Any person 'adversely affected or aggrieved' by agency action . . . including a 'failure to act,' is entitled to 'judicial review thereof,' as long as the action is a 'final agency action for which there is no other adequate remedy in court,'" 470 U.S. at 828, *citing* 5 U.S.C. §§702 & 704, and further noting that "before any review at all may be had, a party must first clear the hurdle of §701(a)," which provision expressly states that such review is not applicable where "(1) statutes "preclude judicial review; or (2) agency action is committed to agency discretion by law." *Id.*

71 The Court refused to hold reviewable the refusal of the Food and Drug Administration to issue a finding that certain drugs were "safe and effective" for human executions before they could be distributed; however, it carefully articulated the limits of that holding.

72 470 U.S. at 832. Emphasis added.

73 *Id.* at 832-33. Emphasis added.

74 *Id.* at 829.

75 *Id.* at 830.

76 *Citing* Abbott Laboratories v. Gardner, 387 U.S. 136, 141 (1967).

> history of the Administrative Procedure Act indicates that *it is applicable in those rare instances where 'statutes are drawn in such broad terms that in a given case there is no law to apply.*'"[77]

The NLRA is patently not such a statute.

The foregoing judicial precedents establish that if the General Counsel refuses to issue a complaint involving members-only minority-union collective bargaining, and thus prevents the Board from ruling on this critical issue, it seems clear that such inaction would violate the APA and provide sufficient basis for a district court to issue a mandamus-type order requiring issuance of a complaint. For these purposes, the district court would thus be the reviewing court granting relief under Section 702 of the APA to persons suffering "legal wrong" because of agency action or inaction; and, pursuant to Section 706(1) of that Act,[78] such court could "compel agency action unlawfully withheld" and set aside the General Counsel's refusal to issue a complaint as "arbitrary, capricious, an abuse of discretion . . . not in accordance with law."[79]

Although such a determination would be fully supported by the cases noted above, its logic is independently compelling and elementary. Congress intended for the National Labor Relations Board to interpret the Act and issue decisions under that Act, and it provided for judicial review of those decisions.[80] It didn't confer final interpretative authority on a General Counsel as to whom there would be no judicial review. Notwithstanding that logical conclusion, if it were to be decided that the General Counsel does have unreviewable authority to issue this complaint, regardless of the considerations discussed above, it would follow that such a determination would constitute a *final order* of the Board under Section 10(f).[81] Accordingly, because "[a]ny person aggrieved by a *final order* of the Board granting or denying in whole or in part the relief sought may obtain a review of such order in [an appropriate] United States Court of Appeals,"[82] such direct appellate action would provide another route to judi-

77 *Citing* S. Rep. No. 752, 79th Cong., 1st Sess., 26 (1945). 401 U.S. 410 (footnote omitted). Emphasis added.

78 5 U.S.C. §706(2).

79 5 U.S.C. §706(2)(A).

80 §§ 10(e) & (f), 29 U.S.C. §§160(e) & (f).

81 29 U.S.C. § 160(f).

82 *Id.* Emphasis added.

cial relief. Although the appellate court might exercise any of several remedial options under those circumstances, it is most likely that it would remand the case to the Board for initial hearing and consideration.

Whatever the judicial route taken, a remedy is bound to be available to correct a refusal by the General Counsel to issue a complaint on such a critical issue of law. Professor Bernard Schwartz's observation is here appropriate:

> [T]here is no place for unreviewable discretion in a system such as ours. Provided that the case is justiciable, all discretionary power should be reviewable to determine that the discretion conferred has not been abused. What the English courts call the *Wednesbury* principle[83] is just as valid in American administrative law. Under it, the reviewing court should always be able to determine that the discretion has not been exercised in a manner in which no reasonable administrator would act.[84]

2. Picketing for Members-Only Recognition

Although the just-described judicial process is probably the most logical route for obtaining NLRB review, and also the most likely to be followed, another possible scenario for obtaining direct judicial intervention if the General Counsel refuses to issue a complaint involves picketing for members-only recognition and bargaining. Such picketing would of course be directed at an employer and workplace where there's currently no exclusive majority-union representative. The key to such an action lies in Section 8(b)(7),[85] the Landrum-Griffin amendment that restricts organizational and recognitional picketing, and Section 10(l),[86] the Taft-Hartley mandatory-injunction provision that applies to picketing where there's "reasonable cause to believe [that] Section 8(b)(7) has been violated.[87] To activate this approach, a minority union would request recognition and bargaining on behalf of its "members only"—being careful not to

83 Named after Associated Provincial Picture Houses, Ltd. v. Wednesbury Corp., [1948] 1 K.B. 223. *See* Council of Civil Serv. Unions v. Minister for the Civil Serv., [1984] 3 W.L.R. 1174, 1196, 1200. (Footnote in original.)

84 Bernard Schwartz, ADMINISTRATIVE LAW 495 (3rd ed. 1991).

85 29 U.S.C. § 158(b)(7).

86 29 U.S.C. § 160(l),

87 Inclusion of §8(b)(7) coverage was added to §10(l) of the Act in 1959 when §8(b)(7) was added.

claim representation of a majority of the employees in any appropriate bargaining unit or to seek bargaining on behalf of all employees in such a unit. The employer, in accordance with latter-day conventional wisdom, would presumably deny that request, whereupon picketing could begin. Such picketing should simply protest the employer's refusal to recognize and bargain with the union for its employee-members only. To assure this critical limitation of intention, I recommend that the picket-sign expressly disclaim any organizational purpose and any intent to represent all of the employees in a likely bargaining unit, or any employees who aren't presently members of the union.

Obviously, the target of such picketing should be an employer and location where picketing can be reasonably effective—perhaps at customer entrances of a retail establishment, or at a loading-dock of an employer's primary place of business,[88] or at both such locations. After picketing has continued for "a reasonable period of time,"[89] the employer will likely file a ULP charge with the Labor Board alleging violation of Section 8(b)(7). (The alternative would be for the employer to recognize and deal with the minority union, which would be a surprise but certainly welcome.) Section 8(b)(7), in pertinent part, basically prohibits picketing

> where an object thereof is forcing or requiring an employer to recognize or bargain with a labor organization *as the representative of his employees* or forcing or requiring the employees of an employer *to accept or select such labor organization as their collective bargaining representative*, unless such labor organization is currently certified as the representative of such employees [and] such picketing has been conducted without a petition being filed within a reasonable period of time not to exceed thirty days . . . .[90]

After the charge is filed, it will either be dismissed because the necessary elements for violation of Section 8(b)(7) will be perceived to be lacking, or a determination will be made to issue a complaint, in which event the Regional Director, on behalf of the General Counsel, would likely file an action for "appropriate injunctive relief" pursuant to Section 10(l) to restrain the picketing

88 *See* NLRB v. International Rice Milling Co., 341 U.S. 665 (1951). To avoid violating §8(b)(4), 29 U.S.C. §158(b)(4), secondary locations should not be picketed.

89 §8(b)(7)(C).

90 §8(b)(7) and ¶(C) thereof. Emphasis added.

pending Board determination, for such filing is mandatory where the NLRB officer "has reasonable cause to believe such a charge is true and that a complaint should issue . . . ."[91] Of course the proper legal determination should be dismissal of the charge entirely, because the picketing would have neither an *organizational purpose* nor a purpose to obtain *exclusive recognition* for all the employees in the bargaining unit—which is what the provision prohibits—in which case the minority union would retain its right to picket.[92] But if a petition for a 10(l) injunction is in fact filed—which would be the more likely occurrence inasmuch as this General Counsel will have refused to issue a complaint on behalf of a minority-union seeking to bargain—the issue in question would then be presented to the court for interim adjudication. The union's defense to the petition and charge will be that its picketing was for members-only recognition and bargaining, not for recognition as an exclusive representative of all the employees in the bargaining unit, which is the only recognition proscribed by Section 8(b)(7).

Not only is the latter reading of all bargaining-unit employees the natural interpretation of "employees" in the provision, it's also the only meaning intended by Congress—as the legislative history makes unmistakably clear and as settled case law confirms. Section 8(b)(7) was enacted as part of an extensive package of new and amended labor-reform legislation in 1959. The sole public purpose of this provision was to ban "blackmail picketing" and "top-down" organizing.[93] And the Board and the courts have indicated that only picketing to obtain recognition for *all* the employees in the bargaining unit—i.e. exclusive recognition—is proscribed by the *recognition* part of Section 8(b)(7). As the

---

91 §10(l).

92 *See infra* at notes 93-98.

93 The provision was the favorable response of Congress to item 12 of President Eisenhower's 20 point program of proposed labor-management legislation. 1 LEGISLATIVE HISTORY OF THE LABOR-MANAGEMENT REPORTING AND DISCLOSURE ACT OF 1959 (1959) (hereinafter 1 LMRDA LEGIS. HIST.) at 81. The proponents of this proposed amendment cited the facts of Curtis Brothers (Teamsters Local 639 (Curtis Bros.), 119 NLRB 232 (1957), *rev'd*, 274 F.2d 551 (D.C. Cir. 1958), *aff'd*, 362 U.S. 274 (1960)) as the prime example of conduct they sought to prohibit. They described the problem as follows: "Organizing from the top rather than persuasion of the employees has become the standard organizing procedure of many unions–in particular the racket-ridden Teamsters Union. The union seeks to bring economic pressure directly upon the employees to force them to join the union in order to protect their jobs....Such picketing also has the purpose of coercing the employer into recognizing the union and signing a contract with it . . . ." 1 LABOR MANAGEMENT REPORTING AND DISCLOSURE ACT LEGISLATIVE HISTORY (1959) at 472-73.

Supreme Court explained in *Iron Workers (Higdon Contracting Co.),*[94] the interpretation of that provision "is rooted in the generally prevailing statutory policy that a union should not purport to act as the collective-bargaining agent for *all* unit employees, and may not be recognized as such, unless it is the voice of the majority of the employees in the unit."[95] The reader is here reminded that the Wagner Act's goal and ultimate objective was mature bargaining based on majority and exclusive Section 9(a) representation, but that's not to be confused with the Act's broad protective umbrella in Section 7 that guarantees a wide range of collective action, including *stepping-stone* minority-union bargaining that precedes majoritarian-exclusivity bargaining. The *Higdon* Court also noted with approval that Section 8(b)(7) "has not been literally applied"[96] and offered the example of Board rulings that a recognized (but not certified) union that pickets an employer to require bargaining to enforce an already executed collective-bargaining contract does not violate the Act.[97] Another example of a non-literal reading of the provision is the confirmed recognition that picketing to protest a nonunion employer's failure to pay area-standard wages does not violate the Act.[98]

Clearly, picketing to require an employer to recognize and bargain with a minority union for its members only wouldn't violate Section 8(b)(7), for, as Professor Alan Hyde rightly summarized the applicable law, "picketing to seek 'members-only' recognition is not organizational, recognitional, or in derogation of an incumbent union."[99] Accordingly, a federal district court faced with that issue in a Section 10(l) injunction proceeding should deny the injunction. But if the court were to hold otherwise its order would be appealable, and the issue would be on its way to final resolution. It's also likely that a determination that such picketing does not violate the Act would be appealed by the

94 NLRB v. Local 103, Iron Workers (Higdon Contracting Co.), 434 U.S. 335 (1977).

95 *Id.* at 344. Emphasis added.

96 *Id.* at 342-43.

97 *Id.* at 343, *citing* Building and Constr. Trades Council of Santa Barbara County (Sullivan Elec. Co.), 146 NLRB 1086 (1964); Bay Counties Dist. Council of Carpenters (Disney Roofing & Material Co.), 14 NLRB 1598, 1605 (1965).

98 *See* Building & Constr. Trades Council (Houston) (Claude Everett Constr. Co.) 136 NLRB 321 (1962).

99 Alan Hyde, *After Smyrna: Rights and Powers of Unions that Represent Less than a Majority,* 45 RUTGERS L. REV. 637, 655 (1993), *citing* Douds v. Local 1250, Retail Wholesale Dep't Store Union, 173 F.2d 764, 769-71 (2nd Cir. 1949), a decision by Judge Learned Hand, joined by Judges Swan and Clark, which held, regarding the earlier statutory provision, §8(b)(4)(C), 29 U.S.C. §158(b)(4)(C), that "members-only" recognition was not the recognitional objective reached by the Act.

employer or submitted to the Board for its full consideration. In either event, judicial review would be available.

C. Implementation Through a Piggy-Back Motion to Amend a Section 8(a)(3) Complaint

The next approach could be labeled the "accidental traveler," an approach that uses a *piggy-back* motion to achieve judicial recognition. As many readers are aware, in the normal course of a union's organizational campaign employees are often discharged to discourage union membership, which is—needless to say—a violation of Section 8(a)(3). If that should occur to an employee who is a bona-fide member of a minority union, that union should not only file an unfair labor practice charge with the NLRB, it should also request that the employer engage in good-faith bargaining regarding that discharge, for discharges are mandatory subjects of collective bargaining.[100] If the employer refuses, which is likely, the charge should thereafter include not only an allegation of a Section 8(a)(3) violation but also a separate claim of refusal-to-bargain under Sections 8(a)(1) and 8(a)(5). If the General Counsel declines to include the latter allegation in the complaint and the discharge case proceeds in due course to a hearing before an ALJ, during the hearing the union should present a piggy-back motion pursuant to Section 102.17 of the NLRB Rules and Regulations[101] requesting the ALJ to amend the complaint to include the refusal-to-bargain allegation; and appropriate evidence or offer-of-proof should be presented to make the necessary record. From then on, regardless of the action of the ALJ or the Board on this matter—and one would hope that either or both would find a separate violation of Sections 8(a)(1) and 8(a)(5)—the issue will have been joined and will thus eventually become ripe for a final order, which if adverse would be appealable to a Court of Appeals.

D. Implementation Through Substantive Administrative Rulemaking

A last-resort alternative means of securing implementation would be for the union to petition the NLRB for issuance of a substantive rule in accordance

100 *See* National Licorice Co. v. NLRB, 309 U.S. 350 (1940).

101 "Any such complaint may be amended upon such terms as may be deemed just...at the hearing and until the case has been transferred to the Board...upon motion, by the administrative law judge...." NLRB RULES AND REGULATIONS AND STATEMENT OF PROCEDURE, Series 8, 29 C.F.R. §102.17,

with Section 6 of the National Labor Relations Act,[102] As described above, such a rule was previously filed with the Board in two union-based petitions which resulted in long delays and no final decision.[103] Accordingly, this procedure isn't now recommended. Not only is this process exceedingly slow, unless it's affirmatively considered by a strongly supportive Board, it's not likely to produce a fully-satisfactory product for judicial review or validation. Accordingly, this procedure isn't now recommended for the proposed reaffirmation of minority-union members-only bargaining.

E. Proceedings in the Court of Appeals

Following completion of applicable requirements in accordance with one or more of the above described procedures, when the case is ready for appellate action or review, should that be necessary, the union should proceed to file the appropriate petition "in the circuit wherein the unfair labor practice in question was alleged to have been engaged in or wherein such person resides or transacts business, or in the United State Court of Appeals for the District of Columbia."[104] Needless to say, that choice of Circuits will probably be based on the guess as to which Circuit's panel might include the most favorable judges; however, that choice might already have been partially determined by the location previously chosen for the test case that would now be ready for appellate consideration—I say "partially" because the D. C. Circuit would still be an alternative choice of venue.

The relief sought may depend on whether the Board has already ruled on the issue. But whether it has or hasn't, the Circuit Court will take whatever action and/or provide such relief as it deems fitting, which won't necessarily include a remand to the Board for its decision. This is so because, as was explained in

102 5 U.S.C. §§551-559. The general requirements for *notice-and-comment rulemaking*— as this procedure is called—are contained in the following excerpt from 5 U.S.C. §553(c): "After notice required by this section, the agency shall give interested persons an opportunity to participate in the rule making through submission of written data, views, or arguments with or without opportunity for oral presentation. After consideration of the relevant matter presented, the agency shall incorporate in the rules adopted a concise general statement of their basis and purpose . . . ."

103 See notes 15-32 *supra* for history of these petitions and note 22 *supra* for text of the proposed rule

104 Text in Section 10(f) [29 U.S.C. § 160(f)].

Chapters 1[105] and 4,[106] the matter in issue—i.e., the right of employees who are members of a minority union to engage in collective bargaining—is authorized, indeed "guaranteed"[107] by *unambiguous* text in the Act, thus this would not be a review of a discretionary permissive agency determination that purports "to fill any gap left implicitly or explicitly by Congress,"[108] for we are here dealing with clear statutory text that, in the words of Justice Scalia "is the law, and it is the text that must be observed."[109]

105 *See* chap. 1 *supra* at notes 12-13 & 19-23.

106 *See* chap. 4 *supra* at notes 34-40.

107 § 8(a)(1).

108 *Chevron, supra* note 41at 843.

109 See chap. 4 *supra* at note 35.

Appendix: Objections and their Refutations

Inasmuch as this book's purpose is to provide complete information needed to accomplish re-validation of the concept of non-majority collective bargaining (NMCB)—at least to the extent that I've been able to secure it—this appendix purports to contain all of the legal objections to that concept of which I'm aware, plus appropriate responses. As the materials in chapters 1, 4, and 6 have already demonstrated, there are actually no valid legal objections to this concept because this NMCB process is based entirely on unambiguous statutory text and strong and consistent legislative history. Various objections, however, have been raised and publically asserted, but they have been based mostly on former General Counsel Meisberg's invalid asserted reasons for dismissal of the charge in *Dick's Sporting Goods, Inc.*[1] Accordingly, the first part of this appendix presents responses to all of the reasons he asserted for that dismissal, much of which necessarily repeats material already contained in prior chapters, especially Chapter 4. In addition, a brief response to former General Counsel Griffin's asserted reasons for his dismissal in the SCA Tissue case appear, both in Chapter 6 and here.[2] The remainder of this appendix treats other known objections and their refutations, whereupon, with all of these responses thus readily available, no further major research should be necessary prior to beginning the validation process described in Chapter 6.

I. Inadequacy of General Counsel Meisberg's Reasons for Dismissal in the *Dick's* Case

A. His Failure to Dispute Unambiguous Meaning of Pertinent Statutory Text and Legislative History

The following discussion represents direct refutation of the asserted grounds for dismissal of the charge in *Dick's*.[3] Although the General Counsel's *Advice*

1 NLRB case 6-CA-34821 (2005). .

2 *See* chap. 6 *supra* at notes 37-39.

3 Contained in Advice Memorandum from Barry J. Kearney, Associate General Counsel (on behalf of

Memorandum (Advice Memo or Memo) in that case asserts and reasserts mantra-like that such dismissal of the unfair labor practice was "based on the statutory language, the legislative history of the Act, and well-established Board and Supreme Court doctrine,"[4] those assertions are never supported in the Memo.

1. Inaccurate Reading of Statutory Text

The Advice Memo begins with the assertion that the employer "had no obligation under the Act to recognize the Charging Party in the absence of a Board election establishing that it represented a majority of the Employer's employees."[5] It then asserts that this conclusion is "*based on the statutory language*"[6] and reiterates that it "*is clearly supported by the statutory language.*"[7] However, notwithstanding those unqualified repetitive assertions, not one sentence or one phrase in either the Memo or the Regional Director's Letter (Letter)[8] presents any discussion of statutory language (other than its unrefuted reiteration of the charging party (Union's) review and analyses of applicable statutory text. The General Counsel in the *Dick's* case (*Dick's* GC) thus expressed no disapproval of or disagreement with the Union's interpretation of the text of the pertinent statutory provisions.

The discussion that follows demonstrates: (1) that the *Dick's* GC failed to identify any provision in the Act that mandates that only majority unions have an enforceable right to engage in collective bargaining; (2) that he omitted entirely any critical reference to the key fourteen-word provision in Section 7 that *guarantees* through Section 8(a)(1) that all "[e]mployees shall have the right to bargain collectively through representatives of their own choosing;" (3) that he did not dispute that Section 9(a), by its unmistakable terms, is a *conditional* provision that applies only *if, when,* and *after* a union achieves majority status in an appropriate bargaining unit, and until that occurs, Section 9(a) is totally

General Counsel Ronald Meisberg) , to Gerald Kobell, Regional Director, Region 6, June 22, 2006, in *Dick's Sporting Goods, Inc.* NLRB case 6-CA-34821. Hereinafter Advice Memo.

4 Advice Memo p. 2. *See also* pp. 1 & 18.

5 *Id.* p. 1.

6 Advice Memo pp. 1, 2, & 6.

7 *Id.* p. 18. Emphasis added.

8 July 26, 2006, letter of the Regional Director formally dismissing the Charge in *Dick's Sporting Goods, Inc., supra* note 1.

inoperable; and (4) that although he asserted that "Section 8(a)(5) is fundamentally premised on Section 9(a),"[9] he provided no textual or historical support whatever for that bald assertion.

Indeed, the *Dick's* GC misread Section 9(a) as if it contained an added phrase, such as shown in **bold type,** as follows:

> Representatives designated or selected for the purposes of collective bargaining by the majority of the employees in a unit appropriate for such purposes, shall be the exclusive representatives of all the employees in such unit for the purposes of collective bargaining **and shall be the only representatives of employees with whom the employer has a duty to bargain collectively**.

Of course that added phrase isn't contained in the statute. The drafters didn't add it, or its equivalent, for the same reason they declined to add the "smoking gun" language to Section 8(a)(5)[10]—because they did not want to confine collective bargaining to majority unions only. Even though majority bargaining was deemed the ideal format for mature bargaining, they recognized that less-than majority bargaining must also be protected, for it would often be a part of a union's developmental process. Inasmuch as Section 9(a) must be read without the bold-face addition—as it actually reads—it's a conditional clause operable only if and when a union achieves majority status in an appropriate bargaining unit. Until that event occurs, employees have the right to engage in collective bargaining through a minority union for its members only. Exclusive representation, the recognized goal for mature collective bargaining, is solely a function of majority status. The *Dick's* GC thus erred in his reading of Section 9(a).

His Advice Memo does recognize, however, that the Steel Workers' (Union's) claim "that employers have a duty to recognize and bargain with minority, members-only, unions is based in large part on two interrelated premises: the clear and plain text of the Act and the legislative history of that text."[11] With regard to that "clear and plain language," the Memo acknowledges and repeats the Union's position—supported by eight cases cited by the Supreme Court,[12] but without raising any question as to their relevance: that "general principles

9 Heading, in Advice Memo p. 11.

10 *See* chap. 4 *supra* at notes 79-80.

11 Advice Memo p. 3.

12 *Id.* n. 6.

of statutory construction mandate that the provisions of the Act be read broadly, and that the language of those provisions be given its plain, ordinary meaning."[13]

The Memo likewise doesn't dispute the accuracy of the Union's literal reading of Section 8(a)(5). And it acknowledges and doesn't question the accuracy of the "smoking-gun" feature of Section 8(a)(5)'s legislative history that confirmed the nonrestrictive meaning of that provision, for it repeats *without any dispute* the Union's contention

> that the drafters intentionally rejected a version of Section 8(a)(5) that in the Charging Party's view, would have explicitly excluded minority unions from Section 8(a)(5) protection. The rejected language would have made it unlawful for an employer only to:
>
> [R]efuse to bargain collectively with employees through their representatives, chosen as provided in Section 9(a).[14]

Instead, as the Memo concedes, Congress adopted the other proffered version of Section 8(a)(5)—the existing version.

Not only does the Advice Memo not refute the obvious conclusion to be drawn from the drafters' selection of the present text of Section 8(a)(5) and their simultaneous discarding of alternative language that would have confined Section 8(a)(5) bargaining only to majority unions, it notes Supreme Court authority reinforcing that conclusion, to wit, the Court's statement in *INS v. Cardoza-Fonseca,*[15] intending it, however, for use where it wasn't applicable:[16]

> Few principles of statutory construction are more compelling than the proposition that Congress does not intend *sub silentio* to enact statutory language that it has earlier discarded in favor of other language.

The Advice Memo also acknowledges, without any effort at refutation, the Union's reading of the text of Section 8(a)(5), including the conclusion that "the presence of the comma in Section 8(a)(5) is evidence that the drafters of the

13 *Id.*

14 Advice Memo p. 5. Underscoring in original.

15 480 U.S. at 442-43 (1987). *See* Advice Memo p. 7, n. 23

16 *See infra* at notes 38-47.

Act intended that Section 9(a) restrict only the *process of bargaining*, not the *bargaining representative*.[17]

The Advice Memo never questions the Union's reading of the language of Section 9(a), that it only provides a *conditional* limitation on the right of employees to bargain "through representatives of their own choosing" and that it applies only *after* a union has been "designated or selected" by a majority of the employees in an appropriate unit. Notwithstanding, the Memo repeatedly asserts that the refusal to issue a complaint was "based on statutory language."

2. Inaccurate Reporting of Legislative History

Disregarding the truism that legislative history without statutory support is meaningless, the *Dick's* GC attempted to present a legislative-history rationale for not issuing a complaint. His historical references, however, were inaccurate, misleading, and irrelevant. The Memo's discussion of his historical premise opens with two headings: that "Industrial Democracy is Fundamentally Based on Majority Rule" and that "The Drafters of the Act intended collective bargaining to be based on majority rule."[18] That *majority* theme runs throughout the Memo—indeed, it's a "Johnny-One-Note"[19] theme alleging that it was the framers' desire that majority-exclusivity bargaining would be the intended form of collective bargaining. That postulate is certainly true for *mature* bargaining, but is beside the point here in issue. Indeed, the Union never disputed that objective—in fact, it stressed it, just as it is stressed in this book.

The Union specifically reminded the *Dick's* GC that Section 9(a) was the provision of the Act

> that was expressly designed to establish what Congress deemed to be the ideal form of mature collective bargaining, to wit: majority and exclusive representation and bargaining covering employees in an appropriate bargaining unit.[20]

---

17 Advice Memo p. 4. Emphasis added.

18 *Id.* p. 6.

19 BABES IN ARMS, music by Richard Rogers, lyrics by Lorenz Hart (1936).

20 Union's initial Statement of Position in the *Dick's* case at p. 20, quoting from CHARLES J. MORRIS, THE BLUE EAGLE AT WORK: RECLAIMING DEMOCRATIC RIGHTS IN THE AMERICAN WORKPLACE, (2005) at 102 (hereinafter BLUE EAGLE).

That same proposition is noted repeatedly in the BLUE EAGLE AT WORK[21] and is emphasized in this book.[22] The concept of majority bargaining, however, was simply the *ultimate* objective of the NLRA and its framers. It wasn't intended to exclude earlier stepping-stone stages of collective bargaining. As previously noted, the framers of the Act took pains to protect such pre-majority bargaining.[23] That's what members-only bargaining is all about. It is not about substituting plurality and proportional representation for majority representation, as the *Dick's* GC attempted to portray in his dismissal of the charge in *Dick's*. Members-only minority-union bargaining was and should be simply viewed as a means to an end—the end being majority/exclusivity bargaining. However, the end should not be confused with the means.

The Advice Memo devotes most of its discussion of legislative history to the irrelevant issue of *post-election* plurality-bargaining, failing to note that all of its references were so limited, hence inapplicable to pre-majority bargaining. Its examples consist of statements touting the advantages of *post-majority* exclusivity bargaining contrasted with *proportional representation*[24] or *plurality bargaining*, which employer witnesses in the Congressional hearings had been advocating.[25] Those opponents of the Wagner bill preferred plurality-bargaining because it would have ensured that after a majority union had been selected in an election, the employer could continue to deal with a minority union—which was expected to be a union that's friendly to the company.[26] That was the post-election position that employers had urged in the *Denver Tramway*[27] and *Houde Engineering*[28] cases, but which was rejected by the National Labor Board (NLB)

21 *Id.*, at 10, 11, 57, 61, 65, 69-71,76, 85, & 102.

22 *Supra* at note 18.

23 *See* chap. 4 *supra* at notes 78-79. The Advice Memo conspicuously ignores available documentations that show the consistent efforts of the drafters, in both their 1934 and 1935 drafts, to protect preliminary minority-union bargaining that would precede the establishment of majority and exclusivity bargaining. *Id.*, at note 84.

24 *E.g., see* statement by Senator Wagner, 2 LEGISLATIVE HISTORY OF THE NATIONAL LABOR RELATIONS ACT OF 1935 (1949) at 2491.

25 *See* chap. 4 at notes 86-87.

26 *See* BLUE EAGLE, *supra note 20* at 69 .

27 1 NLB 64 (1934).

28 1 NLRB (old) 35 (1934).

[29] and the old NLRB,[30] and again by Congress when it inserted Section 9(a) in the Wagner Act.[31] Minority-union bargaining *prior* to the selection of a majority representative was not even an issue in the Congressional debates.[32] All of the legislative-history statements to which the Advice Memo refers, as indicated by their content and their timing in relation to the Section 8(5) amendment, were directed to the bargaining process *after* a union had been designated by a majority of a unit's employees, not before such designation.[33] Those expressions were simply reiterating that the ideal format for mature and effective collective bargaining was bargaining by a majority union in a bargaining unit where the employer was not permitted to deal with any other union.

The only three statements from the Act's sponsors that are quoted verbatim in the Advice Memo show on their face that they were indeed referring to exclusivity-bargaining *after* designation of a union's majority in an appropriate bargaining unit—*not before.*[34] They referred to *Section 8(1)* bargaining—Section 8(5) having been a late-added amendment—within a *unit,* which is a product only of Section 9(a) and majority representation. The *first statement,* a quotation from a radio broadcast by Senator Wagner, stressed the advantage of an employer dealing with "a consolidated *unit*" rather than with "various minority groups."[35] The *second statement* was from the Senate report that explained the advantages of exclusivity *after* designation of a majority representative in an appropriate *unit,* noting that it's almost "universally recognized that it's practically impossible to apply two or more sets of agreements to one *unit* of workers at the same time, or to apply the terms of one agreement to only a portion of the workers in a single *unit* . . . ."[36] The *third statement* was from the House Report, which observed that there "cannot be two or more basic agreements applicable

29 *See* chap. 4 at note 68.

30 *Id.*, at note 70.

31 BLUE EAGLE, *supra note 20* at 35-38 & 70-72.

32 *Id.*, at 69.

33 BLUE EAGLE, *supra note 20* at 74-80, particularly 77-79.

34 In fact, the very concept of an appropriate bargaining unit is tied to the need to establish parameters for determining the existence of a union's majority; an appropriate unit has no essential reason to exist at earlier informal stages of bargaining with not-yet-mature minority unions.

35 Advice Memo p. 8. Emphasis added.

36 *Id.* p. 9. This statement was actually clarified later in the corresponding House committee report. *See* BLUE EAGLE, *supra* note 20 at 76-79.

to workers in a *given unit*; this is virtually conceded on all sides."[37] Indisputably, all three of these statements referred to conditions *following* designation of a majority representative in an *appropriate bargaining unit. Dick's* GC actually conceded the wedding of *majority* and *unit* by his summary statement that "the Act's sponsors believed that collective bargaining simply could not work if the system required more than one minority union to represent different parts of the *same unit.*[38] It is thus undisputed that his cited statements referred only to post-Section 9(a) *unit* and *majority* designations, which are irrelevant to the issue of pre-Section 9(a) bargaining with NMCB unions.

The *Dick's* GC also failed to note the undisputed historical fact that Section 8(a)(5) was not a part of the original Wagner bill, that when it was finally added it was only intended to amplify and not limit the requirements of Sections 7 and 8(a)(1).[39] Legislative history is indeed here important—but not the asserted history of a Section 8(a)(5) that would inaccurately seek to confine bargaining to Section 9(a) majority unions only, as the Advice Memo contends. The truth is just the opposite.

Indeed, the most vital piece of legislative history was conspicuous by its absence, to wit, the previously noted "smoking-gun," i.e., the rejected version of Section 8(a)(5) that would have limited bargaining to unions "chosen as provided in section 9(a)."[40] Although the Advice Memo, as noted above, acknowledges the occurrence of this signal event in the drafting process, the *Dick's* GC opted to omit it in his presentation of legislative history.[41]

That Advice Memo did, however, cite another "rejected" provision in the drafting process—though incorrectly— to wit, an early tentative proviso that was never a part of either the original Wagner bill or any amendment. Regarding that proviso, it falsely stated that the enacting "Congress *considered* and *rejected* a proviso to Section 9(a)[42] that would have protected the status of minority-supported unions."[43] Although the assertion was false, the subject-matter actually

37 Advice Memo p. 8. Emphasis added..

38 *Id.* p. 8. Emphasis added.

39 *See* chap. 4 *supra* at notes 71-81.

40 *Id.*

41 Advice Memo p. 5.

42 29 U.S.C. § 159(a). Advice Memo at p. 8. Emphasis added.

43 The tentative proviso read "that any minority group of employees in an appropriate unit shall have the right to bargain collectively through representatives of their own choosing when no representa-

supports the minority-union bargaining thesis. The reference was to a tentative clause in Keyserling's very first draft of Senator Wagner's 1935 bill that would have expressly authorized an oddly-worded version of "minority group" collective bargaining. The Advice Memo asserts, erroneously, that "Congress considered and rejected" this provision, whereas—unlike the "smoking gun" version of Section 8(5)[44]—*it was never even presented to Congress, hence not considered by Congress, or much less rejected by Congress.* Although the early-draft proviso in question contained two odd or problematic phrases,[45] the clause was *replaced*—not "rejected"—for an obviously important reason *prior* to the bill's submission to Congress. That reason, which is self-evident from the drafts, was that this clause was but one of a *pair* of related first-draft clauses, both of which were later replaced by their inclusion in a broader, relatively problem-free, provision, to wit, Section 7, which at the time of the first draft had not yet been composed.[46] The other clause in the related pair was a tentative Section 8(5), which read: "To refuse to bargain collectively with the representatives of his employees."[47] The next draft bill was the one Senator Wagner introduced in the Senate, which now included Section 7. Its all-encompassing duty-to-bargain language rendered both the minority-group bargaining proviso (with its problematic phrases) and the tentative Section 8(5) duty-to-bargain clause redundant, hence inappropriate. The comprehensive bargaining language in Section 7—including the broad passage that "Employees shall have the right . . . to bargain collectively through representatives of their own choosing"—was a key part of the successful effort by Wagner and Keyserling to "recast the measure in a simple conceptual

---

tives have been designated or selected by a majority in such unit . . . ." Advice Memo p. 7.

44 *See* chap. 4 *supra* at notes 78-81.

45 Those textual problems, which Keyserling and his colleagues probably noted, were the following: (1) It would have allowed collective bargaining—a well-understood process when conducted by and with *unions*—to be conducted by and with any amorphous or ad hoc *group* of employees—an unworkable scenario for both employers and unions. And (2) this process would occur "in an appropriate bargaining unit," a concept that was either *meaningless*, because the only purpose of such a unit is to define the parameters of an aggregation of employees for the designation of an employee-majority, or else *ambiguous and unnecessary*, because unit determination—which is ultimately a function performed by the Board—would have to be made *prior* to such bargaining. This pre-introduction tentative proviso can best be characterized simply as a *drafter's preliminary doodling*.

46 "SEC. (7) [Note by Keyserling]: to be dictated," Kenneth M. Casebeer, *Drafting Wagner's Act: Leon Keyserling and the Precommittee Drafts of the Labor Disputes Act and the National Labor Relations Act*, 11 Indus. Rel. L. J. 73, 76 , 123 (1989). *See also* Blue Eagle, supra note 20 at 59-60 & 238-239.

47 Blue Eagle, *supra note 20* at 59-60.

pattern,"[48] which was how historian Irving Bernstein described the newly compressed format of the final draft of the bill that Wagner introduced in the Senate. It should also be noted that the *pre-introduction* draft upon which the *Dick's* GC sought to rely when he pointed to the deletion of the tentative minority-group bargaining proviso, *didn't yet contain the text of Section 8(5)*[49] on which he based his "Johnny One-Note" majority-only bargaining thesis.[50] When Keyserling deleted the pair of tentative provisions, he and Senator Wagner left no doubt as to what they intended. And when Wagner and the Senate committee finally agreed to add the revised Section 8(5) duty-to-bargain amendment ten weeks later, they were careful—as previously noted—to reject the version that would have required bargaining only with representatives "chosen as provided in section 9(a)." The full story of the deleted proviso to which the *Dick's* GC sought to call attention thus actually confirms the drafters' consistent[51] intent to protect minority-union bargaining as an essential preliminary stage in the development of mature collective bargaining.

The Advice Memo also miscites a secondary source of legislative history, an article by Ruth Weyand, for the proposition that

> by enacting Section 9(a) of the Act, which sets forth the majority rule, Congress explicitly rejected other forms of representation, including plural and proportional representation which were permitted under Section 7(a) of the NIRA.

As the statute indicates, and as the Weyand article confirms, majority rule was intended to apply only *after* a union had achieved majority status, which was the state of the law under the NIRA following the *Denver Tramway*[52] and *Houde Engineering*[53] cases that she cited. Her article neither "explicitly" nor by implication indicated Congressional rejection of "other forms of representation" *prior* to establishment of a Section 9(a) majority representative, as the Memo alleges.

48 Irving Bernstein, The New Deal Collective Bargaining Policy 88 (1950)

49 Designated as § 8(5) prior to 1947.

50 *See* Advice Memo, at p. 11, where the General Counsel asserted that "Section 8(a)(5) is fundamentally premised on Section 9(a)" and that "the Board has never construed Section 8(a)(5) as operating independently from Section 9(a)."

51 *See* drafts of Senator Wagner's 1934 bill (Blue Eagle, *supra note 20* at 231-237), which reveal additional confirmation of intent to protect minority-union collective bargaining. *See also id.*, at 41-46.

52 *Supra* note 27.

53 *Supra* note 28.

Likewise, none of the Memo's quotations from other labor law scholars[54] are relevant, for they all referred to bargaining *after* selection of a majority representative in an appropriate bargaining unit. They were simply reporting, as the BLUE EAGLE and this book also report, that the drafters of the Act made a conscious choice to reject *plurality bargaining* as the ultimate goal for *mature* labor relations. They consciously chose to make exclusive representation by majority labor organizations the standard for fully established mature collective bargaining. The same is true regarding the Advice Memo's quotations from contemporary proponents of the Wagner bill and the Congressional committees,[55] which were only expressing the rationale for the majority/exclusivity principle that was expected to prevail in bargaining units *after* a majority of the employees had chosen their representatives.[56]

With reference to another of the Union's contentions,[57] the Advice Memo correctly noted that Section 9(a) was "merely a codification of the old NLRB's 1934 decision in *Houde Engineering Corporation*,"[58] but it failed to acknowledge the significance of that fact, which was that enactment of this subsection, like the *Houde* decision, carefully left untouched the employer's duty to bargain with minority unions *prior* to the establishment of majority/exclusive representation.[59]

The bottom line of the *Dick's* GC's treatment of the language in the Act and its legislative history in the *Dick's* case is that he never questioned the accuracy of the charging Union's reading or its recitation of legislative history;[60] and he offered no statutory reading or relevant legislative history to counter those well-established conclusions. Having left the Union's statutory conclusions

54 Advice Memo pp. 7-9.

55 *Id.*

56 *See* chap. 4 *supra* following note 86.

57 Advice Memo pp. 5-6.

58 *Supra* note 28.

59 *See* BLUE EAGLE, *supra note 20* at 48-52.

60 His only questioning of the Union's account of legislative history was based on a misconception of the law under the NIRA: Regarding the three cases the Union had cited to demonstrate the acceptance of nonmajority bargaining under § 7(a) of the NIRA (see footnotes 13 and 35 of the Advice Memo), that in none of those cases was the employer ordered to bargain with the minority union; however, that observation is irrelevant and misleading, for *it was not the NLB's authority or practice to order bargaining, either for minority or majority unions.* What was relevant in each of these cases is that the NLB *ruled that the employers were in violation of NIRA § 7(a) when they refused to bargain with those minority unions.* Passage of the NLRA was intended to cure this lack of enforcement authority. BLUE EAGLE, *supra note 20* at 64-65.

unrefuted, he apparently felt compelled to resort to the contention—in effect—that regardless of what the plain language of the Act requires, the Union's minority-bargaining thesis had already been decided and rejected by the Board.[61] That erroneous perception is treated in the discussion that follows.

B. Absence of Applicable NLRB and Supreme Court Cases and Inapplicability of Cases Relied Upon

The Advice Memo attempts to convey the impression that the issue of minority-union bargaining has already been decided by Supreme Court and Board decisions. Nothing could be farther from the truth. With no citation of authority—for there were no cases to cite—it alleges that

> it is *firmly established* under Board and Supreme Court cases that the duty to bargain under the Act is based on *the principle of majority representation*, to the *exclusion* of compulsory minority union recognition. [T]he Board has *consistently* refused to interpret the Act as according minority unions the same bargaining rights as majority representatives.[62]

That statement is inaccurate on several counts.

In the *first place*, there's no statutory language to that effect and *not a single case has ever excluded minority union recognition where the union was not claiming, either overtly or covertly, exclusive Section 9(a) recognition.* On the other hand, recognition and protection of nonmajority bargaining where there's no exclusive majority representative, as previously demonstrated, is protected directly by unambiguous language in the statute. Furthermore, as previously noted, there are several Supreme Court and Board cases[63] which have upheld and approved nonmajority members-only collective bargaining contracts, including the previously discussed foundational Supreme Court decision in *Consolidated Edison Co. v. NLRB*,[64] where Chief Justice Hughes declared that the NLRA "contemplated the making of contracts with labor organizations," including contracts for union

61 The allegation: "The issue is not an open one . . . it is well settled." Letter p.3.

62 Advice Memo p. 11. Emphasis added.

63 *See* chap. 4 *supra* at notes 101-108 and BLUE EAGLE, *supra note 20* at 93-97.

64 305 U.S. 197 (1938). *See also infra* at note 122.

members "*even if they were a minority*."[65] Although the "principle of majority rule" is protected when it is established under Section 9(a), all collective bargaining—including preliminary nonmajority bargaining—is protected by Section 7 and implemented by both Sections 8(a)(1) and 8(a)(5). There are no cases that have ever "established"—"firmly" or otherwise—an exclusion of compulsory members-only minority-union recognition.

In the *second place*, the Board cannot have "consistently refused" to interpret the Act to accord non-majority unions the same rights as majority representatives when it has never been requested to do so except in cases where a minority union was improperly seeking or claiming recognition as an *exclusive* Section 9(a) majority representative, such as in *International Ladies Garment Workers v. NLRB (Bernhard-Altmann Texas Corp.)*[66] and other "false majority cases,"[67] including intentional employee-discrimination cases such as *Don Mendenhall, Inc.*,[68] discussed below, on which the *Dick's* GC relied so heavily.

In the *third place*—directly to the point in issue—the BLUE EAGLE and the charging party Steel Workers Union never claimed that minority unions are entitled to "the same bargaining rights as majority representatives." Unambiguous language in the Act specifies that they are not entitled to the same rights, nor were the "same" rights sought in the *Dick's* case. Section 9(a) expressly denies nonmajority unions the right of *exclusive* representation, thus confining them to representation of their members only—which is what the Union in the *Dick's* case was seeking. And another provision in the Act, Section 8(a)(3), expressly denies minority unions the right to enter into compulsory-union agreements, specifying that such agreements are permitted only "if such labor organization is the representative of the employees *as provided in section 9(a.)*"[69] Thus, as previously noted,[70] Section 8(a)(3) represents further statutory recognition of the expected presence of nonmajority unions and their right to bargain collectively about other subjects of bargaining. For those same reasons, the General Counsel's unwarranted observation that "the Charging Party's view would create the anomaly of granting *greater* recognitional and bargaining rights to

65 *Id.* 305 U.S. at 236-37. Emphasis added.

66 366 U.S. 731, 736, 742-43 (1961).

67 *See* BLUE EAGLE, *supra note 20* at 159-162 and cases cited in note 78 *infra.*

68 194 NLRB 1109 (1972). *See infra* at notes 70-78.

69 § 8(a)(3). Emphasis added..

70 *See* chap. 4 *supra* at notes 28-32

minority unions than those granted to majority representatives"[71] is unrelated to the reality of the Act, which, as noted, expressly specifies *lesser* rights for minority unions.

In the absence of any cases actually holding that Section 8(a)(5) cannot operate independently of Section 9(a), the Advice Memo presents a single paragraph[72] that summed up *Dick's* GC's effort to explain his refusal to issue a complaint. That paragraph (1) presents an inaccurate rendition of the Charging Party's assertion in the *Dick's* case, (2) seeks to make a positive holding out of a negative allegation, and (3) misstates the contents of *Don Mendenhall,* his leading Labor Board case. Here's that entire paragraph with its inaccuracies *italicized*:

> The Charging Party contends that the plain language of Section 8(a)(5) is not limited by Section 9(a) and therefore, an employer's duty to bargain does not hinge on exclusive majority status. However, *contrary to the Charging Party's assertion, the Board has never construed Section 8(a)(5) as operating independently from Section 9(a).* The Board will therefore not find a Section 8(a)(5) violation for refusing to bargain, and will not issue a bargaining order, where a members-only union is not the majority representative. Indeed, in Don Mendenhall,[73] *the Board dismissed a Section 8(a)(5) allegation based on the employer's alleged refusal to bargain over subcontracting affecting union members because the union operated as a members-only union, and was not the exclusive bargaining representative.*

As to the Advice Memo's inaccurate rendition of the Union's assertion, it's simply not true that the Union contended that the Board has construed Section 8(a)(5) as operating independently from Section 9(a). Although the Board should—and if it follows the law it will—it has not done so yet.

---

71 Advice Memo p. 18. Emphasis added. Regarding the Advice Memo's inaccurate reading of Linden Lumber Div. v. NLRB, 419 U.S. 301 (1974), id. pp. 17-18, it should be noted that elections are not essential for Section 9(a) representation. Indeed, the Act does not even permit the holding of an election unless the "employer *declines to recognize*" a union that claims to be a Section 9(a) representative (§ 9(c)(1)(A), emphasis added). Nor is an election always required by *Linden Lumber,* which held only that an election could be required when an employer refused to acknowledge the accuracy of an authorization-card majority; that decision left untouched an employer's voluntary acceptance of other evidence of a union's majority, and nowhere within the language of Sections 7, 8(a)(1), 8(a)(5), or 9(a) is an election mandated for majority-union bargaining.

72 Advice Memo pp. 11-12.

73 *Supra* note 68 at 1110. (Footnote in original)

As to the attempt to turn a negative into a positive, the assertion that "the Board has never construed Section 8(a)(5) as operating independently from Section 9(a)" is not the equivalent of saying the Board has construed Section 8(a)(5) as not being applicable to minority-union bargaining—which would of course be an untrue statement, for the Board has never had occasion to make that determination one way or the other.

As for the cryptic but inaccurate rendition of what occurred in the *Don Mendenhall* case, the quoted statement is simply untrue as to both of its assertions, as the following discussion of that case demonstrates.

In the *first place*, the subcontracting for which the union in *Don Mendenhall* had sought to bargain was not "subcontracting affecting union members" only; rather, it was intended to affect *all employees in the bargaining unit.* As the Board's opinion notes, both union and nonunion employees were laid off as a result of the employer's unilateral decision to subcontract traditional bargaining-unit work.[74] When the union sought to bargain about that decision, it believed—as did the General Counsel—that it was a party to an existing contract that named the union in its recognition clause as the exclusive "*collective-bargaining representative for all work performed by 'tile layers, marble masons and terrazzo workers, whether for interior or exterior purposes, in any public or private buildings' within the Union's jurisdiction.*"[75] That recognition clause— which had an earlier incarnation in a valid Section 8(f) prehire-agreement— confirms that the union, by its effort to reverse the employer's subcontracting, intended Section 9(a) coverage for all the employees in the unit, not just union members. The employer never questioned the contract's coverage; in fact, as the Board's opinion noted, he "paid the union wage scale to both union and nonunion employees;" however, in accordance with his *private* understanding with the union, he didn't pay health and welfare benefits to the nonunion employees. Such discriminatory conduct by the union—to which the employer acquiesced—was an obvious violation of the duty of fair representation[76] that would certainly not be approved by the Board. Inasmuch as the union and the General Counsel were seeking a Section 9(a) bargaining-order applicable to the entire bargaining unit, the Board

74 194 NLRB at 110 ("employees who were not members of the union . . . were also laid off.")

75 *Id.* Emphasis added.

76 However, no charges of §§ 8(b)(2) and 8(b)(1)A), i.e., duty-of-fair-representation violations, were pending in the case, although the reported evidence indicated the existence of such violations. *See generally* John E. Higgins, Jr. ed., THE DEVELOPING LABOR LAW: THE BOARD, THE COURTS, AND THE NATIONAL LABOR RELATIONS ACT (7th ed. 2017) (hereinafter DLL7th) at chap. 25.

had no choice but to conclude that "*in the context of events*, the [employer's] action cannot be held violative of Section 8(a)(5)."[77] This was no different from the Board's refusal to find a violation of that section in other *false majority* cases where a union was *seeking to act on behalf of all bargaining-unit employees* when in fact it didn't represent a majority of the employees in the unit.[78]

In the *second place*, the contract the union in *Don Mendenhall* signed, and to which the employer agreed, *expressly* recognized the union as exclusive representative of all the employees in the unit. The fact that the union never achieved majority representation in that unit following its first contract simply meant, as the Trial Examiner observed, that pursuant to Section 8(f) it was thereafter no longer entitled to bargain as a Section 9(a) representative. By its unwavering adherence to the Section 9(a) recognition clause in that contract—which both the union and the General Counsel claimed to be still in effect—the union was clearly seeking to bargain about subcontracting that would have affected *all employees* in the unit described in the recognition clause. It is thus no surprise that the Board dismissed the charge, for the union did not represent the employee-majority for whom it was purporting to bargain.[79]

77 Emphasis added.

78 *See* BLUE EAGLE, *supra note 20* at 159-62 and the eight *false majority* cases there discussed, to wit, *International Ladies Garment Workers v. NLRB (Bernhard-Altmann Texas Corp.)*, 366 U.S. 731, 736, 742-43 (1961);Segall-Maigen, Inc.,1 NLRB 749 (1936); Mooresville Cotton Mills, 2 NLRB 952 (1937), *enforced as modified*, 94 F.2d 61 (4th Cir. 1938) (modification unrelated to issue); Wallace Mfg. Co., 2 NLRB 1081 (1937); Brashear Freight Lines, Inc., 13 NLRB 191 (1939), *enforced*, 119 F.2d 359 (8th Cir. 1941); National Linen Service Corp., 48 NLRB 171 (1943); Olin Industries, Inc., 86 NLRB 203 (1949), *enforced*, 191 F.2d 613 (5th Cir. 1951), *cert. denied*, 343 U.S. 970 (1952); Agar Packing & Provision Corp., 81 NLRB 1262 (1949); *International Ladies Garment Workers v. NLRB (Bernhard-Altmann Texas Corp.)*, 366 U.S. 731, 736, 742-43 (1961).

79 Some of the Board's careless language and inaccurate assertions about existing law in *Don Mendenhall* may have contributed to the misunderstanding of that decision. For example, the opinion states without citation of authority that "It has been settled since the early days of the Act that members-only recognition does not satisfy statutory norms." 194 NLRB at 1110. Considering the facts in *Don Mendenhall*, this awkward syntax could only mean that when a minority union represents its members only, granting *exclusive* recognition to that union doesn't satisfy the statutory norm of §9(a), which is the only meaning that makes sense, for that was the only relevant legal conclusion that had been "settled since the early days of the Act." *See* cases cited in note 78 *supra*. The opinion compounded its unfounded rendition of the law by stating that: "Although the Board has never ruled squarely on the legality per se of a members-only contract, the insufficiency under the Act of such recognition has been well established." That statement is patently inaccurate, for both the Board and the Supreme Court had squarely approved the concept of members-only contracts, and *Dick's* GC even acknowledged the legality of such contracts. *See infra* at note 202. Furthermore, the cited authority for the Don Mendenhall Board's supposition of "insufficiency," Golden Turkey Mining Co., 34 NLRB 760 (1941), actually recognized the legal reality of members-only bargaining by its reliance on McQuay-Norris Mfg. Co. v. NLRB, 116 F.2d 748 (7th Cir.), *enforcing* 21 NLRB 709 (1940), *cert. denied*, 313 U.S. 565 (1941), where a minority members-only union had grown into a majority

Another inaccuracy in the rendition of *Don Mendenhall* is the Regional Director's assertion that in that case "the Board refused to find 8(a)(5) violation *where the union asserted that the employer had an obligation to bargain under a members only contract*."[80] That's not true. No such assertion by the union is recorded or implied in either the Board's opinion or the Trial Examiner's decision. The union never requested the employer to bargain for or sign a contract *for its members only* and the Board never ruled on such a request that had never been made.

It was also inaccurate for the General Counsel to have concluded that in *Don Mendenhall* "the Board did not rely on a putative claim of majority representation,"[81] for the Board expressly noted that its refusal to find the employer guilty of refusing to bargain about subcontracting was made "*in the context of events*," which included the union's claim to be the representative of all the employees described in the contractual bargaining unit. The union was not claiming that the employer had refused to bargain for a contract applicable to its members only, and that was not what the General Counsel in *Don Mendenhall* was charging in his allegation of a Section 8(a)(5) refusal to bargain. Accordingly, *Don Mendenhall* cannot be distorted to represent a holding that the Board never made and had no occasion to make.

In fact, every Board decision that the General Counsel cited in connection with *Don Mendenhall*[82] that involved an alleged refusal to bargain under Section 8(a)(5)[83] concerned situations where there was either a current or an expired *Section 9(a) collective bargaining contract that spelled out a precise appropriate bargaining unit*. In each of those cases, both the union—which did not represent a bargaining-unit employee majority—and the employer discriminated against nonunion employees by agreeing and providing that certain contractual benefits would be given only to union members. Like *Don Mendenhall*, those cases describe a violation of a union's duty of fair representation under Section 8(b)(1)(A) and an employer's violation of Sections 8(a)(1) and 8(a)(2) by recognizing a minority union as a Section 9(a) representative of an entire bargaining

union, for which the Board and the Seventh Circuit Court of Appeals held that it was therefore entitled to §9(a) exclusivity recognition.

80 Letter p. 3, n. 5. Emphasis added.

81 Advice Memo 12.

82 *Id.*, at 11-13.

83 *Id.*, at 12, n. 37.

unit. All of those cases involved unions purporting to represent *all* employees in designated *bargaining units*, whereas the members-only bargaining at issue in the *Dick's* case was wholly unrelated to the bargaining-unit concept. None of those cases cited in the Advice Memo involved a union that was openly seeking to bargain for and sign an agreement for its members only, or an employer that was recognizing or contracting with such a union only for its members or was refusing to so recognize and bargain with such a union only for its members.

The *Dick's* GC's apparent confusion in the Advice Memo as to the role of bargaining units in relation to members-only bargaining was further illustrated by his citation of *Manufacturing Woodworkers Ass'n*[84] and *Reebie Storage & Moving Co.*[85] Those cases, like several other unit-definition cases,[86] simply held that a history of members-only bargaining is not controlling as to the make-up of an appropriate bargaining unit, which is a sensible conclusion inasmuch as members-only bargaining is not dependent on the appropriateness of a bargaining unit, notwithstanding—as the Board has acknowledged—that it "has sometimes accepted a members-only contract as indicative of the feasibility of the scope of the unit."[87] Furthermore, *Dick's* GC's quotation from *Reebie Storage* for the proposition that the "Board does not issue bargaining orders in 'members only' units,"[88] referenced an oxymoron, for by definition members-only bargaining is not based on or directly relevant to Section 9(a) "units." His emphasis on units, however, underscores what the Board was asserting in the *Don Mendenhall*-type cases: It was simply insisting that if a union seeks to bargain for comprehensive coverage of a Section 9(a) *unit*— whatever its purpose might be—it must first represent a majority of the employees in that unit. Which is an accurate and uncontested conclusion.

To his credit, *Dick's* GC acknowledged through the Regional Director that "the Act permits employers to recognize and bargain with minority unions on a members-only basis where there is no majority representative,"[89] thereby agree-

84 194 NLRB 1122 (1972). *Id.*, at p. 12.

85 313 NLRB 510 (1993), *enforcement denied on other grounds*, 44 F.3d 605 (7th Cir. 1995). *Id.*, at p. 13.

86 *E.g.*, Greyhound Lines, Inc., 235 NLRB 1100 (1978); Crucible Steel Castings Co., 90 NLRB 1843 (1950); Kansas Power & Light Co., 64 NLRB 915 (1945).

87 Crucible Steel Castings Co., *Id.*, at 1843 (*citing* Tennessee Coal, Iron & Railroad Co., 39 NLRB 617 (1942)), which is also illustrative of the respect and acceptance which the Board displayed regarding the then-common member-only contracts, including renewal of such contracts. *Id.*, at 621-625.)

88 313 NLRB at 510.

89 Letter p. 3. *See also* Advice Memo p. 11 where *Dick's* GC concedes that "In the early enforcement of

ing with the basic Supreme Court and Board decisions[90] that establish that such bargaining and resulting members-only contracts do not constitute unlawful *per se* discrimination against nonunion employees under Sections 8(a)(1), 8(a)(3), and 8(b)(1)(A), or violate Section 8(a)(2), the company-union provision of the Act. He failed to explain, however, how minority-union bargaining, which was commonly practiced during the early years of the Act,[91] could have been affirmatively permitted—in fact encouraged[92]—if the Act was based on majority bargaining only, as he repeatedly contended, such as when he professed to reading the mind of Congress—but actually misreading—by asserting that "Congress *understood* that minority union bargaining would *undermine* the very purpose for which the Act was passed."[93]

He also (through the Regional Director) misstated the Union's position with his assertion that the "Charging Party argues that Section 7 of the Act establishes the right of all employees, organized and *unorganized,* to engage in collective bargaining."[94] The Union did not so contend and Section 7 does not so provide.

---

the Act the Board held that an employer may recognize and bargain with a minority, members-only union, as long as the employer does not extend that union exclusive status," citing Consolidated Edison Co. of New York, 4 NLRB 71, 110 (1937). It's noteworthy that the employer in the *Dick's case* also agreed that such minority-union bargaining is lawful under the Act. In its leaflet to employees dated July 28, 2005, the employer asked: "Can the union actually negotiate just for a minority of associates?" To which it replied: "The answer is "yes…." if Dick's *wanted to,* it could voluntarily recognize the Steelworkers and negotiate a contract just for those associates who are members of this [union] 'council.' Under the law, the concept is called a 'minority union.'"

90 *See* Consolidated Edison Co. v. NLRB, *supra* note 64; International Ladies Garment Workers v. NLRB (Bernhard-Altmann Texas Corp.), *supra* note 66; Retail Clerks v. Lion Dry Goods, Inc., 369 U.S. 17, 29 (1962); Solvay Process Co., 5 NLRB 330 (1938); The Hoover Co., 90 NLRB 1614 (1950); and Consolidated Builders, Inc., 99 NLRB 972, 975, n. 6 (1952).

91 *See supra* at notes 79-96.

92 Supreme Court cases: Consolidated Edison Co. v. NLRB, *supra* note 64 at 236 ("The Act contemplates the making of contracts with labor organizations…and in the absence of…an exclusive agency, the employees represented by the [union], even if they were a minority, clearly had the right to make their own choice."); International Ladies Garment Workers v. NLRB (Bernhard-Altmann Texas Corp.), *supra* note 66; *Retail Clerks v. Lion Dry Goods, Inc.*, 369 U.S. 17,29; NLRB cases: The Board pointed out in *Consolidated Builders, Inc., supra* note 90, that since "an employer may grant recognition to each of two rival unions on a members-only basis [citing The Hoover Co., 90 NLRB 1614 (1950)], *a fortiori,* [it] may grant recognition on a nonexclusive basis to a minority union, whereas here, there is no rival union claim." 99 NLRB at 975, n. 5. *See also The Solvay Process Company, supra* note 88. In NLRB v. Lundy Mfg. Corp., 316 F.2d 921 (2d Cir. 1963), *cert. denied,* 375 U.S. 895 (1963), *enforcing* 136 NLRB 1230 (1962), the Board held that a group of unorganized employees had a right to deal with their employer as a group regarding their grievances.

93 Advice Memo p. 10. Emphasis added.

94 Letter p. 2. Emphasis added.

By its terms, it only grants collective-bargaining rights to those employees who choose to be represented for purposes of collective bargaining—i.e., by labor organizations—which was the clear intent of the Act and what the text plainly states.[95]

Dick's GC also misstated the position of the Union when he referred to *NLRB v. Lundy Mfg. Corp.*[96] as no longer being a viable basis "to establish a duty to bargain under Section 8(a)(1)." It was never the Union's position that a minority union's right to bargain is based on the *second part* of Section 7—i.e., protected concerted activity for "mutual aid or protection"—which was the basis for support of the ad hoc group-employee negotiations in *Lundy*. Rather, the Union's position in *Dick's* was, like the position expressed herein, that the protection of union-based pre-majority collective bargaining is premised on the *first part* of Section 7, i.e., the "bargain collectively" part, which is enforceable by both Sections 8(a)(1) and 8(a)(5).

Another inaccuracy in the Memo is its assertion that "the Board has consistently declined to find Section 8(a)(1) violations when employers refuse to recognize and bargain with unrepresented employees over grievances,"[97] which is untrue, because the Board found such a violation in the *Lundy* case and it has never overruled or disavowed that finding. And regarding the three cases that are relied on to support the "consistently declined" assertion,[98] the Board had no occasion in any of those cases either to find or not to find a Section 8(a)(1) violation, which in any event would have been based on the "mutual aid or protection" language of Section 7, not on the affirmative duty-to-bargain-collectively language in the first part of that section or on Section 8(a)(5). The three cited cases contain only tiny bits of pure dicta that casually repeated latter-day erroneous conventional wisdom without any legal support.[99] Thus far, the Board has heard no cases on any issue relevant to the issue in *Dick's* and has made no holding such as the Memo claims. Regardless, however, the position in this discussion, like the BLUE EAGLE's thesis, is based on the mandatory Section 8(a)

95 *See* BLUE EAGLE, *supra note 20* at 155-59.

96 *Supra* note 89.

97 Advice Memo p. 15.

98 Charleston Nursing Center, 257 NLRB 554, 555 (1981); Pennypower Shopping News, 244 NLRB 536, 537 n. 4, 538 (1979), supp. decision 253 NLRB 85 (1980), enforced, 726 F.2d 626 (10th Cir. 1984); Swearingen Aviation Corp., 227 NLRB 228, 236 (1976), *enforced* (but not with regard to the dictum in issue), 568 F.2d 458 (5th Cir. 1978).

99 *See* BLUE EAGLE, *supra note 20* at 162-69 for detailed analyses of these cases.

(1) "guaranteed" "right" "to bargain collectively" contained in the first part of Section 7, plus the text of Section 8(a)(5), and not on the ill-defined "mutual aid or protection" language of Section 7.[100]

Furthermore, *Dick's* GC's assertion "that an employer has no obligation to discuss grievances with a union, once that union has lost majority support"[101] is misleading and wholly unsupported by the case he cites, *Mooresville Cotton Mills.*[102] That case involved a union that had been active at the plant for a number of years, and there was reason to believe that it represented a majority of the employees. When the union's grievance committee sought to settle several discharge grievances with a request for reinstatement of the dischargees, and a request that the employer "adopt a fair rule for the hiring and discharging of workers"—a proposal clearly intended for the *entire* plant (or unit)—the employer terminated the settlement discussion. As a consequence, 48 hours later "approximately a thousand of respondent's 1400 employees went out on strike."[103] In its decision, the Board stated in *dictum*—for it did not decide whether the employer had refused to bargain about the grievances—that the employer had no duty to discuss the grievances because it was determined that at the time of the request the union represented only a minority of the unit employees. This was thus only a garden-variety *false majority* case where a union was seeking to represent an entire bargaining unit—not just its members—when in fact it represented what was presumed to be only a minority of the unit *when the grievance negotiation was attempted.*[104] It's undisputed that an employer has no obligation to negotiate unit-wide grievances with a minority union that purports to represent a majority of employee in the unit.

100 *Id.,* at 155-56.

101 Advice Memo p. 17.

102 *Supra* note 75.

103 *Id.,* 2 NLRB at 955.

104 *Mooresville Cotton Mills* is unique, however, because the Board used that case to clarify—for the first time—that a union's majority must exist, i.e., be provable, at the time the union makes its request to bargain. Obviously the union and the Regional Director both thought that a majority existed at the time of the meeting when the grievance request was made—and the overwhelming support for the strike that followed suggested that it did, *but there was no way to prove that fact with objective evidence.* At the settlement meeting, the union leaders probably had no idea as to exactly how many dues-paying members they had, and they had no reason to believe—if they had thought about it at all—that the large numbers who would strike would not be sufficient to prove majority representation. Nowhere in the Board's factual discussion of the dispute does it appear that the union claimed to be acting as anything other than the *exclusive* representative of all the employees.

C. Summation of Response to Dick's Dismissal

The *Dick's* GC failed to present any statutory basis for his refusal to issue a complaint. As demonstrated by unambiguous statutory text and legislative history, that refusal was contrary to the intent of Congress. In addition, there are absolutely no cases—indeed, he could cite none—where the Board had ever ruled on the issue of an employer's duty to bargain with a minority union for its members only where and when there was no Section 9(a) majority representative. *The few cases that he cited were unrelated to that issue.* Nevertheless, even if the Board were to conclude that it had already determined that the Act does not protect that right of less-than-majority employees to bargain collectively—which is unlikely considering the absence of decisional evidence, as shown above—a fresh look at this issue would have been in order and an accurate declaration of statutory text supporting non-majority collective bargaining would have been appropriate for issuance of a complaint so that the Board could officially issue its decision to that effect.

II. OTHER OBJECTIONS

A. Preview

Inasmuch as the thesis of the proposed "*Blue Eagle*" interpretation, i.e., the NMCB concept, has been highly visible for the last several years, the objections that have been voiced against it (in addition to the foregoing raised by the General Counsel in the *Dick's* case) are now fairly well known. Anticipating that some of those arguments might be presented in any validation action—or that some readers might still have questions stemming from one or more of those objections—a review of those contrary positions and their refutations is appropriate. It is significant and noteworthy that except for one weird "chicken-little" interpretation of English words by one observer, there's not a single assertion from any of the known objectors that disputes the accuracy of the *reading* of the *specific wording* of the critical statutory text that's advanced throughout this book. Consequently, inasmuch as the *wording* of the statutory provisions so obviously indicates that a contrary reading would make no grammatical sense, it's not surprising that all of the objections, including those espoused by the *Dick's* General Counsel noted above, and other objections noted below, have instead focused the opposition elsewhere. The responses to those opposing arguments, which are treated below, fall into three categories: (1) Responses to objections that rely generally on the Advice Memo in the *Dick's* case but concentrate on a specific untruthful presentation of legislative history contained in that Memo. (2) Responses to objections that simply reiterate parts of the Advice Memo in the *Dick's* case and/or erect a "chicken-little" distortion of members-only bargaining in order to demonstrate that the sky is falling. (3) Responses to objections focused on other provisions of the Act—especially Sections 8(a)(2) and 8(a)(3)—with the erroneous contention that *any* NMCB agreement must be illegal *per se* because it would constitute unlawful Section 8(a)(2) employer-support of a union and/or unlawful Section 8(a)(3) employer-discrimination against nonunion employees.

The astute reader might note the absence of objections contained in law-review and other scholarly journal sources. The reason for such absence is that none of those sources but one disagreed with the final reading of statutory text asserted in my book, *The Blue Eagle at Work,* and that was a brief book-review in a Canadian journal[105] that lacked any substance worthy of commentary.

B. An Untruthful Source of Alleged Legislative-History

In 2014 the United States Chamber of Commerce (Chamber) published a 40-page report that employed dishonest legal assertions in order to discourage or prevent re-validation of members-only collective bargaining. Any doubt as to the objective of that widely circulated report was dispelled by its prescient title, *"The Blue Eagle Has Landed: The Paradigm Shift from Majority Rule to Members-Only Representation;"*[106] that title was obviously borrowed partially from my book's title. With reference to minority, or members-only collective bargaining, the report opened with the dishonest assertion that "Congress *considered* such a system during its *debates* over passage of the NLRA [which] was *expressly rejected*." And it closed with the similar dishonest assertion that such "a system that allows for members-only representation . . . reflects a major paradigm shift in direction that was *expressly rejected* by Congress."

---

105 Alan Hyde, The Blue Eagle at Work: Reclaiming Democratic Rights in the American Workplace, 58 LABOUR/LE TRAVAIL 230 (book review).

106 U.S. Chamber of Commerce (April 14, 2014).

Any doubt regarding the untruthfulness that was responsible for those key assertions has been silently dispelled by the three attorneys of the Littler-Mendelson law firm[107] who supplied those assertions. When confronted with the actual facts regarding the invalidity of those statements, which had their origin in the *Dick's* Advice Memo noted above,[108] and presented with an opportunity to deny or clarify them, they evidently chose not to deny their authorship or the inaccuracy of the offending statements; nor did they agree to provide any corrective action. Thus, through their silence, they in effect conceded that the aforesaid lead-off and closing assertions in the report, which comprised a major feature of the report, were blatant falsehoods.[109] As the reader is aware from the above review of the *Dick's* Advice Memorandum, Congress never even *considered* that proviso, and certainly never *debated* or *rejected* it, *expressly* or otherwise.

Among the other falsehoods in the Chamber's report for which those attorneys were responsible was one that might be the most egregious of all because it involved the *text* of the Act itself, not just *legislative history.* That assertion was that: "The *majority representation* phrasing of Sections 7 and 8(1) of the Wagner Act was carried over almost verbatim from the Norris-LaGuardia Act via section 7(a) of the National Industrial Recovery Act [NIRA]"—which is an outright lie, for the word "majority" or its equivalent does not appear anywhere in Sections 7 and 8(1) of the Wagner Act or in Section 7(a) of the NIRA.

The reason I highlighted the Chamber's report and the role that the Mittler-Mendelson attorneys played in its creation is because that report and/or its contents might have played a role in encouraging the General Counsel in 2015 not to issue a complaint in another case that raised the minority-union bargaining issue as noted in Chapter 6 above.[110]

C. Chicken-Little Opposition

Two noteworthy instances of opposition, which were presented alongside favorable analyses, were voiced at meetings of the Labor and Employment Law Section of the American Bar Association. The first was by Professor Samuel

107 Stefan Marculewicz, Erik Hult, and Brendan Ftizgerald.

108 *See supra* at notes 42-51.

109 All of which is clearly spelled out and supported by e-mail files in the author's possession.

110 *See* text in chap. 6 *supra* following note 39.

Estreicher of the New York University School of Law;[111] the second was by Mark M. Schorr, a prominent management attorney.[112] The latter will be addressed first.

Lacking credible legal objections, Mr. Schorr erected a "chicken-little" description of members-only bargaining based on a reading of the law that was obviously grounded on unsupported assumptions, irrelevant cases, and inaccurate legislative history, for he totally ignored the ordinary meaning of words in the critical statutory provisions, giving them a meaning unrelated to their conventional definitions and lack of ambiguity . For example, he stated: "The language of § 8(a)(5) and § 9(a) is clear, and when read together, preclude **compulsory** minority (members-only) bargaining"[113]—which is just the opposite of what that language actually says. Section 9(a), by its unambiguous text, doesn't apply *unless and until* a union represents a unit's majority. He also ignored the true state of the law when he asserted, entirely without authority, that it is "well settled that a bargaining obligation under Section 8(a)(1) can likewise only exist when the union represents a majority of employees." He also repeated the conclusions in *Dick's* GC's Advice Memo regarding irrelevant statements in legislative history about avoiding multiple unions *after* a majority union has been chosen, whereas verified legislative history reveals an unchallenged acceptance of minority-union bargaining *prior to* such majority determination. His presentation also contained a litany of the same irrelevant cases cited by the Advice Memo, but differed as to the application of key Supreme Court cases that had approved minority-union collective agreements. Although the *Dick's* GC recognized the validity of those agreements, Mr. Schorr dismissed that concept as pure "dicta," which was contra to the text of the opinions.[114] Mostly, however, he simply relied upon and repeated the arguments contained in the Advice Memo.

In accord with his chicken-little approach, he announced in effect that if minority unions were allowed, the sky would fall—i.e., that "the proposed rule on minority bargaining is <u>completely unworkable</u>, under any set of

111 On the subject of *Minority Recognition and the Members Only Contract: A Possible Solution? What Issues Need to be Resolved?*, in Naples, Florida, on February 21, 2008. Although Professor Estreicher did not present a paper, his bullet points were graciously provided to the author, who appeared on the same program.

112 A bullet-point presentation on *Minority Bargaining* at a conference at Manele Bay, Hawaii, Feb. 28, 2011, a copy of which was graciously provided by the presenter to the author. (Emphases noted in the quotations are contained in the original.) *See also* 41 Daily Lab. Rep. (BNA) C-1 (3/02/2011).

113 *Id.*

114 *See infra* at note 126 where the Supreme Court dispelled that blind concept.

circumstances....In the end, this would truly undermine the overall purpose of the Act." On the contrary, it would do just the opposite, for as Section 1 clearly indicates, the overall purpose of the Act is the *encouragement of collective bargaining*, which minority-union members-only bargaining would certainly further. Regarding his chicken-little prediction that the sky would be falling, that "[m]ultiple unions in one workplace representing employees who work side-by-side is a recipe for disaster" that it would result in competition among competing unions, create undue tension, and allow employers "to preclude/avoid meaningful collective bargaining, by playing the different minority unions off and against each other," the reader is directed to the contrary view in Chapter 4 above.[115] The sky won't fall when democracy functions in the workplace.

Professor Estreicher, though more delicate in his rhetoric, also painted a picture of the sky falling. He did not, however, because he could not—honorable scholar that he is—dispute the unmistakable English-language meaning of the text of the applicable provisions, to wit, Sections 7, 8(a)(1), 8(a)(3), 8(a)(5), and 9(a). He even joked about—but didn't dispute—what he referred to as the "punctuation theory of labor law" regarding the meaning of Section 8(a)(5)." Unable to mount a response to the plain language of the applicable provisions, he looked for other statutory straws to grasp. None, however, refuted the clear meaning of the applicable provisions. For example, his reference to the presence in Section 8(a)(3) of "*representative of the employees* as provided in section 9(a)," actually underscored the meaning of the provisions he sought to disprove, for it shows positive Congressional recognition and expectation of minority-union bargaining.[116] And his citing of the absence of a reciprocal duty to bargain for members-only unions under Section 8(b)(3) is irrelevant, for that provision was added in 1947, whereas the 1935 Act only needed to reference an *employer's* duty to bargain. Furthermore, it would make no sense to require minority-unions to bargain before they had made a request to bargain. Likewise, the reference to Section 8(d)[117]—also added by Taft-Hartley—was an irrelevant effort to squeeze a square peg into a round hole. The 8(d) definition of the procedural aspects of collective bargaining covers *all bargaining* except when a Section-9(a) representative supersedes another Section 9(a) representative by "intervening

115 Regarding competing unions, *see* chap. 3 *supra* at notes 65-73.

116 Emphasis added. *See* chap 3 supra at notes 28-32.

117 29 U.S.C. § 158(d).

certification." However, even if there were another interpretation, it would not affect what Congress wrote or failed to write in the applicable basic provisions in 1935.

Finally, Professor Estreicher's assertion that the required limited recognition of the duty to bargain with minority unions would create "Practical Problems" was but another assertion that the sky is falling. More to the point, the contemporary majority-application of the duty-to-bargain has created even greater "practical problems." Regardless, it's the Board's function to solve problems that arise under the Act. And problems will undoubtedly arise under this renewed recognition of what the Act requires, but they will be manageable problems. Whatever they are, almost anything would be an improvement over the problems that now exist.

III. INAPPLICABILITY OF SECTIONS 8(A)(2), 8(A)(3), AND 8(B)(1)(A)

An early objection about members-only bargaining—which was actually raised prior to publication of any detailed analysis of the concept[118]—was the contention that a minority-union collective agreement must be illegal *per se* because it constitutes employer support of a union in violation of Sections 8(a)(1),[119] and 8(a)(2)[120] and/or discrimination against nonunion employees in violation of Sections 8(a)(3)[121] and 8(b)(1)(A).[122] Although that conclusion is wholly inaccurate, it's understandable why some observers might have taken that position, because if one hastily compares those provisions without also noting the presence of their statutory limitations, those conclusions might seem reasonable. However, inasmuch as both the Supreme Court and the Board long ago recognized the legality of non-majority *voluntary* members-only contracts[123]—thereby confirming the

118 *See* Julius Getman, *The National Labor Relations Act: What Went Wrong; Can We Fix It?*, 45 B.C. L. Rev.125, 136-37 (2003), which was two years before the appearance of The Blue Eagle at Work, *supra* note 20..

119 29 U.S.C. § 158(a)(1).

120 29 U.S.C. § 158(a)(2).

121 29 U.S.C. § 158(a)(3).

122 29 U.S.C. § 158(b)(1)(A).

123 *See supra* at note 64.

legality of the concept—such a negative conclusion is surprising. This objection evidently resulted from misreading the statutory provisions and/or misreading, or failing to read, key related Supreme Court and Board decisions. Although this line of opposition hasn't been voiced recently, in view of this book's plan to revalidate members-only bargaining it seems appropriate to address this possible objection, analysis of which begins with a review of settled case law (even though this repeats some cases previously noted and discussed[124]).

The foundational case is *Consolidated Edison Co. v. NLRB,*[125] where the Supreme Court unequivocally ruled that the execution of members-only collective bargaining agreements doesn't violate Sections 8(1) and 8(3)[126] and that such agreements "in the absence of . . . an exclusive agency" are valid under the Act even if the covered employees "were a minority."[127] Not only has that ruling never been withdrawn or overruled, the Court expressly reasserted that conclusion in later cases, i.e., in *International Ladies Garment Workers v. NLRB (Bernhard-Altmann Texas Corp.),*[128] and in *Retail Clerks v. Lion Dry Goods, Inc.,*[129] and it implicitly acknowledged it again in *Radio Officers Union v. NLRB.*[130] Furthermore, the NLRB in its original *Consolidated Edison* decision expressly held that the involved companies "have not engaged in unfair labor practices within the meaning of Section 8(2) of the Act."[131] The Supreme Court's decision in that case thus expressly addressed only the Section 8(1) and 8(3) issues.[132] Soon after, in *The Solvay Process Co.,*[133] the Board reaffirmed its prior dismissal of

124 *See* chap. 4 *infra* at notes 101-112.

125 *Supra* note 64.

126 Now §§ 8(a)(1) and 8(a)(3). It was a clear ruling rather than mere dicta, for the Court chose to describe its action as follows:

> [T]he contracts...simply constitute the Brotherhood the collective bargaining agency for those employees who are its members. [T]here is nothing to show that the employees' selection as indicated by the Brotherhood contracts has been superseded by any other selection by a majority of employees of the companies so as to create an exclusive agency for bargaining under the statute, and in the absence of such an exclusive agency the employees represented by the brotherhood, even if they were a minority, clearly had the right to make their own choice.

127 *Id.* at 237.

128 *Supra* note 66.

129 *Supra* note 90, 369 U.S. at 29.

130 347 U.S. 17 (1954).

131 Now § 8(a)(2). Consolidated Edison Co. of New York, *supra* note 89.

132 Now §§ 8(a)1 and 8(a)(3).

133 *Supra* note 90.

the Section 8(2) charge in the *Consolidated Edison* case, expressly holding that an employer's recognition of a minority union "as the sole bargaining agency for its members only"[134] wasn't a violation of Section 8(2). And in *Consolidated Builders, Inc.*,[135] the Board again held that recognition of, and a collective agreement with, a members-only minority union doesn't violate Section 8(a)(2) and likewise doesn't violate Section 8(a)(1).[136] In an earlier case, *The Hoover Co.*,[137] the Board also indicated that an employer faced with rival recognition demands from two unions "may, without violating the *Midwest Piping*[138] doctrine, grant recognition to each of the claimants on a members-only basis."[139]

The next pertinent case, the Supreme Court's 1954 *Radio Officers*[140] decision—which is especially relevant for what it says to the naysayers—is treated separately and extensively below. Six years after *Radio Officers*, the Court revisited the minority-bargaining issue in the *Bernhard Altmann* case,[141] which concerned an employer's signing of a collective bargaining agreement with a minority union, and recognizing it as the exclusive bargaining representative of all the employees in the unit. That conduct was deemed a Section 8(a)(2) violation by the employer and a Section 8(b)(1)(A) violation by the union. Justice Douglas's partial dissent elegantly reviewed the history, nature, and rationale of members-only minority-union bargaining, finding the process to be lawful, noting that "The aim–at least the hope–of the [NLRA] legislation was that majority unions would emerge"[142] from this members-only bargaining process; he thus articulated the stepping-stone role of minority bargaining on the path toward Section 9(a) majority/exclusive bargaining. The Court's majority opinion also acknowledged the validity of those minority-union contracts. Not only did the

134 *Id.*, 5 NLRB at 338.

135 *Supra* note 90.

136 *Id.* at 975.

137 *Supra* note 90.

138 *Supra* note 64. *See* Midwest Piping Co., 63 NLRB 1060 (1945) (it is an unfair labor practice under §8(2) for an employer to recognize one of two competing unions after a representation petition had been filed with the Board).

139 The Hoover Co., *supra* note 92, 90 NLRB at 1618.

140 *Supra* note 130.

141 *Supra* note 66.

142 *Id.*, 366 U.S. at 742-743.

majority opinion not question the accuracy of Justice Douglas's observations—disagreeing only as to his appropriate remedy—it expressly explained that the Section 8(a)(2)

> violation which the Board found was the grant by the employer of *exclusive* representation status to a minority union, *as distinguished from an employer's bargaining with a minority union for its members only.* Therefore *the exclusive representation provision is the vice in the agreement* . . . .[143]

The Court thus recognized that members-only agreements with minority unions don't violate Sections 8(a)(2) or 8(b)(1)(A). A year later, in Lion Dry Goods,[144] the Court again reasserted the validity of minority-union contracts, reminding that "members-only contracts have long been recognized."[145] And as the following discussion will demonstrate, established case law further confirms that the proposed rule would not violate Sections 8(a)(1), 8(a)(2), 8(a)(3), or 8(b)(1)(A).

The objection that minority unions cannot lawfully bargain for their members only because the resulting agreements and their benefits wouldn't be granted to nonunion employees and therefore would constitute discrimination in violation of Section 8(a)(3) is apparently based on a misreading of a statement by the Second Circuit in *Gaynor News,*[146] which the Supreme Court reviewed in *Radio Officers.*[147] This objection is patently erroneous, but in the unlikely event that it were to be deemed valid, it would thereafter be appropriate for the Supreme Court to reverse *Consolidated Edison* and disavow all of its subsequent assertions in the cases that reconfirmed the legality of members-only bargaining. The Board would likewise have to do the same, at least implicitly, regarding its several decisions that also affirmed the minority-bargaining practice. Such reversals would be required because the alleged violation would obviously apply equally to both *voluntary* and *mandated* non-majority members-only bargaining. Although the following discussion demonstrates the total absurdity of this objection, it can't be overlooked that if this objection were ruled valid it would stand *stare decisis* on its head.

---

143 *Id.,* at 736-37. Emphasis added.

144 *Supra* note 90.

145 *Id.,* at 369 U.S. at 29.

146 *NLRB v. Gaynor News Co.,* 197 F.2d 719 (2d Cir. 1952).

147 *Supra* note 130.

The place to begin is *Gaynor News*, which was a case where a majority union that purported to represent an entire bargaining unit signed a contract containing an exclusive recognition clause but thereafter proceeded to represent its members only. In compliance with the union's demands, the employer retroactively paid wage increases and vacation benefits to the union members but not to other employees in the bargaining unit. The apparently-misread Second Circuit statement was that the "[d]iscriminatory conduct, such as that *practiced here* is inherently conducive to increased union membership."[148] That statement, however, wasn't expressed as an indictment of members-only bargaining contracts. Indeed, the Supreme Court in its review of *Gaynor* recognized that the referenced conduct "practiced here" was discriminatory only because it occurred where the union was the *exclusive* Section 9(a) bargaining representative. The Court provided four explanatory bases for its conclusion:

First, it cited explicit legislative history from the House committee report on Section 8(3) of the Wagner Act that shows it was only discrimination by a *majority* representative that was in issue, for the report stated that "agreements more favorable to the *majority* than the *minority* are impossible."[149]

Second, the Court emphasized the significance of the *exclusivity* factor, noting that "the court below held that the union was *exclusive* agent for both union and nonunion employees."[150] Furthermore, it stressed the following limitations, which the Second Circuit had itself expressed in its *Gaynor* opinion:

> According to the reasoning of the Second Circuit . . . disparate payments based on contract are illegal only when the union, as *bargaining agent for both union and nonunion employees,* betrays its trust and obtains special benefits for the union members. That court considered such action unfair because such employees are not in a position to protect their own interest. Thus, it reasoned, *if a union bargains only for its own members, it is legal for such union to cause an employer to give, and for such employer to give, special benefits to the members of the union for if nonmembers are aggrieved they are free to bargain for similar benefits for themselves.*[151]

148 *Supra* note 146, 197 F.2d at 722. Emphasis added. *See Radio Officers, supra* note 127.

149 347 U.S. at 44. Emphasis added.

150 347 U.S. at 46. Emphasis added.

151 347 U.S. at 47. Emphasis added. The Court also quoted from the Second Circuit's opinion distinguishing the Third Circuit's decision in NLRB v. Reliable Newspaper Delivery, Inc., 187 F.2d 547 (3rd Cir. 1951): "there discrimination resulted from what the court considered entirely legal action of

Third, with reference to the foregoing statement by the Second Circuit, the Court pointedly noted that its decision had nothing to do with disparate treatment of union and nonunion employees under members-only contracts. It explicitly limited its ruling as follows:

> We express no opinion as to the legality of disparate payments where the union is not exclusive bargaining agent since that case is not before us. We do hold that *in the circumstances of this case, the union being exclusive bargaining agent for both member and nonmember employees*, the employer could not, without violating § 8(a)(3), discriminate in wages solely on the basis of such membership even though it had executed a contract with the union prescribing such action.[152]

That statement thus implicitly, yet clearly, recognizes the legal validity of members-only contracts—which is not surprising in view of the Court's earlier ruling in *Consolidated Edison.*

Fourth, the Court obviously viewed the union's conduct in *Gaynor* to be a de facto violation of its *duty of fair representation* toward nonunion employees in the bargaining unit. Although this was not an issue directly before the Court, it was obviously an important consideration, for the opinion quoted Senator Wagner's statement that "*exclusive* bargaining agents are powerless 'to make agreements more favorable to the majority than to the minority'"[153] and expressly cited *Steele v. Louisville & Nashville R. Co.*[154] and other duty-of-fair-representation related cases[155] to drive home the point about a Section 9(a) m*ajority* union not being

the minority union in asking special benefits for its members only. The union made no pretense of representing the majority of employees or of being the exclusive bargaining agent in the plant. The other nonunion employees, reasoned the Court, were quite able to elect their own representative and ask for similar benefits. Not so here. The union here represented the majority of employees and was *the exclusive bargaining agent* for the plant." *Gaynor, supra* note 241, 197 F.2d at 722, quoted in *Radio Officers* at 347 U.S. at 37 (emphasis added).

152 347 U.S. at 47. Emphasis added.

153 *Id.* Emphasis added.

154 323 U.S. 192, 202-203 (1944) (holding that an exclusive union representative has a duty to represent all employees in the class or craft [Railway Labor Act terminology for appropriate bargaining unit] "fairly [and] without hostile discrimination").

155 Wallace Corp. v. NLRB, 323 U.S. 248 (1944); J. I. Case v. NLRB, 321 U.S. 332 (1944); Railroad Telegraphers v. Railway Express Agency, 321 U.S. 342 (1944); Ford Motor Co. v. Huffman, 345 U.S. 330 (1953).

permitted to discriminate against the nonunion employees whom it is obligated to represent.

Clearly, *Gaynor/Radio Officers* doesn't hold, or even imply, that a minority union cannot bargain for its members only because a collective agreement that applies only to union members, and not to nonunion employees, and thus would violate Section 8(a)(3). Notwithstanding the clarity of that conclusion, one may ask: Whether there's any other basis for contending that a disparity between the greater benefits that a minority-union might achieve through negotiation, compared with the lesser benefits, if any, that the employer might voluntarily choose to give or not to give to its nonunion employees, would be a violation of that provision? This question doesn't imply, however, that all such contracting employers would choose to withhold union-negotiated benefits from nonunion employees; that is and should be the employer's own business decision, not one dictated by law—especially a law that encourages collective bargaining.[156]

The key factor in the foregoing question is the *employer's purpose.* The critical language in Section 8(a)(3) is that it's an unfair labor practice for an employer "by *discrimination* in regard to hire or tenure of employment or any term or condition of employment *to encourage or discourage membership in any labor organization.*"[157] It's again *Radio Officers* that provides the answer to the posed question, for the Supreme Court there defined—in the following oft-quoted passage—the features in Section 8(a)(3) that are critical to this determination:

> The language of § 8(a)(3) is not ambiguous. The unfair labor practice is for an employee to encourage or discourage membership by means of discrimination. Thus this section does not outlaw all encouragement or discouragement of membership in labor organizations; only such as is accomplished by discrimination is prohibited. Nor does this section outlaw discrimination in employment as such; only such discrimination as encourages or discourages membership in a labor organization is proscribed.[158]

As the Court explained: "That Congress intended the employer's *purpose* in discriminating to be controlling is clear."[159] Indeed, that *purpose* is the reason why

156 § 1.

157 Emphasis added.

158 *Supra* note 127, 347 U.S. at 42-43.

159 *Id.* at 44. Emphasis added.

an employer's grant of additional benefits to union employees in a members-only collective bargaining agreement wouldn't be a *per se* violation of Section 8(a)(3). Even if that conduct were to be deemed "discriminatory in regard to [a] term or condition of employment," its *purpose* would not be "to encourage . . . membership in any labor organization," for American employers, almost universally, don't encourage or intend to encourage such membership. Rather, the employer, having presumably bargained in good faith, would likely have as its purpose simply the fulfilling of its bargaining obligation—which the Act is designed to promote—and perhaps also to spend as little of the company's money as possible or to advance some other business-related purpose. That such conduct may have the incidental effect of encouraging some nonunion employees to join the union doesn't brand the employer with an unlawful purpose.

NLRB v. Great Dane Trailers, Inc.,[160] doesn't indicate otherwise. A careful reading of that case reinforces the conclusion that an employer who grants collectively-negotiated economic benefits to employees who belong to a members-only union and chooses not to grant the same benefits to similarly situated nonunion employees doesn't violate section 8(a)(3). Nevertheless, some naysayers might hastily—but groundlessly—assume that *Great Dane* doesn't permit the granting of such union-only benefits. That assumption is evidently based on an erroneous reading of an incomplete statement in the *Great Dane* opinion, where the Supreme Court was defining a *procedural* evidentiary rule—not a *substantive* requirement—applicable to the statutory provision. The statement was:

> [I]f it can reasonably be concluded that the employer's discriminatory conduct was "inherently destructive" of important employee rights, no proof of an antiunion motivation is needed and the Board can find an unfair labor practice even if the employer introduces evidence that the conduct was motivated by business considerations.[161]

That statement doesn't eliminate the need for *proof* of unlawful motive, for it implicitly incorporates the Court's statement in the preceding paragraph of the opinion that confirms—as the statutory language mandates—that to support a finding of an 8(a)(3) violation there must be proof of *motive* "to encourage

160 388 U.S. 26 (1967).

161 *Id.* at 34.

or discourage membership in any labor organization."[162] That proof might be shown by the conduct itself, but not necessarily so. The Court had previously explained in *NLRB v. Erie Resistor Corp.*[163] with reference to certain conduct deemed to be "inherently destructive" of employee rights, that such "conduct *does speak* for itself."[164] It was thus invoking the age-old doctrine of *res ipsa loquitur* to affirm the Board's treatment of an employer's grant of permanent super-seniority to striker replacements as "conduct which carries its own indicia of intent."[165] Regardless, there must still be a showing of unlawful purpose. In the referenced preceding paragraph in *Great Dane,* the Court reaffirmed that requirement, which it had spelled out earlier in *Erie Resistor,* to wit:

> If the conduct in question falls within this 'inherently destructive' category, the employer has the burden of explaining away, justifying or characterizing 'his actions as something different than they appear on their face,' and if he fails, 'an unfair labor practice charge is made out.'[166]

Accordingly, what the Court in *Great Dane* was saying—albeit awkwardly, was simply that "[s]ome conduct is so 'inherently destructive of employee interests' that it carries with it a *strong inference* of impermissible motive."[167] That's exactly how the Supreme Court in *Metropolitan Edison Co. v. NLRB* later reworded the foregoing incomplete *Great Dane* statement. That prescription, however, doesn't define the unfair labor practice, it only defines the *procedure* to determine which party—the employer or the General Counsel—has the evidentiary burden of proof where there's a showing of employer conduct that adversely affects employee rights. The prescription concludes that whether such conduct is *inherently destructive* or *comparatively slight,*

162 § 8(a)(3).

163 373 U.S. 221 (1963). The Court in *Great Dane* also relied on its prior decisions in American Ship Building Co. v. NLRB, 380 U.S. 300 (1965), and NLRB v. Brown, 380 U.S. 278 (1965).

164 *Id.,* Emphasis added.

165 *Id.* at 231, repeated by the Court in *Great Dane,* 388 U.S. at 33.

166 388 U.S. at 33, citing *Erie Resistor,* 373 U.S. at 228. Emphasis added. The Court also stated that "even if the employer does come forward with counter explanations for his conduct in this situation, the Board may nevertheless draw an inference of improper motive from the conduct itself and exercise its duty to strike the proper balance between the asserted business justifications and the invasion of employee rights in light of the Act and its policy." *Id.* at 33-34.

167 Metropolitan Edison Co. v. NLRB, 460 U.S. 693 (1983). Emphasis added.

> in either situation, once it has been proved that the employer engaged in discriminatory conduct which could have adversely affected employee rights to some extent, *the burden is upon the employer to establish that he was motivated by legitimate objectives since proof of motivation is most accessible to him.*[168]

In other words, the employer bears the burden of establishing a legitimate lawful motive—this is a *procedural requirement*, not a per se *substantive determination.* When an employer negotiates economic benefits with a minority union for its members only, such benefits are not *given* to those employees—rather, they are the natural product of the collective-bargaining process, hence they are the result of the employer's legitimate business activity. That union has no authority to bargain for non-members, and the employer has no legal obligation to give collectively-bargained benefits to nonmember employees.[169] Such conduct is thus not inherently destructive of the rights of nonunion employees, for they are free to join the union or not, or to negotiate for themselves, or perhaps to join another union. Yet even if such conduct were construed to be inherently destructive, it would still not violate Section 8(a)(3) because, as previously noted, the employer can easily demonstrate that it wasn't motivated by a discriminatory intent to "encourage . . . membership in any labor organization" but rather by a legitimate obligation to bargain collectively in accordance with the declared policy of the Act or for some other non-discriminatory business-related objective. Thus, the fact that some employees may join the union to obtain those benefits is not evidence of the employer's unlawful motivation.[170]

The foregoing reading of *Great Dane* is consistent with the established interpretation of Section 8(a)(3), as demonstrated in the Supreme Court's decision in *Metropolitan Edison* and by the D.C. Circuit's opinion in *Contractors' Labor Pool, Inc. v. NLRB.*[171] In the latter case, the court concluded that based on "the Supreme Court's long-standing interpretation of section 8(a)(3),"[172] "[i]ndispensable to a determination of a violation of §8(a)(3) . . . is a finding that an employer acted out of an anti- (or pro-) union motivation."[173] Indeed, numerous Board and

168 388 U.S. at 34.

169 Although some employers may voluntarily choose to do so.

170 *See also infra* at note 179.

171 323 F.3d 1051 (D.C. Cir. 2003).

172 *Id.* at 1059.

173 *Id.*

court decisions illustrate the necessity of an express showing of unlawful motivation.[174] Thus, even in a case where an employer's conduct is so inherently destructive of employee interests that it carries a strong *inference of* unlawful motive, it is but an inference for which the employer must be afforded an opportunity to rebut with appropriate evidence. Accordingly, if successful pre-majority members-only union representation and bargaining encourages employees to join the union, the union's engagement in such statutorily approved activity would be rendered meaningless by treating it as unlawful conduct under Section 8(a)(3) on the part of the employer. And it follows that if there is no Section 8(a)(3) violation by the employer there can be no violation of Sections 8(b)(1)(A) and 8(b)(2) by the union.[175]

Furthermore, in the unlikely event that any two or more of the referenced statutory provisions, i.e., Sections 8(a)(2), 8(a)(3), 8(b)(1)(A), 8(b)(2), and the duty-to-bargain provisions of Sections 7, 8(a)(1), and 8(a)(5), were deemed to be in conflict, such conflict would be easily resolved in favor of members-only minority-union bargaining in accordance with the Act's policy declared in Section 1 of favoring the "practice and procedure of collective-bargaining." The Supreme Court recognized such a potential conflict when it evaluated the alleged discriminatory application of a hiring hall provision in a collective agreement in the 1961 case of *Local 357, Teamsters v. NLRB (Los Angeles-Seattle Motor Express).*[176] After repeating the above quoted language from *Radio Officers,*[177] the Court emphasized that "[i]t is the 'true purpose' or 'real motive' in hiring or firing

174 *E.g.*, NLRB v. Brown, *supra* note 163 (in a strike against one employer of a multi-employer bargaining group, it is not a violation for that employer to hire temporary replacements); NLRB v. Harrison Ready Mix Concrete, 770 F.2d 78 (6th Cir. 1985) (no evidence of discriminatory intent where employer reinstated economic strikers with less seniority than that assigned to replacements); Illinois Coil Spring Co., Milwaukee Spring Div., 268 NLRB. 601 (1984), *aff'd sub nom.* Automobile Workers v. NLRB, 765 F.2d 175 (D.C. Cir. 1985) (transferring bargaining-unit work to unorganized plant during the term of a collective bargaining agreement and laying off affected unionized employees held not a violation of §8(a)(3) because the relocation was not a violation of §8(a)(5)); Suburban Transit Corp., 276 NLRB. 15 (1985) (employer's removal of employees from office payroll thereby depriving them of cafeteria access was not evidence of discriminatory motivation); Evening News Ass'n, 166 NLRB 219 (1967), *enforced sub nom.* Teamsters Local 372 v. NLRB, 404 F.2d 1159, *cert. denied,* 395 U.S. 923 (1969) (conduct of two employers, bargaining with the same union, who locked out employees pursuant to a mutual-aid agreement held not unlawful). *See generally,* DLL 7th, *supra* note 76 at 7-10 to 7-12.

175 § 8(b)(1)(A) prohibits a union from restraining or coercing employees in the exercise of the rights guaranteed in § 7. § 8(b)(2) prohibits a union from causing or attempting to cause an employer to discriminate against an employee in violation of § 8(a)(3).

176 365 U.S. 667 (1961).

177 *Supra* note 130.

that constitutes the test."[178] Observing that successful collective bargaining that encourages union membership shouldn't be confused with discriminatory conduct motivated by an unlawful purpose, the Court stated that

> It may be that the very existence of the hiring hall encourages union membership. We may assume that it does. The very existence of the union has the same influence. When a union engages in collective bargaining and obtains increased wages and improved working conditions, its prestige doubtless rises and, one may assume, more workers are drawn to it. When a union negotiates collective bargaining agreements that include arbitration clauses and supervises the functioning of those provisions so as to get equitable adjustments of grievances, union membership may also be encouraged. The truth is that *the union is a service agency that probably encourages membership whenever it does its job well.*[179]

By the same token, it is the employer's *true purpose* or *real motive* in withholding union-bargained benefits from nonunion employees that would constitute the appropriate test in a members-only bargaining situation.

Moreover, treating nonunion employees less favorably as a result of members-only collective bargaining—if that were the employer's voluntary decision—wouldn't interfere with the Section 7 right of employees "to refrain from any or all" union and collective bargaining activity.[180] By not joining the union, nonunion employees will be exercising their right to refrain from collective bargaining, voluntarily choosing instead to engage in *individual bargaining*, a status that would continue unless and until a majority of the employees in an appropriate unit select union representation, whereupon the familiar rule of Section 9(a) exclusivity would become effective.

---

178 365 U.S. at 675.

179 *Id.* at 675-676. Emphasis added.

180 § 7 text added by Taft-Hartley Act.

TABLE OF CASES

TABLE OF STATUTORY PROVISIONS

National Labor Relations Act—specific provisions: